Copyright © 2015 by King Pharaoh
Holyoke, Mass.
All Rights Reserved
Printed and Bound in the United States of America
Published by:
Biz-e-Bee Book Group
8549 Wilshire Blvd. Suite #139
Beverly Hills, CA. 90211
www.bebpub.com
Library of Congress Cataloging-in-Publication Data
ISBN# 978-0-9817074-4-0
Cover Design: Biz-e-Bee Book Group
Formatting: Biz-e-Bee Book Group
First Printing, April 2015
10 9 8 7 6 5 4 3 2 1
King Pharaoh

Publisher's Note

No part of this book may be reproduced, stored in a retrieval system or transmitted by any means, electronic, mechanical, photocopying, recording or otherwise without written permission from the publisher or author.

This book is a work of fiction. The names, characters, places and incidents are either the product of the author's imagination or used fictitiously without intent to describe actual conduct of any persons living or dead. Any resemblance is purely coincidental. Sale of this book without a front cover is unauthorized. If this book is without a cover, it may have been reported to the publisher as "unsold or destroyed" and neither the author nor the publisher has received payment for it.

Author's Note:

Since my last book I've been through a Lot of shyt. I've been rushed again by a Task Force and been to more jails in more states. Because I can give you another novel from home is how I know that God has my back. God must've given me a lovable personality because he knew I would be in the world alone with no real family as a safety net.

Since my last book I've also had more new cars, trucks, girls and houses, even moved to Atlanta. I've gained a new respect as a great author and I've gained new friends. Life is still shitty and complex and good at the same time. I wouldn't trade it for anything else, lol.

Above all I try not to be too busy making a living or dwelling on things that haven't gone right that I forget to live my life.

My stories come from the fuzzy line in people where anyone can be a different way on a different day. I love everyone who loves me and none who don't, Fuck 'em.

I wanna thank everyone who supported my first effort as an author. I can only Apologize for making you wait longer than you thought you would for part two, life got in my way. If you wanna make God laugh just tell him your plans. To my boys and girls locked up, the hard copies are for yall. Everybody on the streets are downloading this shyt. I thank my children with everything in me for loving Daddy unconditionally.

It's still one thang for certain and two thangs for sure, either you gonna hate me or love me. And thank you to everybody who truly gives a fuck about me.

P.S. I wrote half of this book with my thumbs. Enjoy!

KING PHARAOH

KING PHARAOH
A
Novel

written by
KING PHARAOH

ACKNOWLEDGEMENTS

While most people idolize and worship celebrities, sports icons, movie stars, gangsters and the wealthy, I idolize my Ma, Alice Mae and my Pop, Doc Shaw. They are my heroes for real. My Ma has the will power of a thousand bulls. She had cancer and beat it, fought her demons and beat them too. She raised me and my two sisters as a single mother while working two jobs. She made sure every Christmas we had something under the tree, even when she couldn't afford it. We never went without food and she made sure we always had new clothes and new shoes on our feet. I can't begin to tell you the sacrifices she's made for me and continue to make for me. It's because of her I know what unconditional love is. It's because of her I believe that there's nothing I can't do. Tell me that's not the greatest gift a mother can give her child. Mommy, I love you shorty.

My Pop is the smartest man I know, hands down. Our relationship wasn't always the smoothest. But at no point have I ever hated you Pop, never. I understand now why you were so hard on me. I get it. You were preparing me for life, because life can be hard. Regardless, looking back on it all, I wouldn't change a thing. You set the bar high from the door, and that's why a lot of dudes can't get in my business now. I want to thank you for that. I want to thank you for making me sit at my desk until 3 in the morning studying. I want to thank you making me read the encyclopedia when I was on punishment. I want to thank you for making me ask my teachers for extra homework. Thank you for teaching me how to play chess in the fourth grade. Thank you for making me the beast I am today.

To all the Incarcerated Authors still in jail trying to get your first book off the ground, keep doing what you do. I'm one of you. I'm in the jail library day in and day out putting in work. I spend long nights at my desk in my cell with the night light on. I read all the writing books. I've bought hundreds of packs of pencils, pens, typing ribbons, and paper. I'm constantly thinking about my characters, plot twists, and new scenes. I'm one of you, so keep doing what you're doing because if I can do it so can you.

I have to shout my brothers I never had; Scotty "Little C" Carpenter, you already know what it is between me and you bro. Jose "Cheo" Castro you're the most honest and good hearted person I know, meeting you made me a better man, Biz Nolastname, you've been there from the moment we met and have kept it so fuckin' real it's crazy. While I'm in here I live through you. It's because of you a lot of this is possible. Hands down you're That Fuckin' Dude! Jamal "Jah Jah" Blake, I haven't spoke to him since I been locked up, but he is the only one I'll forgive for that because that's how much love I have for my boy. Victor "Streetz" Epps I see a lot of me in you, just stay focused, the world could be yours.

To the big head nigga with the right phone number, that conversation in your cell on Christmas has changed the way I view things now. That was the biggest jewel anybody had given me. It's because of that conversation I can see beyond the trees now. Thanks yo.

Finally, I'm King Pharaoh. Get used to hearing my name, this book is just the beginning. So without no further hold ups,
The reign of KING PHARAOH has just begun.

DEDICATIONS

To my enemies for keeping me on my toes.

To my Desert Eagle and bulletproof vest that kept me alive during all those shootouts. Without you two I wouldn't be here today.

To all the crackheads and dopefiends, I need to thank you for keeping my pockets fat and my bills paid, for the exotic vacations I took and for the fly cars I bought, for the expensive clothes I wore and finally thanks for allowing me to live a lifestyle most people can only dream about.

To all my Dominican Papis in Washington Heights who stayed with the fish scale coke. Thanks for playing fair, but those last two birds I got, you're going to have to charge those to the game.

To the weed growers of Purple Cush, Sour Diesel, White Widow, Train Wreck, Mother's Milk, Lamb's Breath and all the other great weed strains out there, it's because of y'all I come up with the wild shit I write.

To Keon "Mujee" Smith, you possess a very special gift when it comes to this writing shit. You're still in the tiger stages of your creativity, but when you finally become the dragon I know you will be... I'm going to have to step aside.

To all the chicks out there that take it in the ass and suck dick on the first date, love ya'll.

To all my sex slaves, thank y'all for allowing me to use your bodies and minds to explore the dark side of my sexual desires.

Also I want to give a special shout out to all the girls down for ménage trios, gang bangs, orgies and all the super freak bitches that crossed my path, (Tina, Bootie, Ann, Terri, Sandy, Melissa, Colleen, Cheryl, Kate, Halle, Debbie, Inga, Cookie, Patricia and Hedi) thanks for the memories. They come in handy in here.

To the person who evented the x-pill, you're a beast for real.

To my best friends in the world, my Mom and Dad. Thanks for being there when everybody else left me for dead. Thanks for coming into the darkness to rescue me when I thought there was no hope.

To all my cellies that put up with me while I wrote KING PHARAOH. Thanks, but you're still not getting a cut off this book.

To all the thorough soldiers in the FEDS who have their paperwork and to all the ones that blew trial, keep your head up because nothing bad lasts forever.

For all of you that turned your back on me when the judge gave me 20 years. Thank you! Now I don't owe none of you sorry muthafuckas shit. So don't ask me for shit, if I give you anything you better duck.

To my man Gorilla Olay, rest in peace, my nigga!!!

To my Gorillas... much love y'all, much love!

For all y'all still in the streets getting money, here's the only advice I got for you.

"Prepare for the worse when you're at your best."

To the snitch in my case, a soldier dies one honorable death and a coward dies a thousand deaths every time he looks in the mirror!

Remember that you FUCKIN' COWARD!!

KING PHARAOH
A
Novel

written by
KING PHARAOH

Chestnut Park, Holyoke, Massachusetts.

We hustled in the park on the corner of Chestnut and Sergeant. Chestnut Park was the heart of the neighborhood. The alleyways and streets that led to and from it were the arteries that pumped life into this fucked up place. It was in this park that drug addicts hooked on crack and heroin roamed like zombies in a horror flick.

The park itself was littered with tiny shards of broken glass. They sparkled like a bed of diamonds whenever sunrays or moonbeams fell upon them. The empty crack vials scattered throughout the park, along with the dirty syringes used to administer lethal dosages of heroin, was as common sight as birds flying through the sky.

Surrounding the park were eight rundown apartment buildings with wooden, termite - infested fire escapes. Six of the buildings were packed with poor families and single mothers on Section 8. Even with reduced rent, some occupants still struggled with the pressures of everyday life. These dilapidated buildings were a constant reminder of their status in society.

Two of the eight buildings were no doubt victims of arson orchestrated by landlords to collect insurance money.

Now, the half-gutted apartment buildings were covered with modern-day hieroglyphics; by day they looked like any other abandoned building in a lower class neighborhood.

When night fell on Chestnut Park, these same buildings took on a different look. It was as though they came alive. The hollowed out windows staring back at me, watching my every movement, made me feel uneasy. The smell of trash, vomit and the occasional corpse was the buildings breath that I inhaled.

As a kid, I always imagined death living there, within the darkness, and somehow I knew me and those buildings would cross paths one day.

The actual park was divided into three sections. The northeast part, on the handball court, was where the Latin Crowns hung out. Painted on the handball wall was a mural of Angel, the slain founder of the West Massachusetts chapter of the Latin Crowns. Around that time, gangs were new to Holyoke. Don't get me wrong, we had gangs, but we called them street crews. None of them had clout like the Crowns.

Angel was the first gang member I knew in Holyoke. Eventually, Angel accumulated a following. It was kinda easy since Holyoke was flooded with Puerto Ricans. Within six months, the Latin Crowns grew to 350 members and were making their presence known. Not by gang violence, although there was some, but by organizing food drives for the homeless. Every Friday and Saturday, Angel rented the high school gym. He'd throw parties, and all the proceeds were used to clean up the neighborhood.

Mayor Santiago, in his quest to clean up the Holyoke Police Department, scheduled a public meeting. He solicited public opinion about the police department. At the meeting, Angel was supposed to present evidence of specific detectives who were involved in murder, extortion, and drugs. Well, before Angel had a chance to meet with the mayor, he was murdered and his body was dumped in Chestnut Park.

Rumors circulated about who murdered him. Some say it was rival gangs, jealous of the attention the Latin Crowns were getting. Others suspected that members of his own gang killed him because they didn't approve of Angel snitching, regardless if it was dirty cops he was telling on. The mayor suspected the detectives implicated in Angel's evidence and even though he couldn't prove it, he still suspended them from duty.

After Angel died things changed dramatically for the Latin Crowns. Some dude named Jose took over as their leader, and no longer did they do positive things for the community. Matter of fact, they did the opposite by selling heroin at dangerous levels of purity.

My crew and the Crowns beefed on and off because the number of overdoses rose considerably. They brought a lot of heat to the park every time the meat wagon came and scooped up a dead body. Angel's death went unsolved, and anybody that inquired about it ended up dead or went missing.

The playground in the southwest section of the park had all the traditional things: a swing set with only one good swing, a broken merry-go-round tilted to one side, preventing it from turning and in the center of the playground was a giant set of monkey bars. The only thing missing were the kids playing on the equipment.

I used to hang out as a kid at this playground. Back then everything seemed so simple. The sky was bluer; the grass was greener, and the entire playground had that Sesame St. feel to it.

Sometimes, when I get high off some real, real good weed I could see ghostly figures of me and my childhood friend Jo-Jo playing on the monkey bars. It always felt like I was watching a movie of my past. The scene that kept replaying in my mind was a nightmare.

It was the summer of '88 around 7:30 p.m., the sun had just dipped behind the buildings. I had just entered the fourth grade with my best friend, Jo-Jo. He lived in the same building that I did, and we had known each other since kindergarten. That day we were playing tag with the twins, Jasenia and Jeanette.

All of a sudden, we heard gunshots in the distance.

"What was that?" Jasenia asked, looking around.

"Gunshots. Somebody's shooting," I replied.

"Look, over there!" Jeanette pointed to the entrance of the park.

From the top of the monkey bars we could see a tall, slender, black teenager. He came into the park runnin' at full speed. Right behind him were three white men with black leather jackets.

The shortest of the three was slightly overweight and balding. His face was beet red and covered in sweat. He was out of breath. If it was up to him to catch the kid, the kid would have gotten clean away.

Then there was a taller white guy built like a football player, he was on the heels of the kid. His blond hair was pulled back in a ponytail that went slightly past his shoulders.

As the teenager got closer, I noticed it was Tyran. He lived on the sixth floor with his mother and aunt. My grandma told me to stay away from him because he dealt drugs. At that time, I didn't know what drugs were, but I thought it couldn't have been all that bad since Tyran kept a pocket full of money.

All of a sudden, the tall, blond man reached in his jacket and pulled out a gun.

"BOOM! BOOM! BOOM! BOOM! BOOM! BOOM! BOOM!"

Bullets whizzed by our heads as we scrambled down the monkey bars and hid behind some low cut bushes. I could hear the bullets ricocheting off the playground equipment while we lay flat on the ground. When the shooting stopped, I got up the courage to peek from behind the bushes. Tyran was face down in the dirt, screaming.

"Please! Oh, God, don't kill me!"

The short, fat man finally caught up and kick Tyran in the face.

"That's for making me run, you fuckin' nigger!" The fat man gasped for air as he leaned on the monkey bars to keep from falling down.

We weren't far from where Tyran lay. His face was bruised and swollen while his white baggy shorts quickly turned red from the bullet he took in the thigh.

I had never heard a guy cry like that. It scared the hell out of me for some reason. Looking to my right, I saw the twins as they held each other. I put one finger over my lips in hopes they got the point and shut up. Jo-Jo lay flat on the other side of them. I knew he was scared, he hated guns. When I turned back to look, the third guy came walking up. He was a little older than the other two, with brown hair and tiny streaks of gray. His face was slightly wrinkled, but his eyes had a remorseless glow to them.

"Tyran, Tyran, Tyran, tsk, tsk, tsk."

"Valentine, I'm sorry man, I don't know what I

was thinking… I… I…

"It's a little late for the sorries." Valentine said in a deep Irish accent.

His skin was so pale white that he could have passed as a ghost.

"We must make an example out of you, Tyran, so we don't have any problems like these out of your monkey friends."

When Valentine reached into his jacket, I saw a badge clipped to his belt. "They're police officers," I whispered over my shoulder.

Valentine pulled out his gun and pointed it at Tyran's head. My heart started beating faster. Sweat poured down my face, stinging my eyes. Tyran stopped begging and a strange calmness overtook him. He turned his head to the bush, and I swear he was looking right at me. Valentine pulled the trigger and Tyran's head exploded like a watermelon. Bits of Tyran's skull landed near the bush we were behind. Instantly, my stomach started to bubble. The smell of blood, human flesh and brains was too much to take. I threw up everything that was in my stomach. When I looked up, the three white men were gone.

"Come on, let's go before they come back." I whispered.

Jeanette and Jasenia got up and ran out of the park.

"Come on, Jo-Jo. Let's go, man."

Jo-Jo didn't move. I knew he was scared, so I went to pick him up. When I grabbed the back of his shirt, it was soaked. I thought it was sweat, but when I looked at my hand, I saw it was blood. At first, I thought it was Tyran's blood, but there was no way Jo-Jo's shirt could've gotten that soaked. I gently nudged him again.

"Hey, Jo-Jo, are you a'ight? Come on, we have to go."

Finally I turned him over on his back. He gasped for air, and his eyes were the size of golf balls.

"Aw, shit, no, Jo-Jo... shit, hold on, man... help, somebody, help!"

I tried to comfort him the best I could by cradling his head in my lap. He tugged at my shirt, trying to talk, but every time he tried to say something, he choked on his own blood.

"Don't talk right now, Jo-Jo, help is coming... you're going to be okay."

As I looked into his eyes, I felt like they were trying to talk to me.

What happened? Why are you crying Pharaoh? There's so much blood... it's getting cold... I want my mom... I'm scared Pharaoh... I'm scared.

I looked up to see if anybody was coming, but everybody was moving around in slow motion. There were people screaming and running around, but no one was coming to help.

Just then a blue four door crept by slowly. The window on the passenger side came down. Valentine partially stuck his head out of the window. He placed one finger over his lips and made his other hand into a gun and pretended to shoot me.

Jo-Jo's tight grip on my shirt began to give.

"No... no, Jo-Jo! You got to fight it! Don't die... Don't die on me, don't die, don't die... not like this!"

Tears poured down my face as I stared at Jo-Jo.

All the shaking and screaming I did didn't help. I was losing him, bit by bit. My best friend was dying in my arms. Time seemed to stop as a hush fell over my ears. I watched Jo-Jo take his last breath. I swear I could see his life leaving through his eyes, and felt his soul pass through me. Since that day, I never set foot back in that playground.

The Gorillas

We got our names from the old heads in the neighborhood. They called us Gorillas because we wore all black and sat in the park all day, gettin' money. They said we looked like Gorillas in the zoo. To me the name fit us perfect. The reason was we had to use guerilla tactics to hustle. See, we didn't have a building to work out of, like other, more established, crews. We were outside in the open, and that meant nothing but problems on top of problems.

First, we had to find spots to stash the coke without crack heads or petty hustlers looking for a quick come up. We also had to watch out for the detectives driving around in unmarked cars, jumping out and chasing us during street sweeps.

Then you had the confidential informants, or C.I.'s, as we called them. The police sent them to make controlled buys from us. Then they'd turn around and appear in court to testify against us.

Last, but not least, we had to deal with special units, like C-Pac, MT, or the deep cover agents. These police squads were put together to go after drug organizations. They weren't bound by the same rules as the regular police. Matter fact, them muthfuckas played by their own rules, and you can best believe they weren't fair. Then again, nobody played fair on these streets.

We had stacked $31,000. All we needed was another four grand and we'd have enough to cop two kilos of coke off my Uncle Dante. To us, reaching two kilos was like winning the Lotto. Off two birds, we stood to make $150,000, and from there, the sky was the limit.

"Yo, the block is jumping, kid! If these fiends keep coming like this, we'll be copping those two bricks tomorrow."

That's my man Daryl. He was the type of dude always starting shit. Anytime we went anywhere, he was always fighting. It got to the point where I didn't want to take him anywhere with me, but at the same time, he was good to have around because if anything jumped off, Daryl had my back like my muthafuckin' spinal cord. But once we started getting close to our goal of two kilos, Daryl started acting funny. We'd get into arguments over the dumbest shit, which I blew off as a phase, little did I know, there was a lot more to it.

"For real, shit is off the chain, yo. I never saw so many crack heads in my life."

That was Country, he was like my brother. Matter of fact, people have mistaken us for brothers because we were both dark skin with baldies. At one time, we were inseparable. Everywhere he went, I went. When you saw me, Country wasn't too far behind. If he was fighting, I was there, throwing my knuckles with him. If I was fuckin', he was fuckin'. If there was only one bitch, we both fucked her. We were together so much; his mother put an extra bed in his room for me.

"Yo, son, we're getting Bill Gates money tonight."

That's T-money. If every crew has an odd ball, he was ours. T-Money was smart as shit. He spoke five different languages, studied linier mathematics equations for fun, and he was a super beast at that computer shit. He was from India and still had that funny accent, like that dude on the "Simpson," but with street slang.

For real, T-Money didn't have to be out on the block with us. His mother worked at the Bay State Hospital as the chief radiologist and made good dough. Not to mention he once had a scholarship to the Massachusetts Institution of Technology, which is a super nerd college. His stay there didn't last long at all. His first year there, him and a Chinese cat hacked into the United States Treasury Department and transferred $100,000,000 to a hundred different non-profit organizations as a joke. That joke got him kicked out of the school and banned from ever touching a computer again.

I always used to think he was wasting his time with us, but he didn't care. T-Money loved being out on the block. Even though he didn't have any fight skills, he had the heart of a lion. To tell you the truth, without T-Money, we would've still been in the park until this day.

Now, the guy sitting over there on the benches. The one with the hoody on. That was my man, Joey. He was from Brooklyn, New York. I met him through his sister Tutee, who I was fuckin'. After she introduced me to Joey and me and him became cool, I stopped fuckin' her. It just didn't feel right. Joey lived in the building next to mine on Sergeant St. with his mother Madee, and his sister. Tutee told me that Joey was there when his father was murdered. Joey never spoke about his pops. Anytime the subject of fathers would come up, he'd remain silent or walk away. Whatever happened to his father shook him up pretty bad. I think because of it Joey hated violence.

Joey wasn't your average Puerto Rican from New York and didn't speak to you if he didn't know you. I'd always turn to him for advice. Truthfully, he was the only one out of us with common sense. He was the one that kept the balance in the crew.

You're probably wondering who the fuck I am. Well, I'm Pharaoh. I was born and raised in Holyoke, Massachusetts. My mother was killed by a stray in a drive by shooting. I never knew my father and my grandma raised me after my mother's death. We lived right across from Chestnut Park. It was me, my grandma and my uncle Peanut.

My uncle Peanut was a stone cold crack head. One of the funny types that made you laugh all the time. He wasn't always fucked up on crack. At one time in his life, he was a lady's man. You know the pretty boy type. He was light skin with light brown eyes and a decent frame, well, before the crack. Now, everything he did was towards his next hit.

Me, I was the opposite. Crack to me meant money, plain and simple, and money was what I was addicted to. It wasn't just the money, but all the things money could buy. Cash ruled my neighborhood, and if you were from the ghetto like me, it ruled yours too. I wasn't your average drug dealer. To me, the streets was the university I attended and cocaine was my major.

Check it, I'm about to give you some game about this coke shit. Cocaine is one of the most powerful stimulants found in nature. The first use of cocaine as a stimulant goes all the way back to the Incas in Peru. They called it the diving plant. The priest would chew the leaves to enter into a trance-like state during ceremonies. Then the common people started using it to stay up while working.

Albert Neimen was the scientist who extracted cocaine from the plant in the 1800s. After that, it started finding its way into everyday products. One of them was the wine, Vin Marini. I know you heard of Coca-Cola having cocaine in it, right? It was only the stimulant based flavoring. Nobody was getting high off drinking soda,

Cocaine plants grow best in the Andes Mountain and can produce leaves for up to 50 years. You can harvest one plant up to three or four times a year. It takes 150 pounds of leaves to make one pound of powdered cocaine. $C17$, $H21$, $1O4$, and HCl are the elements that make up cocaine powder.

Yeah, like I told you, I wasn't your average crack dealer.

Chapter 1

It's crazy how when I think back, I can pinpoint the exact moment my life changed forever…

It was about 11:30, Friday night, still 75 degrees with a slight breeze. The euphoric feeling of the summer was in the air. We hustled by the light of the moon and one or two street lights that randomly flickered on and off like strobe lights.

Friday night, business was booming. Chestnut Park was alive with every element of street life possible. Front stoops were packed with old ladies gossiping about today's girls wearing next to nothing. All the petty hustlers gambled their profits away, shooting craps.

Every now and then a patrol car crept down Chestnut St. with a spotlight scanning the park. Some people ran and hid like roaches. Others would block their eyes and hissed like vampires. Everybody else gave them the middle finger and shouted, "Fuck The Police!" Yeah, it was a typical Friday night except for this feeling I had.

I was sitting on the back of the benches, smoking a blunt while observing the night's festivities. E-Love and his Southside crew were throwing a party. One of their members had just gotten out of jail, while another was on his way to jail. So I guess it was a going away and coming home party, all in one.

Sounds of clubhouse music thumped from the back of a canary yellow Toyota Camry. The basketball court was full of bodies dancing to the hypnotic beats that echoed off the buildings. Plastic cups were filled with beer from kegs hidden in trash cans covered in ice. Then there was a visible cloud of weed smoke that enclosed everybody over there in their own world.

Phil Collins said it best: "I can feel it in the air tonight." I felt it, but I didn't know what it was or when it was coming… but it was coming.

"Yo, Pharaoh, let's go over there, man," Daryl said, taking a pull off a blunt.

"Nah, yo, I'm straight."

"Yo, they got bitches over there, kid. I'm trying to fuck something tonight."

"Country knocked one of them niggas out last night over some bullshit. They might still feel some type of way about that."

"So, and?"

"So I ain't trying to beef again tonight. I'm trying to get this money."

"For real, those chumps over there don't want it with us, Pharaoh."

What Daryl was saying was true, but 30 to 6, the odds weren't in our favor.

"Yo, Pharaoh, what's up? You look like something is bothering you," Daryl said, changing the subject.

"I don't know what it is, but something don't feel

right. You don't feel nothing?"

"Feel what? I don't feel nothing but this Henrock in my blood and this hydro in my head." He held the blunt out in front of his face. "And my pockets getting fatter. What the fuck are you feeling?"

"I don't know."

"We got about 400 joints left, and the way things are looking, we are going to have that money we need for the two birds, yo."

"That's exactly what the fuck I'm talking about, Daryl. Why are we the only ones getting money tonight? There's a least five more crack spots in the hood. If we're jumping like this, they can't possibly be making money."

"And?" Daryl shrugged his shoulders.

"And let's keep it real. Since we've been out here gettin' money, we've never seen a Friday like this before. Something is up."

"Man, who the fuck do you think you are, Spiderman? What, you got Spidey senses or something now? Yo, cut the bullshit, son." Daryl laughed out loud.

"Whatever, yo. I just know something ain't right."

"Daryl!" Country called from the corner.

"What up, yo?"

"Step over to the bootleg spot with me, right quick!"

"A'ight, yo. Now that's what I'm talkin' about. I bet Country will go over to the basketball court with me."

"Don't start no shit, Daryl."

"Chill, Spiderman, I got this."

"Fuck you, punk."

The air in Chestnut Park was similar to a traveling carnival coming to a small town. Everybody was out doing this and that.

Suddenly, in the warmth of the summer night, I felt a cold chill run up my spine that made me jump.

"Yo, what's up with you?" T-Money looked at me with a puzzled look on his face.

"Man, I've been having this funny feeling that something fucked up is gonna happen tonight?"

"Like what?"

"I don't know, but something ain't right. Check it, you noticed how we haven't seen no D's or undercovers tonight? Plus the block is flooded with fiends. The dope heads we know about, but why does it seem like we are the only ones in West Mass. with crack? What's up with the other spots?"

"So what's up? You want to shut down shop, or what?"

"Not yet, I got to check something out first. Yo, Jessito!" I shouted to the corner where he was sitting on his bike, talking to two chicks.

"What's up, Pharaoh?"

"Come here, yo."

I forgot to tell you about Jessito. He was like my little brother. His mother died in a car accident two summers ago. Jessito lived up by Holyoke High School in a nicer neighborhood with his father, Teddy, and his two sisters. Ever since his wife died, Teddy had to work double shifts to make ends meet. That was the reason he was never home, and gave way to Jessito straying into the streets.

I had taken a liking to the 17 year old kid. In a

lot of ways, he reminded me of myself. He was young, but light years ahead of his time. I treated him like my student and schooled him to the game.

"Take a ride around to the other spots and see what's up. See if their spots are jumping like ours."

"A'ight."

After sending Jessito on that little mission, I felt relaxed. I wanted to twist another blunt, but the fiends were coming too fast. Just when a break came, a brand new dragon flame colored E-Class Benz rolled up. Stopping in front of us, the passenger side window fell without a sound. I could hear the Isley Brother's smooth ballads blowing from the speakers.

"Youngblood," a deep voice called from inside the car.

His name was Artey the Gangsta. He didn't teach me about the coke game, instead, he always schooled me on life and leadership. Artey was a legend. He had put in so much work on these streets in his day that people still talked about it like it was yesterday. He and his crew did it all, from racketeering, extortion, gambling and robbin' banks. They even broke their man out of jail once. Even the Irish Mob didn't want to fuck with Artey.

"What up, Artey?" I said, walking over to the Benz. He got out and leaned against the hood. Even though he was 55 years old, Artey was still a fly muthafucka.

His dress code reminded me of that old show "Miami Vice."

He wore egg shell white Armani pants with a brown silk shirt. His red-bone skin tone made him look like he was from the Bahamas.

"How are you, Youngblood?"

"You know, trying to get this money."

"I can respect that. You finish the book I gave you?"

"Of course, Artey, I don't be bullshittin', yo."

"So tell me about Julius Caesar and why he was a great leader."

"Julius was that muthafuckin' dude, for real, because he took care of his soldiers. If they had to walk thirty miles, he'd get off his horse and walk it with them. When it came to war, he didn't play the back like a punk. Caesar was right on the front lines, putting in work. Julius was one of them, and they loved him for that, that made them go all that much harder for him."

"So what did you learn and how can you apply that to your crew?"

"Don't expect my crew to do anything I wouldn't do. Lead by example, not force."

A smile spread across Artey's face. "Youngblood, you'll be a king before you know it. Here, read this."

I took the book and looked at the front cover. "Genghis Khan?"

"Yeah, him and his sons were vicious muthafuckas, but there was a method to their madness."

"A'ight, who do you got in the car with you?"

Artey whistled and two young, bad shorties got out the back of the Benz.

"Meet the newest addition to my crew, Baby Dee and Pussycat."

"You're always doing it big, Artey."

"Show my Youngblood what you are working with."

Both, Baby Dee and Pussycat lifted their skirts

and pulled their thongs down to their knees.

"Damn!"

Artey was a beast when it came to the bitches. He had them doing things guys wished their girls would do.

"Yo, them some fat pussies."

"You want one for the night?"

"Nah, Artey, business before pleasure."

"That's my Youngblood, money over pussy."

We talked for a little bit longer before he bounced. That was when Joey walked up.

"You remember J-Dog?"

"From Central St., the one who pushed the blue Beamer with those fly ass rims?"

"Yeah," Joey replied.

"What about him?"

"Some Jamaican cats hit him up thirty times in front of his daughter."

"Where were they from?"

"I heard they were from New York."

"That's fucked up. Dudes don't give a fuck nowadays. It's kill or be killed. You know how it is, Joey. Life is fucked up."

"I know… but it feels like we're surrounded by death. Everywhere you look, death takes on a different form. This whole shit is depressing, son. Look around us. You have pregnant girls addicted to crack. 12 year old boys bringing guns to school. Mothers dying like flies because of cancer, and fathers being thrown in jail like it ain't nothing. Life isn't fucked up, our lives are fucked up. The only reason we are comfortable with it is because we're born into it, and if this is all we know, we accept it for what it is."

"So what are you gonna to do about it?"

"I don't know, but I do know I don't want to hustle forever."

"Nothing lasts forever, so don't worry about it."

I passed the blunt.

"I'm trying to bounce for real, yo. There's nothing here for me. The game is fucked up."

"Here we go with that 'I'm trying to bounce' shit again."

Every time me and Joey got into a conversation about the ghetto, he'd always bring up how he was going to leave it and the game. Joey would talk so much shit about the game that it would piss me off. It got to the point that I felt I had to defend it, like now.

"Yo, son, you steady talk shit about the hand that feeds you. How did you get all those fly ass clothes? Blood money, that's how! And still you talk shit. If you want to bounce so bad, bounce! Go head and get the fuck out of here, peace!"

"Trust me, kid, one of these days, I'm gonna be gone."

"Whatever, yo, I ain't trying to hear that shit."

And to tell you the truth, I really wasn't trying to hear that shit. Maybe it was because I didn't want to be left behind in this godforsaken place. It could've been that I didn't know any other life but this coke life. After a moment of uncomfortable silence, Joey finally spoke.

"You don't have a plan after all this?"

"After all of what?"

"After all this hustling shit. Come on, yo, you're the smartest one out of the crew. What, you plan to hustle forever?"

"I don't know maybe," I said somewhat childishly.

"Maybe? Hold up, didn't you just say nothing lasts forever?" he said.

"I did just say that, didn't I?"

"Yo, put it this way, I consider this hustling shit to be a chapter in my life, and at some point, it's got to end. Then I'll begin another chapter in my life. The next chapter in my life I'm going to write word for word."

"Hey, y'all got any crack or what?" A skinny white female called from the corner.

"I got it," Joey said, getting up to serve her.

Gradually, the flow of customers picked up again, and we were back at it. For ten minutes, there wasn't a word spoken between us. I don't know what he was thinking about, but I was deep in thought about my plans afterwards. It never dawned on me what I was going to do after hustling.

Hustling was all I knew. My whole life revolved around the coke game. If I had to compare my life to an animal, it would have to be the great white shark. We both were predators, but in different habitats. Sharks could smell blood from miles away. I could smell money miles away. They prey on the weaker fish. I prey on a person's weakness for crack. Most importantly, great white sharks must keep swimming to survive. Even when they are sleeping, they swim or they die. I felt like if I stopped hustling, I would die. The more I thought about it, the more I realized Joey was right, I needed a plan.

"Tell me about this plan of yours, yo."

"You serious?"

"Yeah, let me hear it. You may've found yourself

a partner."

I could see the excitement in his eyes as he mentally prepared his presentation, and Joey wasn't one to get excited.

"A'ight, check it, I want to move to South Beach, Miami and open a cafe slash restaurant."

"A cafe?"

"Yeah, a cafe right on the beach somewhere."

Joey went on to tell me about his idea. He broke everything down, from the construction costs, inventory, marketing and everything. I was impressed because it seemed he had done his homework.

But while Joey was talking about South Beach and his cafe, I heard, "Yo, Pharaoh! Pharaoh! Look." T-Money pointed over to the basketball court. "Isn't that Country and Daryl over there?"

Sure enough it was, and it looked like Daryl was about to beef with some dude in his face.

I told Daryl not to start no shit!

"Yo, T-Money, come on, let's go Joey!"

"Fuck you, punk muthafucka, you bitch ass nigga. What you tryna do?!" Daryl shouted.

"Yo, Daryl, fuck that. Stomp his ass!" Country instigated.

Before me, Joey and T-Money could reach the basketball court, Daryl hooked off on the dude, knocking him off his feet. After that, all hell broke loose. At least four of them jumped on Daryl. I pointed towards Daryl for T-Money and Joey to go help him. Country was balled up in the fetal position, getting stomped, when I reached him.

Nobody noticed me runnin' up, which gave me the advantage on the first kid. I caught him with all my might, sending him flying into a group of girls.

One of the three on Country tried to square up, but I caught him with two quick blows to the face. I pushed the other two guys off Country and pulled him to his feet. After that, it was a wrap. Me and Country started handling them like we were back in the school yard. Then all of a sudden, there were gunshots.

Chapter 2

"What the fuck! Chill the fuck out!" E-Love shoved and shouted his way through the crowd. "I said chill the fuck out!"

E-Love let off a couple more shots in the sky. He pulled his crew behind him until it was us on one side and them on the other.

"Yo, Pharaoh, this shit gots to stop, bro. This is the second time Country was over here starting shit. This shit gots to end tonight. If not there's going to be problems. I'm warning you, kid." E-Love cocked his gun for added effect.

I took a second before I answered because this shit could turn ugly quick. Artey taught me to never fear the gun, fear the person with the gun. Well, ever since I had known E-Love, he's been a pussy.

Then I said, "What? You think you're scaring somebody with that weak ass cap gun? You don't have the heart to shoot nobody."

"Kill nuthin' let nuthin' die, punk!" T-Money shouted over my shoulder.

"You ain't no killer for real, son. You just out here

faking for your crew. If I remember correctly, I think that's the first time I heard you buss that weak ass cap gun. What fuckin' kind of killer are you supposed to be anyway?" I said, getting all up in his face.

E-Love looked from side to side at his crew. The way I was talking shit to him, I knew he was going to try and save face. He pointed the gun at my forehead.

"You talk a lot of shit, Pharaoh. Maybe I should put a hole in that big ass head of yours. What do you think about that?"

Although I knew E-Love was a pussy, he still had a gun. And my heart pounded so hard, I thought I was gonna have a heart attack. Nobody else could tell because I appeared cooler than a fan on the outside. The ball was in my court, and I had to figure out how much of a pussy he really was. So I looked him in the eyes and saw that they were shifty. That chump was just as scared as I was.

"Yo, peep this pretty boy. I'm a Gorilla. My heart don't pump Kool-Aid. Go 'head and pull the trigger. I ain't Superman. You don't see a "S" on my chest. A bullet will kill me but the question is, do you have the heart to do it?"

"Now, that's a real muthafucka for that ass!" Daryl shouted.

"Shoot that piece of shit, E!"

Even though I knew he wasn't going to shoot, I still didn't like having the gun pointed at my face.

I said, "You don't want it with a Gorilla, you punk. You a pretty boy. Stick to fuckin' bitches. Pretty boys don't kill nuthin."

I turned and walked away, and I thought for sure he was going to blow the back of my head out. My heart was somewhere in my toes, hiding, while my legs felt rubbery. When we got back to our side of the park, my whole crew was amped.

"Gorilla soldiers, muthafuckas!" Daryl, T-Money and Country shouted back towards the basketball court.

"Pharaoh, that was some real gangsta shit you just did, yo! Everybody is gonna be talking about that shit." Daryl said putting me in a playful headlock.

After the urge to vomit subsided, I pushed Daryl off of me and snapped on him. "What the fuck is wrong with you!?"

"Huh? What are you talking about?"

"Didn't I tell you not to start no shit!? There's five of us and thirty of them. The only reason we got out on them was because they were drunk! This ain't a game. This shit is for real, yo! You got to get on point and stop the dumb shit."

"Relax, Pharaoh," Country said as he stepped between me and Daryl.

"Man, fuck that! That shit goes for you, too! Why are you over there two nights in a row, beefing? Them muthfuckas have nothing to do with us getting money!"

"Hold up, you talking like you're the boss or something!" Daryl said, taking a defensive tone towards me.

I knew he'd eventually bring that shit up again. Lately, we beefed on and off about who should be the shot caller for the crew. It was between me, Country and Daryl. There was no question in my mind that I should be boss. It was me that organized the Gorillas. Our coke connection came from my aunt's baby daddy, Dante. He fronted us our first ounce on the strength of me being his nephew. So with none of that, none of this would have been possible.

Daryl and Country couldn't see it that way. They wanted to become boss for all the wrong reasons. To them, it was about the fame that came with it and how many girls they'd be able to fuck.

Before I had the chance to respond to Daryl, Jessito rolled up on his bike.

"What did you find out?"

"Ain't nothing jumping. All the other spots looked like ghost towns. I saw Havie down on Pine St. He said there was a huge bust in New York. Here, he gave me this."

Jessito handed me a folded up piece of newspaper.

I unfolded it and the front page read…

50 Tons of Pure Coke seized on the docks in New York.

"That's why our spot is jumpin'," Joey said.

"That's not all. When I was coming back, I seen Crazy Eddie sitting in his yellow Caddy. He was with one other dude about a block away from here."

Soon as Jessito said the name Crazy Eddie, that unexplained feeling came again.

"You sure it was him?"

"I know what Crazy Eddie looks like, Country. Trust me, it was him without a doubt."

"Of course, he's going to be plotting on us. We're the only ones with work."

Joey looked at me for some type of response.

"Let's shut it down and finish what we got tomorrow."

"Hold up, who are you giving orders to, Pharaoh?"

"Not right now, Daryl. We don't have time for that shit."

"Man, fuck Crazy Eddie. I say we stay," Daryl insisted.

"Listen, I ain't staying out here with that crazy muthfucka. You must didn't hear what happened last week. Up on Walnut Street, on the corner with that burnt up building, some dudes were trying to open up a new spot. Crazy Eddie ran up on them the night they opened."

"I heard about that shit," T-Money cut in. "That was Niko from Limen Terrace. He saw Crazy Eddie coming and swallowed two eight balls. He thought he was slick and started popping shit to Eddie."

"What happened?" Jesstio asked.

"Crazy Eddie snatched Niko by the throat and drug him into an alley. Then he picked Niko up and pinned him against the wall with one hand. He pulled out some type of Rambo knife and stuck it in the bottom of Niko's throat and cut him all the way to his belly, then reached inside Niko's stomach while Niko was still alive and got the two eight balls. Then he just left him there to die."

There was no question in my mind whether I believed T-Money or not. Ever since we'd been hustling in Chestnut Park, we'd heard stories about Crazy Eddie. He was a young black drug dealer's nightmare. He drove a yellow '69 Caddy with no muffler or windows. It had a distinctive sound that could be heard from blocks away. When you heard it, it was your first and last warning he was around.

The first time I saw him, he looked like he could be Shaquille O'Neal's evil twin brother. He was dark as night with red eyes and yellow teeth. He had a scar from his right ear that went across his cheek and chin.

Then he had another scar that went from the top of his head down over his left eye to the top of his lip. I heard his chest was covered with bullet wounds.

Crazy Eddie only terrorized young crack dealers for crack. When he robbed dudes, he never took their money. It was useless because nobody sold him crack anyway. So far to date, I knew of 35 D-boys that he rocked to sleep. The Police didn't bother him because in their eyes he was doing their work for them. I knew, I wasn't trying to go out like that, so I decided to close shop.

"We're shutting down for the night."

"Hold the fuck up, yo!" Daryl shouted.

I didn't pay him any mind. When I turned to leave out the park, Daryl grabbed my shoulder and spun me around. Not thinking, I punched him in the face. He stumbled back a few steps, then charged and tackled me. This wasn't the first time we fought and it damn sure wouldn't be the last. Everybody was trying to break it up. Then, out of nowhere, Crazy Eddie snatched up Joey in a headlock.

"Where's the shit at?" he roared.

"Let him go!" I shouted, getting back to my feet.

T-Money charged him, but Crazy Eddie just batted him away like a fly. Daryl tried to tackle him. Eddie kicked him in the stomach, knocking the wind out of him. Joey's feet dangled at least two feet from the ground. His face turned beet red by the second. His eyes began rolling into the back of his head.

"I'll kill him! Give me the shit!"

Joey thrashed about and was slowly losing consciousness. No matter how many times we charged him,

Crazy Eddie managed to keep us off of him and he kept Joey suspended in the air in a choke hold. I could see the fear in Joey's eyes. They were exactly like my best friend Jo-Jo's before he died. I wasn't going to let death take another one of my friends. My heart raced like a thousand stallions. I wanted to do something, anything, but I couldn't. Crazy Eddie used Joey's body as a shield by swinging him back and forth. I got hit in the face by one of Joey's Timberland boots when I tried to charge in. When I fell back, I noticed one of the bricks were loose. Picking it up, I circled around to the back of him.

"Give me that shit!"

"He's foaming at the mouth!" T-Money shouted, pointing at Joey.

"Fuck! Let him go!" Country shouted, as he charged Eddie with all his might.

When Eddie turned to deal with Country, I got up on him and smacked him with the brick. His grip loosened around Joey's neck. Picking the brick up again, I smacked him on the other side of his head, this time twice as hard as the last time. At the same time, Daryl got close enough to give him a nut shot.

The crack head monster flung Joey like a rag doll into the cement table. Joey's head caught the edge of the table before he slumped to the ground.

"T-Money, Jessito, get Joey outta here!" I shouted, as I picked up the brick, I positioned myself to deliver another blow. Crazy Eddie was in a daze. Both of his hands were holding his head while blood leaked through the cracks of his fingers. I wanted to beat his brains in. I didn't want to stop until he was dead.

As I went to smack him again with the brick,

he caught my wrist and punched me in the face. Now mind you, I had boxed for four years, and never in my life had I been hit that hard. Last thing I remember was floating through the air and everything fading to black.

Chapter 3

When I awoke, I was lying in my bed. If it wasn't for the massive headache I had, I would've figured the whole thing was a dream.

"Pharaoh, you a'ight?" Jessito asked as he sat next to me in my Lazy Boy recliner.

"What the fuck happened?"

My head pounded as I tried to sit up.

"Man, crazy Eddie knocked you out."

"Tell me something I don't know."

"He bruised two of Daryl's ribs, T-Money fucked his wrist up, and Joey, oh… well."

"Well what, what happened to Joey?"

"He's at the Holyoke Hospital. He's in a coma, yo. Last I heard from Tutee, Joey wasn't looking too good."

"Shit, where's everybody at?"

"Home, I guess."

"What time is it?"

"2:34 p.m. You've been out all day."

"Call T-Money, tell him to go pick the fellas up and meet us downstairs out front."

"A'ight, yo."

Jessito got up and left the room, no sooner after he left, my grandma came in. I knew she was going to lecture me, so I got up and started putting on my Tim boots.

"Where do you think you're going, Suga?"

"To the hospital to see Joey, Grandma."

"Suga, you need to get some rest. You don't look so good. Was you out there fightin'?

"You can say that."

"Suga, look at me."

I didn't want to because she had a way of getting to me with her soft brown eyes.

"You know them streets are no good out there. Everything about them is bad, Suga. I thought after your Uncle Greg died, you'd realize and open your eyes. All them drugs, guns, and fast-ass girls are nuthin' but the devil's doings."

"Grandma, I'll be a'ight. I can take care of myself," I said, hoping to cut her lecture in half.

"I know, Suga. You remind me of your Daddy, so thick-headed."

As I finished tying my boots, my Grandma put her hand on my shoulder, and at the same time, I felt her looking into my soul.

"I just don't want to lose another one of my babies to those mean streets again."

I didn't reply. She patted me on my back, kissed the top of my head, and rose from the bed.

"You be safe out there, and tell Madee that I'm going to put Joey in my prayers, God bless his soul."

After she left, I felt bad for cutting her off. She had been there for me ever since my mother passed away. She had seen a lot in her 75 years on earth. Not all of it had been good, especially when you outlive two of your children. When my mother died, she took a piece of my grandmother with her. She hadn't been the same since.

Then, last summer, my Uncle Greg was stabbed to death over a girl. I could remember that night he came home and collapsed right in front of us, and died. That really did it; my grandma had to be hospitalized for six months for depression.

Now all she did was cook, clean and watch soaps. When she was doing none of that, you could find her in church. I often wondered why God would put someone through so much pain if he loved them so much.

"Yo, Pharaoh, everybody is waiting out front," Jessito said, standing at my bedroom door.

The ride to the hospital was a silent one. The only thing on my mind was Joey and the things we talked about that night. I was never the religious type. Shit, I was still mad at God for taking my mother, and when I caught up with him, he'd have a lot of explaining to do. Until then, I felt he was the only one who could help my man, so I prayed.

"God, if you hear me, I got to ask you something. I know we aren't really on speaking terms, but I don't know who else to turn to. You know Joey, the one that lives in the building next to mine? What am I thinking; of course you do, you're God. Well, he's one of the good guys, and right now, he needs you."

"Yo, Pharaoh, you coming in?" T-Money said, knocking on the car window.

"Yeah, give me a minute, son."

"Sorry about that, yo. Anyway, Joey has this plan

and I want to help him with it. The thing is I need him here to do it. So if you can look out for him and do what you do, I'd greatly appreciate it. Oh, tell my mother I said I love her, peace."

When the elevator doors opened on the fifth floor, my heart skipped a beat because I didn't know what to expect. That floor wasn't like the emergency room where all the chaos was at. It was quiet, almost a spooky quiet. Only thing that I heard were respirator machines and heart monitors.

I hated hospitals. I hated everything about them. The pale, white walls, bright florescent lights, the shiny floors, but most of all, I hated the smell. Upon reaching the nurses', desk, a cute Spanish chick looked up.

"He's in room 517. Visiting hours are over in 45 minutes, except for family."

"How do you know who I'm looking for?"

"Your friends came in five minutes ago and said there would be another one coming shortly."

"Is he awake?"

"No, I'm sorry. He's still in a coma."

"Thank you."

I stood in the entrance to Joey's room. I didn't know if I was prepared to see him like that. T-Money, Jessito, Daryl and Country were at the foot of the bed. Tutee and her mother, Madee, were on each side of the bed, holding Joey's hands.

Jessito spotted me first and motion for me to come in. Joey looked dead. He had all kinds of tubes and machines hooked to him. Madee noticed me and said something to Tutee in Spanish.

Tutee said she asked, "Who did this?"

"Crazy Eddie," I said softly.

"Why?"

"He was trying to rob us. We didn't see him coming. Everything happened so fast."

Tutee translated for Madee. Madee broke down crying. Then she started talking sadly. I didn't understand a word but it was full of emotion. Finally, Tutee translated.

"She said Joey wasn't supposed to be out there hustling. She said he wanted to move to South Beach and open up a cafe. My mother was happy he wanted to do something other than deal drugs like his father. The problem was he wasn't going to leave unless you came. You're like a brother to him. It will kill my mother if…"

"Joey's going to make it. Don't talk crazy like that."

Madee started speaking Spanish again. This time, there was a lot of anger in her tone, and I wondered if it was directed at me.

"What did she say?"

"She said the insurance company will not cover Joey's stay here. They want to send Joey to one of those cheap coma care units ran by the state. She doesn't want Joey to go, because she knows he'll die there. Everybody in a coma that goes to that place dies. In order for him to stay here the hospital needs $50,000 in two weeks. If they don't get it they'll move him to the state coma care."

"Tell your mother we'll get the money."

Everybody looked at me like I was crazy. I took one last look at Joey and burned the image of him in my head.

"Don't worry, kid, we'll get the money."

Chapter 4

I had T-Money drop me off on Northampton Street at Dante's crib. I told everybody to meet at the top of my building at 8 O'clock that night.

Dante was my Aunt Joanne's baby Daddy. He was originally from Chicago but moved to Massachusetts after killing two cops... (so he says.) Him and my aunt had two young girls together and separated a few years ago. My Aunt Jo lived on Dwight Street in a brand new townhouse with the girls. Dante had his own apartment on Northampton Street. Dante came up big when crack first hit Holyoke. He was one of the first crack dealers who made a fortune fast. He bought a lot of real estate throughout Holyoke, including the building he lived in. Nowadays, all he sold was cookable cocaine.

The benefit of dealing with Dante was that he got his coke straight from Mexico. That meant we weren't affected by the cocaine climate in New York. So when the coke drought happened, like now, we would be the only ones with coke in West Mass. Besides dealing with him on the coke tip, I couldn't stand him. Just because he had money, he thought he could talk to you any kinda way. Another reason I couldn't stand him was because he liked to beat on my aunt.

Buzzzzzzzzzzz!

"Who is it?" A squeaky voice crackled over the intercom.

"Pharaoh."

"I'm busy, boy, go away."

"It's serious, yo. I got to talk to you."

"It better be negro!"

The door buzzed and clicked.

He let me in the bottom door. Then I had to climb seven flights of stairs because the elevator was broke. Even though the piece of shit knew I was coming, he still wanted me to knock.

"Who is it?"

"It's me, yo, damn."

Dante took forever unlocking the door. It seemed like he had a thousand bolts and chain locks. Finally, tall, lanky, Dante stuck his head out.

"Ain't nobody with you?"

"No, I'm by myself."

"Hurry up and come in."

Dante had been acting funny the last six months. I think he started using his own shit. He always snorted coke here and there, but now he was starting to look like one of my customers back at Chestnut Park.

One thing for sure, Dante's crib was laced the fuck out. He really knew how to put the shit together. Everything was mahogany with gold trim and smoked glass. On one side of the apartment was an antique, tournament-size pool table. In the middle of the room sat a crescent moon-shaped Corinthian leather sofa with matching love seat and Lazy Boys.

Dante wore a silk robe with a Chinese dragon embroidered on the back. His shiny, permed, black hair draped recklessly over his shoulders. I always thought he was on some fag shit, but Country said it was a Chicago thing.

Dante sat in the middle of his sofa like he was a king. I sat directly across from him in the love seat.

"Bless, bring me a drink and a cigar."

Now this was always the best part of my visit to Dante's. Out of the backroom came a fine, caramel colored Bless. Her straight black hair cascaded to the small of her back. She wore a white wife beater tank top that exposed her toned stomach and a pair of boy shorts. She looked like she was mixed with something, but one thing for sure you could tell she had black in her somewhere.

Bless wasn't Dante's girl, so to speak. You could say she sort of worked for him. He found her in the women's shelter and took her in. On occasion, she delivered coke to the block or picked money up for Dante. I'd spit mad game at her, but I could tell she wasn't feeling me. She didn't take me seriously. The one thing that attracted me to her even more than her looks was her loyalty to Dante. Even though he treated her like shit, she never crossed him. A thorough chick was an aphrodisiac to me. Bless would be the perfect one to run my all bitch squad I had been dreaming of. I just had to get her away from this clown.

"Light me one of those Don Tomas cigars."

"What do you want to drink?" Bless asked.

"Pour me a glass of that Chateau Pessac Leognan."

"You want a glass, Pharaoh?" Bless asked.

"Nah, I'm cool, Shorty."

Bless walked past and handed Dante his cigar and his drink. She gave me a perfect shot of her ass as she bent over.

"Get them bitches out here to suck me and my nephew off while we talk business."

Bless disappeared into the back and a minute later two white females came out, completely naked. They both looked barely 18 years old. The female that kneeled in front of me had to be Irish. I admired her tight frame and perky red nipples that sat upon a mouthful of flesh.

She wasted no time in undoing my pants. Looking over at Dante, I saw that his girl's head was already bobbing. That made my dick that much harder to pull out.

"You need some help with that?" I asked.

She smiled.

"Speak. You have until I buss in this bitch's mouth."

"Joey's in the hospital."

"So what does that have to do with me?"

"Nothing, but he's in a coma. Late last night, Crazy Eddie ran up on us and caught us slippin."

"Crazy Eddie. Nobody killed that crazy muthafucka yet?"

"Nah, not yet."

"So what the fuck you want from me?"

"I need a piece."

"You mean to tell me you finally grew some nuts?

Negro, please! You don't have the heart to kill nuthin', punk! I bet your dumb ass think once you pull the trigga, it's over. It isn't that easy, punk!" Dante threw his head back and let out a loud, fake laugh. Then he took a drag from his cigar and blew the smoke in my direction. "Have you killed anything before, a dog, a cat or even a cockroach?"

I didn't bother to answer because I knew he just wanted to hear himself speak.

"You have to be able to deal with demons afterwards, punk. The look in a man's eyes is the scariest thing you'll see before you kill him. Your mind will take a picture that will never go away. You'll see those eyes in your sleep. When you're fuckin' them young bitches. You'll even see them when you look in your kid's eyes years from now. You can't escape the eyes, Pharaoh… you can't escape the eyes. Some people are haunted by the people they murdered. Those are the demons you have to live with. Do you think you can live with the demons?"

Dante's voice became low and deep as if he was trying to scare me like a little kid.

"Listen, Dante, I don't know about all that, demon shit, and, truthfully, I don't give a fuck about it. All I know is my man is in a coma. I'm going to do what I got to do, with or without your help."

"Who the fuck are you talking to like that, punk? I taught you everything you know! Without me, you'd be just another poor Negro running around in them streets!" Dante pointed out the window. "So don't come in here talking all that fly shit. You ain't no gangsta."

Before, when Dante would scream on me, I'd get

scared. Now, I didn't pay him no attention. When he was teaching me the game, he was like a god to me. I overlooked him beating my Aunt, telling myself that she might have deserved it.

Things have changed, and I became more mature in my ways. The student had become the teacher, and the lessons were over.

The girl between my legs began deep throatin' the best she could. Every once in a while, she'd gag, and would have to catch her breath. The shit started feeling so good that I grabbed the back of her head and pushed her down on my dick."

"Pharaoh… You listenin', punk?"

"What?"

He repeated himself. "I said did you get the money up for the two birds?"

"Yeah, but I'm not buying shit from you until we deal with Crazy Eddie."

Dante paused for a second. I knew that got his attention.

"When you're done with that bitch, go look in the back room on the left. On the top shelf in the closet, grab the SIG-9 and the extra clip. That's going to be an additional $500, punk. When are you coming through with the money?"

"Tonight, after I handle my business."

"Cool, well, in that case, enjoy. I'm going to fuck this slut in her ass. When you're done, see yourself the fuck out, punk."

Dante got up and left. His white chick followed close behind him like a puppy. With him gone, I was able to focus on the chick sucking my dick. She relentlessly pumped my dick in her mouth bringing me closer to my nut.

"When I cum, I want you to look me in the eyes, okay?"

She nodded yes.

"A'ight, yo, here it comes."

She fixed her money green eyes on my brown eyes.

"Now, suck, no, no, just suck it. Don't jerk it and don't move your head. Just suck it like a straw in a milkshake. Yeah, like that, that's it, get all of it."

When she was done, she said, "I never done it like that before."

"You liked that, didn't you?"

"Yes, it was different," she said, shyly with a smile.

Bless emerged from the darkness of the hallway and said, "Dante wants you in the back, Colleen."

"Bye, Pharaoh."

"Peace."

I got up to retrieve the gun from the closet. The hallway was filled with howls of pain. Dante was still working the other girl when I passed his room. I stared for a second or two before continuing to the last room on the left.

When I first grabbed the gun, it was cold and heavy. It had an evil beauty to it I liked. Reaching up on the shelf for the extra clip, it managed to slip through my fingers and fall on top of two duffle bags. Both of them were unzipped. One bag had at least 25 kilos of coke. The other was filled with bricks of money wrapped inside plastic. On top was a tiny piece of paper with $300,000 written on it.

Butterflies fluttered inside my stomach and the urge to piss came over me. All my problems would have been solved. Everything I needed was right there in front of me. Coke for the block, money for Joey, and a gun for Crazy Eddie. Only thing that stopped me from taking it was a little voice in my head telling me not to. After staring at the bags for another minute or two, I suddenly felt somebody standing behind me.

"That's a lot of shit, isn't it?"

"It's enough."

"To tell you the truth, I wouldn't know what to do with all of it."

"I doubt that, Bless."

I tucked the SIG-9 in my waist and slid the extra clip in my back pocket. Since Dante was busy with those two chicks, I figured I'd shoot at Bless one more time.

"Yo, check this out."

"What?"

"What do you see in that clown Dante?"

"Nothing, really."

"Yeah, then why are you so loyal to him?"

"I was raised to be loyal to the man that takes care of me. Dante was the one that got me out of the shelter, fed me, clothed me, and gave me a roof over my head."

"But he treats you like shit."

"I know plenty of girls who would love to be in my position," she said, leaning against the door. "You have no idea how hard it is for a young girl on these streets. It is a lot harder than it is for you guys. The abuse is worth the security."

"Yeah, well, I can understand that to a certain extent. I can't imagine how hard it is for y'all girls, but at some point, you got to look to the future. Is this all you want to be?"

"What do you mean?"

"You know exactly what I mean. Is this all you want to do, be Dante's live in pussy?"

"Why, do you got a better idea?"

"Yeah, in fact I do."

"I'm all ears."

"Unlike this dude, I see a whole lot more in you."

"Yeah, tell me what you see in me."

"Thoroughness for starters. You're a real bitch, and you know how to carry yourself. Then there's that loyalty thing you have. That's priceless in this game."

"Is that all you see in me?"

I paused for a second and looked Bless in her eyes. In that second, I realized what I was doing wrong. She had told me what I needed to know to get at her. Her thing was security. Plus, the fact she was in a shelter let me know she didn't have nobody in her life, especially a father figure. That was what Dante was to her. So what I mistook for loyalty was really a love a daughter would have for her father. In order to bag her, I had to become that figure for her.

I thanked Artey with a smile for all those psychology books he gave me to read on women.

"Look, yo, I'll be back at 12 tonight."

Bless rolled her eyes. "So?"

And before she could unroll them, I smacked the shit out of her. That was all it took. In that instant, she became submissive, childlike, as she stared at the floor while holding her cheek.

"You don't get it now, bitch." Her whole demeanor confirmed what I thought. "You belong to me. I own you now, bitch, and like I said, I'll be back at 12 tonight, so pack your shit."

"Wha… what about Dante?" she whined.

I showed her the gun. "I'll deal with him," then I grabbed her chin. "You just be ready."

Chapter 5

I caught a cab to Daryl's; up on the north end of Chestnut St. Around his way, buildings were either burnt up or abandoned. Dumpsters overflowed with trash. Pothole ridden streets and decrepit apartment buildings painted a perfect picture of poverty. Country lived in the same building as Daryl, but on the second floor. I figured I'd go see Daryl first, then drop by Country's afterwards.

I knocked on the door.

"Who is it?"

"Pharaoh."

"What do you want?"

"Let me holla at you a second."

Daryl opened the door and walked away. I waited a second before I pushed it open. Daryl sat on the sofa and picked up the PlayStation controller.

"We need to talk, yo. Shit is getting out of hand between us."

I took a seat on the Lazy Boy.

"Talk."

I could tell that he still felt some type of way

about me punching him in the face.

"What's happening with us? It's like we are spinning out of control. We don't agree on nothing anymore. We stay at each other's throats like pit bulls. That's not us, kid. We are bigger than that."

"You don't act like it. You call the shots like you're the boss. Everything is about you. Like you're so muthafuckin' special."

"Is that how you feel?"

Daryl paused the game to look me in the eyes.

"Yeah, that's how the fuck I feel."

He unpaused the game.

"Is that it?"

"No, it ain't, muthafucka. All that shit Artey feed you about being the next King of West Mass. has gone to your head. You need to come back to earth and realize that you didn't do it alone."

"I know that."

"Then act like it."

Daryl took a swig of a long neck Icehouse. There was a moment of uncomfortable silence. I watched as he played "N.B.A Live" for a couple of minutes. He must've had all this shit built up in him for a while. That was why I gave him a couple of minutes to cool down.

"Yo, shit is about to get serious, Daryl."

"What do you mean serious?"

I pulled out the gun and handed it to him.

"Is this why you went to Dante's?"

"Yeah, plus I got my dick sucked by some white chick."

"Dante still be on that wannabe pimp shit, huh?"

"Yeah, anyway, yo, like I said, it's about to get serious and I need my number one man with me. I can't go at this alone. Plus, it wouldn't feel right without you with me. By the way, if it means anything, my bad for that."

"Yo, forget about it. You hit like a bitch, anyway."

"It's 7 o'clock now. I'm gonna holla at Country. I'll see you at eight."

"A'ight son, I'll be there."

I gave Daryl some dap and left feeling a little bit better.

On the way down the stairs, I saw Cindy. She was a notorious crack head, known for stealing everything under the sun. Cindy was thin as a board, pale and ugly as sin. Her teeth were yellow and brown, and her breath smelled like hot garbage.

She saw me and said, "Hey, there's my baby. Got any candy for Cindy?"

"No."

"Come on, I know you got something for me. You know I like suckin' big, black cocks."

"Bitch, I wouldn't stick my worst enemy's dick in your mouth."

"Hey, you don't have to be mean about it."

What puzzled me was, what the fuck was Cindy doing coming out of Country's crib? When I looked up, I saw Darlene, Country's mother, standing in the doorway. Ayo, Darlene was bad as a muthafucka, for real. She had short, wavy hair like Jada Pinkett had back in the day. Her smooth, ebony complexion was free of scars or blemishes.

Darlene used to be in the army, and retained a nice physique. Her bedroom was next to Country's bedroom. When we were 13, we knocked two nice size holes in to the closet walls. On the other side was a perfect shot of Darlene's bed. She'd bring a different guy home every night. Me and Country would sit up all night and watch his mother get the shit fucked out of her.

I remember one night she came home with two guys. Country was knocked out.

Darlene was like an animal. These dudes had her doing all kinds of wild shit. They pissed on her, had her barking like a dog, they slapped her around, and fucked the shit out of her every way possible. I can still picture her voluptuous titties swinging back and forth. I must've beat my dick a thousand times that night.

I think it was because of that shit I became freaked out. Seeing Darlene so open made me realize that there was more to it than just fuckin' a bitch.

I walked up to her and said, "Is Country home, Darlene?"

I didn't even give her eye contact. My eyes were stuck on her thick ass nipples pushing through her thin t-shirt. It seems the older I got the bolder I got when it came to Darlene. Whenever Country wasn't around I was throwing subtle hints at Darlene. A few times I'd play stupid and walk in the bathroom while she was just getting out the shower. Yeah, I know doing that shit to my man's mom was crazy but fuck it. I wanted to put that dick in her something serious.

"He's upstairs in the shower." she replied in her sexy southern accent.

I don't know if it was me, but I swear she intentionally brushed her tits against my arm when I passed her.

"Hey, Pharaoh, you have anything?"
"What… weed?"
"No, the other stuff."
"Crack?"
"Yeah."
"What do you need crack for, Darlene?"
"Cindy got me a whole bunch of stuff from Lord & Taylor and she don't want money for it."
"Why don't you ask Country?"
"I don't want him to know. You know how he can get sometimes."

I always kept an eight ball on me, because around my way, crack was currency.

"Here, I only have an eight ball."

After that, I went up to Country's room.

"Yo, Country!"

"I'm in the shower. Give me a minute!"

Country's room was always the same, smelly and messy. The walls were covered with old karate posters and holes. Clothes were thrown everywhere, leaving nowhere to sit. Buried under some sweaters was a picture of us when we were 13. In those days, life was so much simpler.

"How much did he give you?" I heard Cindy's voice, coming through the wall from Darlene's room.

"A whole eight ball, girl."

"What do you have to give him back?"

"Nothing, Pharaoh's like a son to me."

"Well, the way your son was looking at your tits, it looked like your son had incest heavy on his mind."

I peeked through the holes in the closet and saw Darlene and Cindy.

"He's always doing that."

Darlene opened the bag of crack I gave her.

"Well, you better milk him while you can. Those jugs should be good for another two or three free eight balls. Then you're going to have to give up that punnany."

"Girl, you crazy."

"Trust me, I know how it goes. It's all good in the beginning, but things get ugly quick. But with that body of yours, we can get all the crack we want. You just got to be willing to suck and fuck when the time comes."

"We'll deal with that when the times comes. Now, break me off a big chunk. I'm trying to blast off for real."

My jaw hit the floor watching Darlene suck the crack smoke out of the can. I wrestled with the thought of telling Country. Then I realized that was my chance to fuck her. The thought alone had my dick hard. Country opened the door to his bathroom while I closed the door to his closet. He was going to have to find out about his mom on his own. Hopefully, after I fucked her.

"I thought the meeting was at 8 o'clock?" Country said as he walked into the room, drying off his face.

"It is still."

"So what's up?"

"I was downstairs at Daryl's crib."

"Yeah, what happened?"

"We squashed the beef."

"That's cool, yo."

"Yeah, for now."

"What do you mean for now?"

"I know this shit is gonna come up again. The Gorillas need a leader, plain and simple. Nobody wants to take sides, so a vote is out."

"I take it you think you should be the leader?"

"Without question. I'm built for this shit."

"Maybe that's your ego talking."

"My ego?"

"Pharaoh, you got the biggest ego I've ever seen. You got to admit you really think you're the shit, don't you? Plus, not to mention all the shit Artey be putting into your head. You got to remember that we're all in this together, right?"

"For sure."

"Then you need to come back to earth, kid."

"Yeah, whatever. Daryl said the same shit. Anyway, you remember when we took this?" I handed him the picture.

"Where did you find that?"

"In one of your thousand piles of clothes."

"Oh, shit, that was the day we both lost our virginity to Wilder beast."

"She was so fat and ugly, yo."

"Remember you thought you were fucking her pussy, but it was really one of her rolls?"

We both broke out laughing.

"Ayo, I busted and everything."

Again we broke out laughing, this time with tears rolling down our faces. He was on the bed, and I was on the floor, trying to catch my breath. It felt good to laugh like that, it had been a while.

When things calmed down, I said, "To answer your question on why I should be a leader, I have big plans for us. When I get done with the Gorillas, they'll compare us to the Freemasons, and that's on some real shit, kid. But, anyway I'm out. See ya at 8 o'clock."

"A'ight Pharaoh."

I turned around at the door and said, "One more thing, yo."

"What's up Pharaoh?"

"Name a King that didn't have an ego."

He couldn't think of one.

"That's what I thought. You have to have a big ego to be a king. It's part of the job description."

Chapter 6

I left Country's crib and headed up Pine St. on foot. It was a nice night out, plus I didn't mind walking.

"Youngblood." I turned to see Artey's 1960 Cognac colored Cadillac Eldorado with the gangsta white walls and a klan white ragtop creep up on me.

The passenger door opened. "Need a ride?"

"Sure."

I climbed in the back seat with Artey. Diamond was driving and Pussycat sat in the front seat.

"I heard what went down with Crazy Eddie. How's your boy Joey doing?"

"He's in a coma."

"So what are you going to do about it?"

I flashed him the gun.

"Are you sure you want to take it to that level?"

"I got no choice, Artey. I'll feel like a piece of shit for the rest of my life, if I don't do anything about it."

Artey pulled out one of his cigars and lit it. He took a couple slow drags and blew the smoke out the window.

"You know there is no going back after you pull the trigger, Youngblood."

"Yeah, I know. Dante gave me the same speech earlier. The truth is, I'm not trying to look back. Besides, there's nothing to look back to."

"So you made up your mind already?"

"A while ago."

"Look at my Youngblood, he's about to catch his first body. You make an old gangsta proud." Artey cracked a smile.

"Hey Artey, I got a problem."

"Shoot."

"Daryl and Country also want to be the leader of the Gorillas. Me, and Daryl beefed about it yesterday in the park. It got so crazy it came to blows between us."

"I told you I never liked Country. He looks like he's holding too much inside. You can't trust a man that can't deal with his own problems. Daryl's too much of a knuckle head to lead anything."

"So what do I do?"

"I could tell you what to do and your problems would be solved. What happens when I'm not around, Youngblood? What will you do then?"

"I'd have to figure it out on my own."

"So pretend I'm gone, so you can figure it out on your own."

"Man, I knew you were going to say some shit like that."

Artey smiled and rubbed the back of my head like a father did a son.

"Youngblood, don't worry, your life has been written already. Just sit back and enjoy the ride."

"So you already know how this is going to play out?"

"Pretty much, Youngblood, pretty much."

We drove around the ghettos of Holyoke. He told

me the story about how he caught his first body and how it felt to kill. He also schooled me on the best way to get rid of the gun and the body if need be. After all that, he dropped me off at my building.

"Youngblood."

"What's up?"

"A man becomes a man from all the things he goes through."

I didn't reply I just nodded and left.

In the darkness of my bedroom, I lay in my bed, staring at the stucco ceiling. Random thoughts flashed in and out of my head. The one that had me feeling sick was killing Crazy Eddie. It was easier to say you'd kill somebody because those were just words. They meant as much as you wanted them to. Now, to actually do it was a different story.

The more I thought about killing Crazy Eddie, the more excuses I made not to. Then the images of Joey flashed in my head. They were of all the good times growing up. Going to parties, talking to bitches, drinking on the rooftop, or just plain chillin' out, doing nothing. The last thought was of him lying in the hospital bed, hooked to all the tubes and machines.

It was then I realized that no matter how scared I was, Eddie had to die. There was no way around it. The unwritten laws of the streets called for it. It was something you accepted and embraced while living it. After that night, I knew things wouldn't be the same for me.

Chapter 7

When 8:00 p.m. finally came, I slowly made my way up the fire escape to the rooftop. The whole crew was there, waiting for me. I walked over to the edge of the building and gazed down at the park.

"Ayo, Gorillas, we're here for two reasons. First, our man Joey is in coma, fighting for his life and the muthafucka that did it is still out there. Something got to be done about it."

Everybody nodded in agreement.

"When I went to Dante's earlier, I got this."

I pulled out the Sig-9mm and passed it around. We all had seen guns before, but none of us had fired one.

"If we don't handle Crazy Eddie, nobody will take us serious. If nobody takes us serious, there is no reason for us to be out here. We'll just be in the way. Besides more important than that, we'd be letting our muthafuckin' man Joey, down. So Crazy Eddie got to go tonight."

"What's the second reason we're up here?" Daryl cut in.

"To choose a leader," I replied.

Artey was right; I did figure it out on my own. It came out of nowhere.

"Since nobody wants to take sides, I came up with a way to solve our problem. Whoever kills Crazy Eddie is the boss."

"You're serious, Pharaoh?"

"Does it look like I'm joking, T-Money?"

I placed the gun on the ground in front of everyone. Everybody just stared at it. I knew the idea would catch them off guard. If I was destined to be the King of the Gorillas, it didn't matter what I did, right?

"Like I said, whoever picks up the gun is boss. That means that his word is final. What he says goes. No arguments. Everybody agrees?"

"No doubt." T-Money said.

"A'ight." Jessito replied.

"Yeah, I'm with that." Country said.

"It's whatever with me," Daryl hissed.

There was a minute or two of silence before T-Money said, "I'm going to keep it real. I'm not cut out to be a leader. I'm more of a team player, yo."

"Me, too," Jessito said.

Both of them took a couple of steps back from the gun. It was only me, Daryl and Country. My heart pounded with anticipation from what was going to happen next.

Another few seconds passed before Country threw his hands up in surrender.

"This is too much for me," he said and took a step back.

"Well, it is on you, Daryl. Here's your chance. You

won't hear shit out of me. You want to be the boss, pick the gun up and kill Crazy Eddie."

And he did. To tell you the truth, I had mixed feelings about him picking up the gun. A part of me was relieved because I wasn't sure if I could kill Crazy Eddie. The other part of me was like, now I got to listen to this dude. Fuck it, he picked up the gun, he was the boss. So much for destiny.

"Here, Pharaoh, take it, yo."

"What?"

"Take it. I don't know if I'm ready to cross that line, yo. I'll beat a muthafucka's ass, but killin' someone is a different ballgame so here, I guess you are the boss."

It was official. I was the King of the Gorillas.

"What's the plan, Pharaoh?" Jessito asked, giving me dap.

"I want you to scout for the police, D's and jump outs. Country, Daryl and T-Money, open up shop. New York is still fucked up on coke, so our spot should be the only spot jumpin' again tonight. Plus, since we're the only ones with coke, Eddie should be paying us another visit. This time, we'll have something for him." I cocked the gun.

Everybody gave me dap and a thug hug and left. I stayed on the roof because there was one more person I had to talk to.

I looked up and said, "Ayo, God, you up there? It's me again. I guess it would be kinda crazy to ask you for the strength to kill one of your children. But for real, he got to go. I hope this don't put me on your bad side. If so, oh well, you're up there, and I'm down here. It's not like I really give a fuck what you think. All that "turn the other cheek" shit don't work down here. The same rules as the jungle apply to the streets. Kill or be killed. All I'm saying is, whatever I do, don't take it out on Joey. That would be some sucka ass shit if you did."

Chestnut Park slowly came alive. The alleyways that led to and from it began to pulse once again. In the air, the smell of fried pork and rice gave the night its scent, while the sound of salsa gave the night its rhythm.

The front stoops, like always, were packed with old, gossiping ladies. No doubt I was going to give them something to talk about for sure after tonight. While T-Money, Country and Daryl were serving the fiends, I chained smoked blunt after blunt.

"Yo, Country, I think Pharaoh is nervous. Look at him," I heard Daryl say.

"Wouldn't you be, yo?"

"Fuck, yeah, yo. I couldn't do it. I'm going to go check on him."

"Chill, Daryl, let him get his mind right."

There was no question I was nervous. My stomach bubbled, my head throbbed, and my heart pounded like a bass drum. Every car with a fucked up muffler had my head turning. And even though I was outside, I still felt like I needed air.

"Yo, fellas, I'm going to take a quick walk. I'll be right back."

Feeling thirsty, I headed up the street to the corner store on Walnut Street.

"Hey, Pharaoh!' A voice called from behind me. I turned to see Cindy pulling up in the back of a cab.

"What the fuck you want?"

"Darlene has been calling you for the last hour."

"My phone is off. Why is she calling me anyway?"

"Uh… I don't know, but it is important."

"Why didn't she call Country if it was so important?"

"I don't know. She just sent me to find you, come on, get in."

Without a second thought, I jumped in the cab. Not because Cindy said so, but because I wanted to get as far away from Chestnut Park as possible.

Pulling up to Darlene's, Cindy jumped out and ran behind the liquor store.

"Wait for me here," I said, handing the cab driver a $50.00 bill.

I climbed the stairs in the dark hallway, and again, Darlene was standing in her doorway.

"What the fuck are you doing sending this bitch, Cindy looking for me?"

My voice was a little more aggressive then she was used to hearing, and I saw that it made her nervous.

"I… I… come in… let me talk to you."

I walked in, closed the door and leaned against it. Darlene was high as a kite, off crack. Her eyes were glossed and dilated. She grinded her teeth together, a typical crack head trait. It was a damn shame to see her like that. But my dick was hard as a muthfucka.

"A… ah, Pharaoh, ummmmm do you have anything?"

"Have what, crack?"

"Yes… um, do you… you?"

"Why, do you still owe Cindy?"

"Yeah," she said, fidgeting with her hands.

"Oh yeah, well let me see what she got you, Darlene."

"…It's not here."

"Why did I have a feeling you were going to say that? I tell you what. I only have an eight ball. Will that be enough?"

Darlene's eyes widened while sweat beaded across her forehead.

"Yes, that should do," she said, trying to clench her butt cheeks together to prevent from farting again. "Yes, tha… that… should do."

I slowly took a step towards her. At the same time, I dangled the eight ball between my fingers. "Is this what you want?"

She didn't say anything.

"How long have you been smoking?"

"I… I… don't smoke."

I continued towards her.

"Cindy is the one that got you fucked up on this shit, isn't she?" I closed the space between us. "Yo, Country is going to flip when he finds out his mother is a crack head."

"I don't know what you are talking about."

"Bitch, cut the bullshit."

Darlene jumped after my sudden outburst and backed herself into the wall. I took my jacket off and tossed it on the back of the sofa.

"Please don't tell Country, Pharaoh."

I didn't say anything, but now we were face to face. Darlene's supple breasts heaved up and down as she took deep breaths. The guilt inside her wouldn't let her look me in the face.

Again, in a softer voice, she said, "Please don't tell Country, please."

I slid the eight ball into the pocket of her miniskirt and said, "I won't tell if you won't tell.

"Tell what?" Darlene got up enough nerve to look me in the eyes.

"This!"

I grabbed her t-shirt with both hands and tore it in half, exposing her huge ass tits. She let out a loud shriek and tried to fight me off. I grabbed her by the throat and backhanded her across the face. When she calmed down, I pinned her against the wall, by her throat.

"Listen, bitch, I'm going to tell you how this works. You want to smoke my crack, cool. I'll give you all the crack you want. But, this pussy belongs to me, yo. Do you understand?"

"Yes," she whispered.

I started sucking on her black, thick nipples real hard on purpose. At the same time I lifted her skirt over her fat ass, and began squeezing both her ass cheeks. I worked my hand into her panties and started playing with her pussy. It wasn't long before that shit was sloppy wet and I had four fingers up in her. This was some unreal shit. I was having my way with my best friend's mom.

I betcha you called me a piece of shit. On the real, I'm not trying to hear that shit. If you had a chance to fuck your friend's mom and she was bad as Darlene, you'd fuck the shit out of her too.

The more I played with her pussy, the more relaxed she got. Her hands found their way to my zipper. She wrestled with it for a second before she got it down. After that, she started jerking my dick and massaging it at the same time.

"Bend that ass over the table, bitch," I said, smacking her ass.

Instead of pulling her panties down, I snatched them off in one motion.

"Ahhhhhhh!" Darlene moaned.

"Spread your legs!"

Darlene's back shot was off the hook. At 42, she had the body of a twenty five year old. She propped herself up on her elbows and arched her ass up to me.

"That's it, that's what I like."

My dick slipped right between her wet pussy folds with ease. Grabbing her waist, I started ramming her as hard as I could.

"FLOP! FLOP! FLOP! FLOP! FLOP! FLOP!'

"Ahhhhhhhh! Ahhhhhhhh! OOOOOOOOh! Shiiiiiit!

Plates, glasses and newspapers crashed to the floor. I thought the table was going to collapse under us. The more I fucked Darlene, the less I saw her as Country's mother and more like a crack whore. After all, that was what she would become.

I smacked her ass harder, pulled her hair and pinched her nipples. When I put my fingers in her ass, it triggered her orgasm, and her milky white cream coated my dick.

"Ummmmmm, ahhhhhhh, fuuccck!" Darlene howled.

"It's about time you put this dick in your mouth."

Darlene went to turn around.

"No, hold up. I'm gonna dip it in some chocolate first."

I pulled out of her pussy, and forced it up her ass, and pumped it five times. Then I pulled out and allowed her to drop to her knees.

"Now you can suck this dick."

Darlene went to work suckin', squeezin', and jerking my dick. When I finally came, Darlene swallowed half of my nut and jerked the other half all over her face.

"Damn, Pharaoh, if I knew your dick was like this, I would've gave you some pussy a while ago."

"Yeah, you suck a mean dick, bitch, no bullshit."

I was even getting off talking to her all crazy.

Looking down at her cum smeared lips, ripped t-shirt and skirt above her waist, I thought to myself, I'd definitely be fuckin' her again.

"So is my secret safe with you?"

"Don't sweat it. If you need something, just call me. I don't want to hear about you fuckin' all these niggas out here for crack."

"Sure, baby," she said too nonchalantly.

I snatched her by the throat. "Bitch, look at me when I talk to you! That's my pussy. Now, say it!"

"This pussy is yours." Darlene said nervously. Then she leaned over and tried to kiss me.

I slapped the shit out of her.

"I don't kiss crack heads, you stupid bitch! If you're going to kiss anything, it's going to be this dick."

I pulled my dick out, and Darlene hunched over and kissed my dick several times. When she was done, I stood up and slapped her in the face with it a few times, just because I could.

Exactly 15 minutes had passed when I got back in the cab. On the ride back to Chestnut Park, running through my head was, I just dogged the shit out of Country's mother!

Chapter 8

"Yo, where you been?" T-Money said, walking up to the cab.

"I had to relieve some stress."

"You good?"

"Yeah , I'm good."

"Pharaoh, I seen a couple of undercovers over by Steffinelli's. Then I saw two patrol cars, but that was it," Jessito said.

"Did you see Crazy Eddie?

"I seen his car over there on Appleton Street, but he wasn't in it."

Sitting back on the bench, smoking another blunt, I thought about Joey. I recalled all the conversations we had before the coma. For some reason, the things he said now made sense. It felt like I was looking at the park through his eyes.

A person who had never been to the ghetto would think this place was hell. So why were we all right with it? I think Joey said it best: "We accept it because we don't know no other way."

A couple of hours had passed, and the park was

in full swing again, like the day before, we were flooded with fiends. Nobody really said anything, and for real, there was nothing to talk about. I sat and watched fiend after fiend come and go. I shook my head in disappointment because soon Darlene would be like them.

"Hey, Pharaoh, what do you got for your Uncle Peanut?"

"An ass whooping, if you don't have my boom box?"

"What boom box?"

"Stop faking, yo. Grandma saw you with it last."

"Oh that boom box. The damnedest thing happened to that. I ran into a street magician that said he could turn your boom box into a fat piece of crack rock. I called him a liar, and guess what? He made a liar out of me."

"You sold my boom box for crack!"

"I like to use the word donated."

"Donated?"

"Yeah, I donated it to the 'Get Peanut High Foundation!'"

I just looked at Peanut and shook my head. Although I should have beat his ass, it wouldn't have done any good. Crack heads have a higher tolerance for pain than the average human being. His crack addiction was punishment enough. I missed the old Peanut. The cool Peanut who always had all the new clothes and fine women. The Peanut who would give me five dollars when I was younger to go buy penny candy. Yeah, I missed the old Peanut. Standing before me was a shell of the man he once was.

"Yo! Peanut, tell us a story. I'll hit you off." Daryl said.

"It better be fat."

"Go ahead, yo, I got you."

Peanut was famous for his crack stories. Shit, he should be the one writing a book. He loved crack so much he even had his own crack dance he'd do after he hit the pipe.

"Okay, okay, well I was down at the 24-hour store, selling my dummies. Now, you know, my fake crack looked better than the shit you're selling. Plus, I had sprayed it with some chemical shit that makes you dizzy when you try to smoke it. Anyway, I'm out doing my thang, and a Puerto Rican cat standing next to me had real shit. I sold this one black guy some shit. Ten minutes later, the same dude came back and started whipping my ass. I mean this muthafucka was fucking me up something serious. I tried to give him back his money. I figured he found out they were dummies. Man, he didn't want the money".

"He didn't want the money?" Country said.

"Hell, no, he didn't want the money. This asshole robbed me for the rest of my dummies! Do you believe that shit?!"

We all broke out into a ridiculous, loud laughter. Peanut started doing his crack dance to put the finishing touches on his story. One thing about Peanut, he was always good for a laugh.

Then the laughter stopped. The sound of Crazy Eddie's Caddy could be heard in the distance. Five minutes after that, we heard it on another street, then another, and another. It was like he was circling closer and closer, without being seen. Finally, the yellow Caddy pulled up on Chestnut Street, about fifty yards away from us. The only thing we could see was the cherry of his cigarette as it illuminated the inside of his car. The orangish glow gave us a faint glimpse of his huge silhouette.

"What do you want us to do, Pharaoh?"

"Chill, Jessito, just act like he's not there."

Everybody kept their eyes on the Caddy. It was impossible to act normal. Nobody wanted to end up like Joey. My palms became sweaty. I suddenly had to take a shit, and my breathing sounded asthmatic. It was like I was going to have a heart attack out that bitch.

Chill out, chill out, chill out. I whispered to myself.

I didn't want to be there. I wished I was in my grandma's house where it was safe. Shit, I wished I was anywhere but inside Chestnut Park.

All of a sudden, the yellow Caddy's engine roared to life. We watched as the beat up Caddy crept towards us. As it drew closer, I gripped the handle of the gun. My grip tightened when it passed in front of us.

"It's not Eddie!" Country shouted.

"Huh."

"That's not him, Pharaoh," Country repeated. I let out a sigh of relief.

"WATCH OUT!" Jessito shouted.

It was Crazy Eddie. He had run up on us from behind. It was a set up. He caught Country in the ribs, slumping him on the first blow. Then he charged T-Money, picked him up and threw him over the five-foot chain link fence.

"SHOOT HIM!" Country yelled.

Eddie turned to face me.

"Who are you going to shoot? You're going to shoot me?" Eddie roared. "Come on! Come on, you little fuck, shoot me!"

Eddie started beating his chest.

"SHOOT HIM!" T-Money screamed.

Eddie stood twenty feet away from me. In that time, a million things flashed before my eyes. My best friend Jo-Jo, my grandma, my uncles, my aunt, the neighborhood, the corner store, the rooftop, the D's, the fiends, Artey, my crew, and, finally Joey lying in the bed.

When I saw the heart monitor flat line, it woke something up in me. My blood pulsed through my veins like hot lava. My breathing quickened, and when the realization of what I had to do hit me, I raised the gun and took aim.

Crazy Eddie charged at me like a wild rhino. I pulled the trigger, and the first slug stopped him dead in his tracks. He looked down at his chest in disbelief, then back at me. He growled, flashed his bloody teeth, and charged again. That was when I emptied the whole clip into his chest. Crazy Eddie collapsed to his knees first, hovered there a second, then fell flat on his face. Not knowing what I was doing, T-Money later told me I was still squeezing the trigger long after Crazy Eddie was dead.

"Come on, let's go, Pharaoh!"

I just sat there, staring at Crazy Eddie's corpse as blood pooled out from his body.

"Pharaoh, let's go, yo!" Daryl said, tugging my arm. "We got to get out of here."

I did it, I killed Crazy Eddie.

"That's for my man, you piece of shit," I said,

backpedaling and disappearing into the darkness of the alley. I told everybody to go home and lie low for the rest of the night. Since T-Money decided to stay the night over and we sat on the rooftop, looking down at the crime scene.

"You think somebody ratted on you?"

"I don't think so. Nobody liked him."

"How does it feel?"

"How does what feel?"

"You know, killing somebody."

"To tell you the truth, I don't know how I feel right now."

"You a'ight, though?"

"Yeah, I'm cool."

"I'm going to call it a night. Peace."

When T-Money left, I was alone with my thoughts once again. I thought about hollering at God, but I knew he wasn't trying to hear shit I had to say. You know what? I lied to T-Money. I did feel something. I wasn't the same kid as before. What innocence I had was gone. I had officially crossed the threshold into the street life. No longer could I recapture what was, but only accept what was to be.

Chapter 9

After, I killed Crazy Eddie, I experienced every single human emotion possible in thirty minutes. At first, I was nervous, and as time passed, I became scared. When Crazy Eddie ran up on us, me being scared turned to fear. As visions of Joey flashed before my eyes, I grew angry. After I shot him the first time, I felt the power of the gun, and I liked it. I wasn't scared no more. Now, after I dumped the rest of the clip in him, I felt evil. I wanted him to get up, so I could do it again.

Then I became scared, all over again, because I didn't want to get caught. So I was anxious to get away. When I made it to the rooftop, I felt safe, like I distanced myself from the guilt. Then when it set in what I had done, my stomach bubbled and I threw up. Once I smoked that blunt with T-Money, I relaxed. I realized I was here, and he was not. Could I do it again? Fuck, yeah, the next time wouldn't be with all the drama.

It was around 11:30 p.m., and I still had thirty minutes before I'd go see Dante for the two kilos of coke. I was waiting for my Aunt Joanne to drop off the

$35,000 we kept stashed at her house. We all figured it would be safer at her house because she lived in a crime-free neighborhood.

It was 11:59 when she finally showed up.

"What the fuck happen to you?" I said, looking at her swollen eye.

Joanne tried to cover the side of her face. So I couldn't see it, but it was too late for that. Just then, Peanut walked in, high as a kite and said, "What in the hell happened to you?"

"Nothing, nothing, it's no big deal," she said, dropping the duffel bag and trying to leave.

"Hold up, Joanne, come here." I got up and followed her into the kitchen. I grabbed her arm before she made it to the door.

"Please, I just want to go home to my girls. Pharaoh, I'm going to be okay."

I spun her around and brushed her hair to the side. Her eye was completely shut and the right side of her jaw was swollen.

"Dante did this to you, didn't he? Tell me what happened."

Joanne sat down at the kitchen table.

"I… I went over to get some money for Talesha's birthday party. I still have the keys to his apartment, so when he didn't answer, I let myself in. I walked in on Bless fucking him with a dildo."

"What!?" Me and Peanut said at the same time.

"He flipped out, charged me, and started beating me. If… if… it wasn't for Bless, he would've killed me."

Joanne broke down, crying uncontrollably. I handed her some napkins for her tears and some ice for her face.

"Sugar."

"Yes, Grandma."

"Who's that doing all that crying out there?"

"It's Auntie Jo."

I heard my grandma getting up, I really didn't want her seeing her daughter like this.

Grandma came in, took one look at Auntie Jo and said, "Oh, baby Jo, what happened? Don't tell me that no good Dante put his hands on you again. Oh, come to momma, come now."

My grandma took Joanne into her arms and comforted her. Then she gave me a look. At first I didn't know what it meant because she never looked at me like that before. When she nodded, it was clear. I didn't need no clarification, her eyes said it all. I went to my room, grabbed the Sig-9, and changed clips. Peanut followed behind me.

"We're going to get that muthafucka, Pharaoh."

As I tucked the gun in my waist, I just looked at him and his fragile self. "Peanut, there is nothing you can do. I'm going to handle this."

I put on my black jean jacket and left. I turned around because something told me to. Peanut stood in the mirror, staring at himself. I could tell he was frustrated with what he had let himself become. Even though it hurt him then, it would help him in the future.

I took Joanne's Saab to Dante's. The only thought on my mind was killing him. With Crazy Eddie, it was out of fear I killed. Dante's death would be out of anger. The rage inside wouldn't allow me to calmly walk up the stairs, so I ran up with the duffel bag in hand. Before knocking, I took a deep breath and wiped the sweat from my forehead. I knocked on the door.

"Who is it?"

"Pharaoh,"

"You by yourself, punk?"

"Yeah!" I growled.

He went through the same unlocking-the-door ritual, then stuck his head out the door, looking me up and down. When he saw the duffel bag, he couldn't help but grin.

"So, is that the money?" he said, as we took our same seats as earlier.

"Yeah count it, $35,000, it's all there." I told him.

"Oh, I will."

I tossed him the bag. What's up, pimp no entertainment?"

"That bitch, Bless, got rid of those bitches for some reason. Maybe she wants daddy all to herself."

"Shit, can a brother at least get something to drink?"

"Yeah, yeah, my bad nephew... Bless!"

Bless came out of the backroom. This time, she was fully clothed. Her hair was drawn back in a tight ponytail. I could see she had a shiner under her eye.

"Get Pharaoh a drink bitch, and when you're done, get him two birds out the bag in the room."

Bless passed me my drink and disappeared into the back. When she came back, she was carrying the two duffel bags from earlier and brought them over to me. She gave me this look, then stood next to me. I guess she had made her decision. Dante was too busy with his face in the bag to notice what Bless had done.

You want to know something crazy? When I spoke to Bless earlier, I was just saying anything. If Dante didn't hit my Aunt Jo, I would've come, bought the two kilos and left like any other time. Bless was under the impression I was coming to kill Dante that night, that was why she brought the bags out. Her actions sealed Dante's fate. He definitely had to die now.

"Bitch, I said two birds, not two duffel bags. Maybe you need another ass whoppin'!"

"Shut the fuck up, Dante. You ain't whoppin' shit." I said.

"What?"

"You heard me, punk!" I pulled the Sig-9 and aimed it at his forehead.

Dante's eyes widened, "Hey, don't point that thing at me. What's going on, Pharaoh?"

I didn't say a word, I just let the whole situation sink in for a second.

"Oh, you a gangsta now, huh? You think you some kind of killer now, punk!? I taught you everything! Without me, you'd be nothing! Now you want to turn on me for this bitch!? That stank ass ho will turn on you, too! We're family, Pharaoh. Don't let this bitch come between us!"

The more he begged, the more pathetic Dante sounded. This man, a couple of years ago was God in my eyes. His words were like scripture from the Bible to me. Now he was on his hands and knees, begging for his life.

"Come on, Pharaoh, please don't kill me, man. Go ahead, take the shit and the girl, just don't kill me."

I didn't feel the least bit sorry for that muthafucka.

He must've seen it in my eyes that he was going to die.

"What about my girls? Who's going to take care of Shaniek and Talesha?"

I stood up. "Don't worry, I'll take care of them, I promise. Bless, turn up the stereo."

Bless walked over and turned up the volume. "Careless Whispers" by George Michael, would be the last song Dante would ever hear. I aimed at his head, and right when I was about to pull the trigger, Bless got in front of me.

"Let me do it. I owe him this."

I gave her the gun, stepped to the side and said, "Handle your business then."

"Aw, shiiittt!" were Dante's last words.

Dante's head snapped back as the first bullet pierced his forehead. It blew out the back of his head, spraying his brains all over the Corinthian leather sofa. The second shot ripped his jaw clean off his face. The last two plunged into his chest.

Bless fell to her knees, throwing up. I grabbed her by her shoulders and picked her up. She was shaking and her eyes were closed.

"Bless! Bless! look at me, Bless. You can't fall apart on me now. Take deep breaths. There you go, breathe with me. You okay?"

"Yes, I'm okay, I'm okay."

"I need you to focus. Bless, we're going to make this look like a robbery, okay? Are you with me?"

"What do you need me to do?"

"That's my girl. Listen, empty the $35,000 into the bag with the $300,000. Then fill the bag with things a burglar might take."

Bless handed me the gun and went to work. I began wiping things down for fingerprints with Windex and a rag. I can't front. Every time I passed Dante's mutilated corpse, I felt like I had to throw up my damn self. Death is so final, especially when you get shot in the face.

Chapter 10

I decided to get a room at the Arrowhead Motel in West Springfield. It was the next town over from Holyoke, about ten minutes away from Dante's crib. Arrowhead was one of those cheap, one-story motels that prostitutes used to turn tricks, mid-level drug dealers went to bag up, and guys took girls they met at the club to get their fuck on. We got there around 1:30am. I got the room for a week and asked not to be disturbed.

"Go take a shower, you'll feel better afterwards."

"Take one with me," Bless said, grabbing my hand so I did.

After the shower, we went straight to bed. We didn't say a word to each other. Bless fell asleep with her head on my chest. I stared at the ceiling, recalling the night's events.

I awoke early the next morning, wanting to catch the morning news. After twisting a blunt up, I laid back and turned on the T.V. Channel 40 was our local channel and "Hard Talk Live" was a hybrid news show that strictly covered stories happening in the West Mass area. Diane Fletcher was the show's only anchor and was known for asking tough questions during her interviews. Even though she was older, I had always had this thing for her. She kind of reminded me of a young Teri Hatcher.

When I flipped to the channel, Diane had just finished mentioning something about Senator Holten. Then a picture of a gun appeared in the upper right-hand corner of the screen.

Yesterday, there was a near fatal shooting in Chestnut Park, one of Holyoke's drug infested areas. A man was reportedly shot 11 times. Although he is still alive, the doctors don't expect him to make it through the night. If he dies he'll be the thirty fifth murdered this summer. In other news, it...

"Anything on the news?" Bless said, waking up.

"Nah, just the shit with Crazy Eddie."

"You shot him, huh?"

"Yeah."

"How did it feel?"

"At first, I was fucked up about it. But now I don't feel shit. I liked the rush I got from pulling the trigger. I can see this killing shit becoming addictive."

Bless noticed my dick rising in my boxers. She slid her hand underneath the elastic band and slowly began massaging my dick to life.

"You want me to tell you how it felt when I killed Dante?" she said, in a soft, sexy voice.

"Tell me."

"It was incredible. I could feel every hair on my body stand up. When I took aim, my nipples hardened."

Bless pulled my boxers down to my knees and removed her thongs and bra. She straddled me, inserting my dick inside her.

"When I caressed the trigger, my pussy got so wet, like it is now."

She grinded her pussy in slow, circular motions, forcing my dick deeper inside her.

"Ahhhhh, ahhhh . . . Mmmmmm. When I squeezed the trigger, ahhhh, ooooh, the sound vibrated throughout my body. Each time I pulled the trigger, I think I came."

Bless picked up the pace with her hips.

"Who do you belong to now?"

"Pharaoh! Mmmmm! Pharaoh!"

"Don't cum until I say. You hear me?"

"Yesssssss!"

I flipped her on her back, put her knees to her ears, and punished the pussy for about ten minutes. By the way Bless thrashed and clawed at the sheets, I figured she hadn't been dicked down this good in a while.

"FLOP! FLOP! FLOP! FLOP! FLOP! FLOP!"

"You better not cum yet!"

"Ahhhhh! Mmmmmmm!"

Holding back her orgasm was driving her crazy. Our bodies, covered in sweat, slapped together as we clashed like two porn stars amped off coke.

"Look at me! I said look at me!"

I snatched her by the throat and begin choking her. At the same time I pulled my dick out.

"Cum!"

Looking down at her pussy, I saw her shaven lips quivering. Gradually, she began to cream. That was when I let go of her throat. She collapsed on the bed, trying to catch her breath.

"Pharaoh, I never came like that in my life," she said, between coughs and gasps for air.

Later that night, I decided to go through the duffel bags. I knew how much money we had already. In the bag with all the coke were twenty kilos of fish scale worth about $500,000 broken down. In the last bag, Bless filled it with Dante's jewelry. I figured I could get at least $250,000 for all of it. It had to be worth a million or more. When I peeked in the bag to see if I got everything, I noticed some papers wrapped up with a rubber band.

"What are these?"

"I thought you might want those." Bless said, coming out of the bathroom wrapping a towel around her head.

"They're the deeds to all of his property."

"Look whose name they are in."

"My Aunt Joanne."

"Did I do good?"

"Shorty, you did better than good."

For the rest of the week, we stayed at the motel. I called T-Money to find out the word on the street. He told me that everything was cool, and nobody was really tripping off Crazy Eddie's murder. I didn't think they would.

Chapter 11

For once, everything seemed to be falling into place. I had money for Joey, coke for the block, deeds to Dante's real estate and Bless as my girl. It was time to form my family.

I didn't want one of those crews that everybody could join. I wanted it to be deeper than that. I was trying to build an empire, not a gang. So I thought back over all of the books that Artey had gave me to read and came to a realization. Ninety percent of the world's greatest organizations, civilizations and religions have some type of book, doctrine or body of instructions they go by. Christians had the Bible, Muslims had the Quran. Communist countries lived by the Marxist manifesto written by Karl Marx. The United States had the Constitution our country was built on. Even corporations have their by-laws and articles of incorporation. In order for the Gorillas to grow, we needed a foundation to grow from.

I sat up day and night thinking about a foundation for the Gorillas. Instead of copying from one particular organization, civilization or religion, I decided to take a little from each one.

From the Jews, I took how they took care of their

own. In Brooklyn, New York, the Jewish Community formed their own welfare system to support struggling Jews coming to America. The Gorillas will do the same for its members and their families. We would own all the buildings we lived in. Also, we'd own all the stores we shopped in and all the parks our kids played in, and that was just the beginning.

From the Romans, I took their sense of pride and honor of being a Roman citizen. Back when the Roman Empire was in power, if you weren't a citizen of Rome, you were considered second class. Rome was held in such high regard because of Rome itself. At the time, Rome possessed the largest armies, greatest philosophers, the best painters and sculptures. Their buildings were works of art and their technology was centuries ahead of its time. So, to be a Roman citizen was to be a part of greatness. That was the feeling I wanted every Gorilla to have and non-Gorilla to dream of.

I went through all the great civilization, such as the Egyptian Dynasties, the Aztecs, The Chinese Dynasties, and not to mention all the secret societies and the top criminal organizations. To take it a step further, in order to become a member, you would have to surrender your faith to the family because nothing would work unless you believed in it.

It would take me two weeks to complete what every Gorilla would live for, and ultimately, die for. I named the two hundred page book,

The Way Of The Gorilla.

Chapter 12

A few weeks had passed before I felt safe venturing back out into the streets of Holyoke. I called T-Money and had him round up the crew to meet me on the rooftop at noon.

"I've got to handle some things. I want you to stay here with all of the shit and wait for my call."

"Okay," Bless replied.

"Here's the gun. Anybody come around acting funny, slump them and get out of here."

Bless nodded and crawled to the edge of the bed. She stood up on her knees and gave me a kiss. "I'll be here."

"I know you will, Shorty." First thing I did was return my Aunt Joanne's car. Pulling into her driveway, I saw her on the front steps, watching the girl's jump rope.

"Boy, where have you been with my car? I was just about to call the cops and report it stolen."

"Joanne, lets go inside for a second."

"Boy, I ain't goin' nowhere. It's too nice out here."

"I'm serious, Joanne. We got to talk." I said, staring in her eyes. Joanne saw that I was serious and got up to follow me inside the house.

"What's wrong, Pharaoh, Grandma all right?"

"Grandma's fine, Jo, just listen for a second."

"What is it?"

"You don't have to worry about Dante hitting you no more."

"Why, did y'all beat his ass? He's a sorry muthafucka, anyway. I can't believe I was ever in love with him. Maybe that's why he ain't answering the phone. He knows I need money for the girls."

"Jo, he ain't never going to answer the phone again."

"Then I'll go over there and..."

"Joanne, listen, Dante's dead."

"Stop playing, Pharaoh... you're joking, right? No! You're serious, aren't you?"

"Yeah."

"Oh, my God... you... you didn't... did you?"

Joanne reclined in her chair and covered her mouth. I could see by her reaction that she'd blame herself for Dante's murder.

"You okay, Joanne?"

"What... what about the girls? What do I tell them?"

"Give them the heaven story Grandma gave me when my mother died."

"But... but how will I take care of them? Dante always gave me money. You know I never had a job. How will I buy them clothes and shoes?"

"Calm down, Joanne. Did you know that all of his apartment buildings and houses are in your name?"

"No, I never asked questions about that stuff. I just signed where he told me to sign."

"Well, they are, Jo. That means you own it all. So from now on, you'll be getting all that money."

"What money? How much is it?"

"Off the apartment buildings alone, you'll be getting $60,000 a month. That's not including the ten houses he owns."

"$60,000."

"Yeah, Jo, Dante was doing it real big."

"I don't know how to manage any apartment buildings, Pharaoh. I'll fuck it up, I know I will," Jo said, getting herself all worked up again.

"Joanne, will you calm the fuck down? I'll hire a management team to take care of your apartments. All you have to do is sit back and enjoy the money."

"They got people to do that?"

"Yeah, don't worry, I'll hook it all up."

I could see a little sign of relief come across her face.

"Hey, Joanne."

"Yeah."

"I need you to do something for me."

"What?"

"You know I be doin' my thing down on Chestnut."

"Yeah."

"Well, Dante has two apartment buildings right across from the park. Then there's another one in North Holyoke."

"What about them?"

"I want you to sign them over to me, along with

100

three houses he has up by Holyoke Mall. I'm going to move Grandma in one of them."

Dante had trained Joanne well. She signed the deeds over without so much as a blink of the eye. She sat back and stared at the picture on the wall of Shaniek and Talesha. We all grew up without fathers. I think she wanted to break that cycle. Even though Dante was a dick, he was still there for the girls. For a second, I thought it might've been selfish killing Dante, but… man… fuck him.

After leaving Joanne's, I caught a cab to my grandma's. I still felt a little uneasy about going back around Chestnut Park. It might have been because I didn't know what to expect. When I got out of the cab, I looked around, and everything was normal.

I was trippin'.

Here I was acting like I shot the president of the United States or something.

Grandma was in her room getting ready for church. Sounds of gospel music blared throughout the three-bedroom apartment. Then there was the smell of good, old, down south cooking that made my stomach growl.

"Suga! That you?"

I don't know if it was a grandmother's intuition, but she always knew when I was in the house.

"Yes, Grandma."

"Come in here and talk to your grandma before I go to church."

This would be the first time I'd seen her since that night I killed Crazy Eddie. When I walked into her room, she stopped what she was doing and stared at my heart.

"Suga, how's your soul?"

"Fine, I guess."

"You sure?"

"Yes, Grandma, everything is okay."

"Then why don't you go get dressed and escort an old lady to church?"

"Grandma, you know I'm not into all that church stuff."

"You know, the best place to look for a girl is in the church."

"Those same girls after church be smoking weed, drinking and doing the nasty. Trust me, I know."

"Suga, you're going to have to let God into your heart one day."

"I talk to him sometimes, but right now, we ain't speaking."

"God is always listening, Suga."

"Yeah, but he ain't always speaking."

"Hand me my black wig over there, Suga."

I got it and handed it to her while I said, "You know, back in the day, I mean way back in the day, they used religion to control the masses. That's where all that fear of God talk came from. If you didn't believe in their God, they would kill you. So it makes it hard for me to trust in religion."

"Suga, you know Grandma don't know about all that history stuff. It's all too confusing to me. But do you know how I know there's a heaven up there?"

"How?"

"I can see it every time I look in your eyes."

Grandma always had a way with words. I could state all the facts in the world, and in one sentence, she could sum up the whole conversation.

"Oh, guess who is going to church with me?"

"Who?"

"Your Uncle Peanut, thank you, Jesus."

"Peanut, are you sure?"

"He's in the bathroom, getting ready right now."

I looked over towards the bathroom. I gave my Grandma a kiss on the cheek and left. As I passed the bathroom, I glanced in, and, sure enough, there was Peanut, getting ready.

"Uh, Peanut, what the fuck are you doing?"

"I'm going to church with my mother."

"Crack heads don't go to church. What are you going to do, steal some dough out of the trays?"

Peanut just looked at me. He didn't laugh or crack a smile. For once, he didn't find my crack joke funny.

"What's up, Peanut?"

"I'm done, Pharaoh. I'm done with the crack, the streets, and the whole life-style. I let myself slip too far. Look at me, I'm a hundred pounds, soakin' wet. I was supposed to be the one to go and handle Dante, not you. Ever since that night, I haven't touched the crack pipe. I haven't even thought about it. Pharaoh, I just want my life back. I know it's going to be hard but I can't live with myself like this. So that's why I'm going to church, to ask God for help."

Out of the corner of his eye, I saw a tear fall.

"Yo, do what you got to do."

I gave him some dap, a hug, and left. I decided to go to the rooftop and smoke a blunt while I waited for the rest of the crew. The sun was out, the sky was cloudless, and the warm breeze felt good against my face.

Suddenly I heard, "What's up, son?"

I didn't have to turn around to know that it was T-Money behind me. His Indian accent gave him away.

"What's the deal?" I said, as I turned around and gave him some dap. "Where's the rest of the crew at?"

"On their way up now."

They all seemed happy to see me, except Daryl. He had an attitude as always.

"Why are we up here?" Country asked.

"Because I wanted to show y'all something."

"Up here?" Daryl said.

"Yeah, look at those two buildings over there."

"And what about them?"

"They belong to the Gorillas now, Daryl."

"What?" everyone said in unison.

I went on to explain what happened at Dante's. I left some things out, like how much dough and coke I got, the rest of the properties, and how Bless was the one who actually killed Dante. I don't know why I only told half the story. It just seemed like the right thing to do at the time.

"Did anybody find the body yet?" Jessito asked.

"Not yet."

"Damn, son, you just going wild on some Billy the Kid shit. What are you, trigga happy or something?" Daryl said sarcastically.

"Nah, I just did what I had to do. Now, because of it, the Gorillas are really going to eat. You got a problem with that?"

"So what are you saying? You want us to recognize you as some kind of killer or something?"

"Yo, Daryl, I'm getting sick of your shit, son!"

"What did you say?" Daryl got up in my face.

"Chill, chill, we family, yo," Country said, pushing himself between us.

"What's up with the buildings, Pharaoh?" Jessito asked, changing the subject.

"We're going to open up shop in the first one. Finally, we're going to get the fuck out of the park. In the second one, each one of y'all can take an apartment for yourselves."

"For real?!" T-Money shouted.

"No bullshit, yo. The first building will be the official Gorilla clubhouse. We'll call it the Jungle. Country, I want you to come up with a way to move the coke.

T-Money, I need you to lace the top two floors. That's where the hang out spot will be. Do it big, kid. I want a DJ booth, pool tables, a mini-stage for throwing shows and everything. Have it all ready for my birthday in six weeks."

"What, are we throwing a party?"

"You fuckin' right we're throwing a party, and do it big, like I said."

"Say no more."

"Daryl, I want you to start recruiting some thorough muthafuckas. We about to get on some Nino Brown shit. All the other crews are going to either cop from us or get the fuck outta the way."

"Okay! Now that is the type of shit I'm talking about," Daryl said, pounding his fist into his hand.

"I'm out, yo. See y'all in six weeks. Jessito, call a cab, you're coming with me.

Chapter 13

We took the cab to the hospital. On the way, I could tell something was bothering Jessito.

"What's up with you, kid?" I asked.

"You gave everybody something to do but me. I'm saying, I'm not a kid anymore. Every book you gave me to read, I read. Everything you taught me, I remembered. I'm tired of being the look out. I want to start putting in some real work. I've just been playing my position until you give me the word."

"That's what I've been waiting for out of you. I didn't want to give you anything. I wanted you to want it. You're my prodigy, kid. I've been grooming you for the big time. When I get this family up and running, I want you to take over the drug operations. You know everything I know when it comes to this game.

All the long talks we had weren't for nothing. Trust me, your time is coming. For now, you can take care of something for me. I want you to go see Giuseppe in the north end of Springfield. Tell him you're speaking on my behalf. I want you to place an order for 20 baby nines, 10 Macs, 10 AK's and 10 S.W.A.T. vests. Do you think you can handle that?"

"Hell yeah."

"Bet."

Earlier, before I left the block, I called Bless and told her to meet me at the hospital. When the cab pulled up to the hospital, Bless was standing out front. She wore some tight, torn daisy dukes and a white sports bra. Her hair was in tiny braids that zigzagged all the way back. Her caramel skin glistened under the evening sun, making her look that much more tasty.

We went to the 5th floor to see Joey. Madee and Tutee were in the same position I'd left them in. Joey didn't look any better, but his heart monitor assured me he was still alive.

Tutee's red rimmed eyes looked up at me. "Hey, Pharaoh."

I could hear how exhausted she was from crying. She managed to get up and give me a weak hug.

"How are you doing girl?"

"I don't know. Nothing has changed, so far. Some administration guy from the hospital came and spoke to us."

"What did he say?"

"He said that if we didn't get the money, he was going to ship Joey out. He said it so heartless, Pharaoh. He didn't look at Joey once."

Tears streamed from her beautiful, brown eyes.

"Bless, the bag."

Bless passed me the back pack she was wearing.

"Here," I said, passing it to Tutee.

"Uh? What is this?... Oh my God... how much is it?"

"Sixty thousand. There's fifty thousand for the insurance company and ten thousand for you."

"Thank you! Thank you!" Tutee said, giving me a thousand kisses.

"Que pasa?" Madee said, with a puzzled look on her face. Tutee exchanged some words in Spanish with Madee, and she looked up and said, "Gracias."

"Hey, let me have a moment alone with Joey,"

Everyone nodded and stepped out.

"What up, kid? Man, its crazy seeing you like this. I'm going to take a picture so we can laugh about this when you wake up. A lot of shit has happened since you been asleep. I took care of Eddie. The same goes for Dante, but I'll tell you about that when you wake up. I miss you, kid. Shit ain't the same without you. Anyway, don't worry about your moms and them, I got them. You just work on trying to wake the fuck up, a'ight? Peace, Joey, Gorilla Family forever."

Chapter 14

Two days after Joanne signed the deeds over to me, I moved into one of the houses up by the Holyoke Mall. It was a gray, three story, four bedroom, contemporary style home with a full basement and a huge backyard. It was in an upper class neighborhood, on top of a hill, away from the other houses. I picked that particular house because it was the farthest removed of Dante's properties from the craziness of Chestnut Park.

The last week of June, I was out back in my hammock, smoking a blunt. I had to take a second to chill the fuck out. Things were moving faster than I was used to but then again, I lived a fast paced life. It was to be expected, I guess.

With everything in motion, it was time to put my team of thorough bitches together. Although I had an idea of what I wanted, I still gave Artey a call for his input.

"Speak."

"What's up, Artey? It's Pharaoh."

"Hey, Youngblood, or should I say, King Pharaoh. How are you doing?"

"Same ole shit, just chilling."

"I heard about Crazy Eddie and Dante."

"Damn, yo, nothing gets by you when it comes to these streets."

"Youngblood, I am the streets, you dig?"

"I can dig it."

"So are you all right with it?"

"Yeah, I'm cool with it"

"Well, in that case, I'm proud of you, kid."

"Thanks, that means a lot to me."

"So what's up?"

"Remember how I always talked about putting together a team of thorough bitches?"

"Yeah, you called them your Gorilla Queens, right?"

"That's right. Well, I'm at that point, and I want you to refresh me on how I should go about it."

"Hold up, Youngblood, this calls for a cigar."

I heard Artey snap his fingers. Without having to be there, I knew Diamond or one of the other girls brought him a lit cigar.

"Okay, first I want you to put this picture in your head," Artey said as he took a couple puffs, no doubt trying to get the cherry on his cigar going.

"What picture is that?"

"Picture the sun and all the planets rotating around it."

"Okay." I locked in a mental picture of the solar system.

"This is how I need you to see things. You're the sun, the center of your universe. Your females are the planets that revolve around you. They need your light to survive. Without you, they'd be lost in total darkness."

"Okay, I'm feeling that."

"Now, since it is your universe, you can pick and choose the females you want to revolve around you. Peep game; you just don't want a group of any old girls around you. There are specific types you're looking for."

"And they are?"

"The first trait you look for in a woman is submissiveness. Submissive women surrender themselves to power, aggression and authority, with the obedience of a trained dog. Most, if not all of the time, that trait is an internal thing that developed during their childhood. It can come from an overbearing parent who constantly yelled at them. It could come from physical abuse. Maybe they saw how their mother was submissive to their father. There are other ways that they could've acquired the trait. Nine times out of ten, it subconsciously followed them into adulthood. You follow me?"

"Yeah, I'm with you."

"Another trait you want in your females is called DMPD."

"What the hell is that?"

"Deep Masochist Personality Disorder. Females with this trait view themselves as powerless and needy. They want you to like them so much they'll do anything to please you. They'll depend on you to make decisions for them. They ask you what they should wear, what to eat, and anything else that requires them to make a decision. They happily hand over their lives to you."

"Word?"

"Word, Youngblood. But it isn't as easy as it sounds. You have to be on point. If you can't recognize what they want, they will look for it elsewhere. Not all females want that traditional romance shit. Love comes in many different shades. You just have to train yourself to recognize the traits. Now I'm about to lay the real heavy shit on you. Once you bring them into your universe, give them a taste of paradise. Make sure it is far beyond anything they have ever experienced. Take them places they never been. Buy them things they couldn't normally afford. Show them how small and insufficient their lives are. At the same time, you gradually cut them off from their friends and family. Have them give up their apartments and move them in with you. Have them sell their cars and buy them new cars. The same goes for their clothes, bank accounts and anything that establishes their independence. You replace all the things they gave up or let go, but nothing is in their name. You own everything. So, at any point you can take it all away from them. You want them to depend on you for everything mentally, emotionally, physically and financially. Then when you have them at that point, snatch it all away, even if they didn't do anything wrong. You have to give them a taste of what life is like without you. They'll do whatever you tell them to do to get back in your universe."

"Yo, Artey, that was some deep shit you just laid on me."

"There's more."

"Okay, hit me."

Artey took a pull on his cigar, and coughed a bit before continuing. "All the traits I told you are important, but there is one trait you have to make sure all your females have."

"Which one is that?"

"The Daddy Syndrome, which is nothing more than females that grew up with some type of daddy issues. It could either come from abandonment, neglect, or death. What happens is you become the father they never had.

In turn, they'll unknowingly transfer qualities they wanted in their fathers into you. And because of that, they become Daddy's girl all over again, or for the first time."

"You a muthfuckin' beast, Artey!"

Artey laughed, coughed a little and laughed some more. "Before I let you go, I'm gonna lay one more thing on you."

"What's that?"

"You need a boss bitch to keep the others in check. She has to be aggressive with them, but, at the same time, she has to play the big sister role. She's the one that's going to reinforce your vision in your other girls' heads. The deeper you get into your boss bitch's head, the better she'll be able to train the other girls. You also have to treat the boss bitch better than you treat the rest, and they got to see you doing it. That is going to cause a little jealousy, but it's going to be the good type of jealousy."

"How?"

"Your other girls are going to see how close the boss bitch is to you, and they'll want to get that close to you, too. They are going to show you they can be a boss bitch, too. The boss bitch, on the other hand, is going to do everything to make sure she doesn't lose her position. What's gonna happen is they'll end up policing themselves. Each girl will watch the other ones around them. The first time one of them does something wrong, another one is gonna tell you. So it's a good idea to continuously play one against the other. You dig?"

"I dig. I think I already found my boss bitch."

I watched Bless walk by in just her panties and bra.

"Yeah, I got my boss bitch."

"Cool, then handle your business, Youngblood, and call me if you need anything."

Chapter 15

One night, while laying in bed with Bless, after some wild, barbaric sex, I asked her, "What is your purpose in life?"

Bless straddled my dick, letting her silky black hair fall in front of her face. "What do you mean, my purpose in life?"

"Exactly what I just asked you. Are you on some day-to-day shit, or do you have a bigger purpose in life?"

"I never thought about it. You're the first person to ever ask me anything like that." Bless paused for a second. "I guess my purpose in life is to be happy," she said, shrugging her shoulders.

"And what is happiness to you?"

"To be taken care of, I guess. Not having to worry about where the next meal is coming from or where I'm going to sleep at night. Hmm… I guess my happiness is nothing more than having some security, huh?"

Even though I understood where Bless was coming from, at the same time, she revealed a way into her psyche. Without a second thought, I moved in like a lion on a wounded deer.

"So that's what you think your purpose in life is, to find happiness in being secure? Damn, Bless, I thought you were different from the rest of the bitches out there. You have a price tag stapled to your forehead, too. It was just hidden by your beauty so well that I didn't see it."

"But… I…"

"Shut up, bitch!" The coldness in my voice made Bless jump. "Damn, I was looking for a Queen, not a gold digger. Get the fuck off of me, yo!"

The soft, golden glow of the candles glistened off of Bless's sweaty body as she sat up on me.

Bless's facial expression went from sexually satisfied to confused. "What's wrong?" she said.

I pushed her off of me, got up, grabbed my robe and walked into the closet.

"Get dressed!"

"Why, what did I do?"

"Get dressed," I said!

Peepin' out of the closet, I saw the lost look in her eyes as she slowly reached for her clothes. A couple of minutes later, I returned with a duffle bag.

"What's your price?"

"What do you mean, what's my price?" Bless said with tears building in her eyes.

"How much does your happiness cost? If you think your only purpose in life is to have security, then I'll give it to you. So how much does it cost? What? $10,000, $50,000, $80,000? Nah, you look like a $100,000 ho! Come on, bitch!" I snatched Bless up by the arm.

"What was I supposed to say? Tell me, Pharaoh, please!"

Bless tried to grab on to anything to prevent from being dragged down the stairs. That pissed me off even more, and I ended up throwing her down the stairs, head first.

I grabbed Bless by the hair and dragged her to the front door. "Stand up, bitch!" I picked her up by the throat. I opened the door, her eyes damn near fell out of her face.

"Please, don't put me out! Please!"

At that point, Bless was crying, flailing hysterically. She stared at the darkness beyond the door like it was the jaws of death.

I grabbed the bag of money and said, "There's enough money in this bag to give you security for a long time." I shoved the bag into her arms. "If this is all you want out of life, here you go, you worthless bitch!"

I pushed her out the door and slammed it behind her.

"NOOOOO!"

Bless's pleas faded as I climbed the stairs to my room. After rolling up a Garcia Vega, I laid down, puffed and relaxed. All I could do then was wait because only time would tell if the game Artey gave me would work. It might just appear that I was putting her out of my house, but, really, I was putting her out of my universe. I was actually taking a gamble. If I lost, I'd be out of $100,000 and thorough bitch. If I won, I'd get my boss bitch.

The next morning, I woke up around 11:30. I went about everything like normal. As bad as I wanted to, I resisted the urge to run to the front door. I ended up holding out another hour or so. I approached the front door. My heart beat like crazy. When I opened the door, the sunlight blinded me for a second. Looking at the ground, a silhouette in a fetal position came into focus.

Bless laid there on the cold cement, using the bag as a pillow. When she heard the door open, she looked up with tear-swollen Bambi eyes. We stared at each other for a second. In that instant, I saw all the qualities Artey told me to look for, staring back at me.

Without saying a word, I held the door open and stepped to the side. Bless picked herself up and came in. She sat down at the kitchen table and put the duffle bag on the floor. I sat across from her. Bless looked like a child that was sorry for breaking her mother's favorite lamp. She sat with her hands folded in her lap, staring down at the table.

"Why are you still here, Bless?"

"I didn't have anywhere to go," she mumbled.

"You have $100,000. You could've went anywhere you wanted in the world."

"You could've gave me a million dollars, and I still wouldn't have gone anywhere."

"Why?"

"Because... I need you."

"Like you needed Dante?"

"No, I never felt this way about Dante. There's something different about you, but I can't explain it. When you kicked me out, I felt so alone and scared, like when my father was murdered. I don't ever want to feel that pain again. Promise me you won't do it again."

I resisted the urge to question her about her father. I figured I'd save that for another time.

"It all depends. I'm going to ask you one more time, what is your purpose in life Bless?"

Bless sat in silence for a few minutes. I could tell she was searching her mind for the answer. When my patience ran out, I stood up and grabbed her arm.

"Okay, okay," she pleaded. Bless stood up and positioned herself in front of me. "I thought about what you asked me, over and over last night."

"And what did you come up with?"

"I believe things happen for a reason. Until that night at Dante's, when you asked me to be your Queen, my life meant nothing to anyone, including me." Bless started unbuttoning her shirt. "You asking me to be your Queen, gave me a purpose. I just didn't realize it until last night." Bless undid her pants and let them fall to the floor. "That night, I could see the ambition in your eyes. There was something about you. I felt like you were destined for bigger and better things in life, and still do. I want to be a part of that."

Bless shimmied out of her thong and kneeled before me.

"Just tell me what I have to do and I'll do it. Tell me what I have to say, and I'll say it. Tell me what you want me to think, and I'll think it. I can't explain this feeling in my heart I have for you, but I know this is where I'm supposed to be."

"So what's your purpose in life, Bless?" I said standing directly in front of her.

She submissively looked up at me. "My purpose in life is to become your Gorilla Queen. To make your dreams my dreams. To see your vision through-my eyes. To serve you, Pharaoh, the King of the Gorillas."

Most guys would have been content with what Bless said. Not me. I'm not going to lie. I was feeling myself like a muthafucka. I wanted to see how far I could take it.

"In order to become my Queen, you must drink from your King."

I pulled my dick out, and Bless opened her mouth. My heart skipped a beat, Bless was really going to let me piss in her mouth. My dick got hard as shit, and I think that was the reason it took a while for it to come out.

Finally, a steady stream of golden shower shot into Bless's mouth. Before it was over, I had baptized her, drenching her face, hair and titties with my watery, yellow fluid. Bless treated my piss like it was holy water, rubbing it all over her body.

"I'll kill for you, like I will die for you. I am a Gorilla for Life," Bless said, staring into my eyes.

As I stood there, staring down at Bless with a demi-god complex, I thought to myself, Yeah, it's on like a muthafucka, it's on!

Chapter 16

Out in my backyard, under a werewolf's moon, Bless and I lay on sex-scented Versace sheets. For the past couple days, I sculpted Bless's mind with words equivalent to the hands of Michelangelo.

"So, what is it you want me to do?" Bless asked, eagerly.

"The Gorilla Queens will be the deadliest weapon in the Gorilla's arsenal. The future of the Gorillas depends on them. So this is what I need from you. I want you to find me four attractive young females. I need one Asian, one white, one black, and one Puerto Rican."

"Why the different flavors?"

"Because not everybody likes chocolate. I want them to be at the lowest point in their lives. They must have a feeling of abandonment. A dysfunctional childhood is a must, and they must be trainable. Do not bring me any bitches that don't know how to listen."

"Okay, Daddy, anything else?"

"Yeah, they have to be fine as hell, no dog-face bitches. Another thing, any bitch that enters the family from here on out is your responsibility. That includes

Queens and other bitches. You're responsible for making them see my vision."

"Don't worry, Daddy. I'll make sure them bitches stay in check."

"That's what's up. Tomorrow, when you leave out, I'm gonna give you $10,000 and a rented Benz truck. The four you choose, take 'em out and dazzle the fuck out of them. Let them know what you're offering is only a taste of what's to come. After a few days of the high life, bring then back to their meaningless lives and leave them to ponder your offer. When you go to revisit them, I bet they won't let you leave without them."

"I betcha they won't either, Daddy."

Five days later, Bless returned with exactly what I asked for. In my living room sat four females, fine as a muthafucka. A hidden camera allowed me to inspect the prospects from my bedroom. Bless sat with them, talking, before leaving and returning with drinks for everyone.

"Here, ya'll, here are some drinks to relax ya'll a bit." Bless said, passing the drinks around.

"When are we going to meet him?" the black chick said.

"Be patient, Lasandra. You'll meet him soon." Bless replied.

They spoke for a while before Bless left and joined me in my bedroom.

"What do you think?

"They got the look I want. Now, tell me about them. Start with the white one."

"I knew you would like her. Her name is Tonia. She's from Hickory, North Carolina. I was in the shelter with her. Matter of fact, I was in the shelter with all of them. Anyway, she's everything you're looking for; wrapped up in that tight, little frame of hers."

Tonia was about 5'7", with short, red hair, light brown eyes and matching freckles sprinkled across her face and chest. She had an innocent country girl appeal, but her body was screaming fuck me like a slut. Her ass wasn't that fat, but when she bent over, it spread beautifully. Her main attractions were her voluptuous titties with thumb-size nipples that could be seen through her shirt.

"What about her childhood?"

"She used to live in a trailer park in North Carolina."

"It figures."

"She told me she used to fuck her father. She said they were in love."

"What?"

"The counselor at the shelter told me her father was molesting her, for real. Tonia didn't see it that way, though."

"She wanted his attention, anyway she could get it."

"She's fucked up in the head, pretty bad."

"That's exactly what I wanted."

"Well, she got it from her dad and his friends, for about three to four years, until she got pregnant. Her mother got her an abortion and put her on a bus to Springfield. She's been in the shelter ever since."

"What about the black one?"

"That's Lasandra. She's from Hartford, Connecticut, and she's a beat freak."

"Beat freak, what do you mean, a beat freak?"

"Exactly what I said. She likes to get beat. I met her in juvie hall. We would sneak off and get high, and all she'd talk about was her father beating her. At first, I felt sorry for her, but then I realized she was getting off by talking about it. When her father died of a heart attack, she ran away from home. Then she had a string of abusive boyfriends that used to beat the shit out of her. Eventually, she came to like the shit and saw her beating as a sign of them showing their love for her. The harder the punch, the deeper the love."

"Just like Tonia, Lasandra transformed the abuse into a form of love to justify the action."

"Is she dysfunctional enough, Daddy?" Bless said, with a smile.

"Yeah, more than enough." Lasandra looked like Janet Jackson for real. Her beautiful ebony complexion looked like it would taste like the finest chocolate ever made. She was by far the curviest of them all. She had nice, thick thighs, a fat ass, a small waist and big, juicy titties.

"The Puerto Rican is Tiffany. She's from New York. She's the only one that had her shit halfway together. She was enrolled in college for accounting. Her father had dough and spoiled her rotten. Then he got drunk one night and got into a car accident, killing himself and the driver of the other car. Her relatives didn't take her in, because they couldn't stand her father. She went from majoring in Accounting, to majoring in sucking dick. When things got too rough for her, she ended up in the shelter. Oh, I almost forgot…"

"What?"

"She has two additional qualities I know you'll like."

"What's that?"

"Obviously, she was a Daddy's girl, and she is going to need a replacement. Another thing she is into is public sex and humiliation."

"Oh, yeah?"

"The last is Akura. She's been in the shelter for over a year. I don't know that much about her, but she's the only Asian I could find in the shelter. Something got to be wrong with her, because you don't find too many Asians fucked up like that."

Tiffany and Akura were both fine as a muthafucka. Tiffany looked like a young version of Sophia Vergara. She had golden-brown, shoulder-length, Shirley Temple styled curls and had an exotic Latin beach sand complexion that heightened her sex appeal. Akura, on the other hand, had that foreign sex appeal. Her straight, black hair fell to the small of her back. She reminded me of that chick in, Crouching Tiger, Hidden Dragon.

"The drinks you told me to fix them should have them feeling good in a few minutes."

I had Bless crush up 15 pills of ecstasy and put it in the wine bottles. It was time to get into their heads, and the ecstasy was going to help.

"What did y'all do the past five days?" I said, walking over to the end table to grab a clipped blunt out of the ashtray.

"First, we went for a girls' day out. We went to one of them expensive spas in Boston and did it big. You know, the facials, nails, skin treatment and full body massages. After being cramped up in the shelter all that time, I wanted them to know how it feels to be a lady, once again."

"And?"

"They fuckin love it. Next, I took them shopping. Everything you see they got on, I bought them. After that, for the next couple of days, I did things with them that they would never imagine doing. Showing them things that they'd never otherwise would have seen. So when it was time to drop them off, none of them wanted to get out of the truck, so we came here."

"A'ight, sounds like they are ready. It's time to go get into their head."

"Okay, Daddy."

Bless walked over and gave me a kiss on the cheek.

"Go handle your business." I said.

I smacked her on the ass as she walked away.

I watched on the TV as Bless joined the girls back in the living room.

"So, how are you all feeling?"

"I feel good, girl." Lasandra said with a big smile.

"Shit, I felt good ever since I knew I didn't have to go back to that stankin' ass shelter," Tiffany said. "Can I have some more to drink? That shit got me feeling good."

"Me, too." Tonia cut in. "That shit got my nipples so hard, they hurt."

All the girls looked at Tonia's nipples and said, "Damn!" in unison. Bless got up and went to the kitchen, returning with the bottle of wine.

"So, when do we meet him?" Akura said, breaking her silence.

"Don't worry, he'll come when he's ready."

"What's he like?" Tonia asked.

"Everything you want in a man."

"Will he be able to take care of all of us?" Lasandra asked.

"Mentally, dickly, emotionally and financially. But your main purpose will be to take care of him. You'll have to put him before everything you know and love. Including yourself."

"You talk about him like he's God or something."

"He is my God, Tonia. He gave me a purpose when I didn't have one. Now I got something to live for. Then, on top of all that, He made me a Queen. I feel like I've been reborn. Everything seems clearer with my Daddy in my life. None of this would have been possible if I didn't make the ultimate sacrifice."

"What was that?" Tiffany asked.

"Me? I had to sacrifice myself to him. I had to put my life into his hands and trust him with it. I let him in my head and my heart. Was I scared? You fuckin' right I was scared. But look at me now," Bless said, sitting back in the leather chair, crossing her legs lady-like and finished with, "I'm a muthafuckin' Gorilla Queen."

Bless wiggled her diamond-covered fingers in the air.

"Y'all could be too if you let my Daddy become your daddy and you are willing to sacrifice yourself like I did."

"Where do I sign up?" Tonia said excitedly.

Bless went on about me to the girls. She had them drooling. Artey was right about having a boss bitch. She was laying it on thick. Her voice was mesmerizing, and captivating her audience like a master story teller. Finally, I made my entrance.

"Daddy, I want you to meet Tonia, Akura, Lasandra and Tiffany. Girls, this is Daddy."

They looked at me with dreamy drug-induced eyes.

"I want y'all to do something for me. I want you to take tonight and think if becoming a Queen is something you really want to do. If you choose to walk out that door, fine. I'll give you $5,000, with no strings attached. But if you decide to stay, your life won't be yours, anymore. Your thoughts won't be yours, anymore. You'll give me your mind, body, and soul. In turn, I'll make you a Gorilla Queen. Bless only gave you a taste of what's to come. Bless."

"Yes, Daddy?"

"Make sure these girls are taken care of."

"Yes, Daddy.

"A'ight, ladies, hopefully, I'll see you in the morning. If I don't, have a nice life… peace."

Chapter 17

The next morning, when I woke, Tonia, Akura, Lasandra and Tiffany were standing at the foot of my bed.

"What's up? Have y'all made up your minds, yet?" I asked.

"We had already made our decision when Bless made the offer." Tiffany said.

"So, all of you realize there's no going back?"

"We have nothing to go back to in the first place." Lasandra replied.

"A'ight then, let me be the first to welcome you to the rest of your lives, as Gorilla Queens."

I didn't waste any time with my Gorilla Queens. Three hours after I woke, their training began. Since the main objective of my Queens would be to seduce men, it was only right that they studied their prey. I sent Bless to the college bookstore at the University of Massachusetts to purchase each girl a male psychology textbook.

We sat around, studying and discussing what we read five hours a day. I had them bring up old relationships and analyze them.

We studied the different egos found in men, then came up with different ways to cater to them. They learned how to turn a man with a lion's ego into a lamb, and, at the same time, to turn a man with a lamb's ego into a lion.

Next, we studied Sirens.

When we got to that subject, Akura asked, "What are Sirens, Daddy?"

"Sirens originated from Greek mythology. They were said to be beautiful women who lured sailors onto rocks with their singing. Vanessa Williams played a Siren in the movie, Odyssey. Anyone see that movie?"

"I did." Tiffany replied.

"Nowadays, Sirens are considered women who have mastered the art of seduction. Females like Halle Berry, Angelina Jolie, and Selma Hayek are the Sirens of today."

"So all a Siren is, is just a beautiful woman?"

"No, Tonia. First of all, beauty has nothing to do with seduction. Seduction is more like a game of psychology. It involves combining the right words with the right actions for a desired result. Seduction is all mental, ladies, remember that. A Siren isn't just a beautiful woman. She's more than that. She's larger than life. Siren's give off vibes of mystery, danger and excitement. They possess the powers to take men beyond their normal limitations into the realm of the forbidden."

"What will be the difference between us and any other girl they fucked?" Lasandra asked.

"You will knowingly and willingly cater to their egos, while most girls will be trying to get into their pockets. They'll be intrigued at this new approach and they will relax, once they realize you're not interested in their money. All of a sudden, all the other girls will seem like they are the same to him. Gradually, with your manipulation, they'll distance themselves from those other girls to spend more time with you."

"So, if we aren't interested in their money, what are we gettin' at them for?" Tiffany asked.

"Each one will be different. Now, I never said we won't be getting at them for their money. I just said we won't appear to be interested in their money. That's just so they drop their guards to let you in. Besides getting their money, you're gonna do a little blackmailing, spying and manipulating for Daddy."

"Kinda like some secret agent shit, huh?" Lasandra asked while the rest of the girls laughed.

"Ya'll laugh now, but that's exactly what it's going to be like. Oh, by the way, while you're laughing, remember this, secret agents die in the real world."

The laughing stopped.

For the next couple of days, we took a break from the books. I had to give them time to soak in all they had learned.

During the day, I took them to a shooting range owned by an ex-drug dealer from the hood. There I taught them how to shoot, load and clean a gun. At first, they were nervous and jumped every time they heard gunshots. But, as time went on, they got more comfortable and started hitting their targets, dead-on.

At night, we sat around, watching porn flicks. I wanted them to see what men like and didn't like. I pointed out the faces men like to see a girl make and the moans men like to hear. From that lesson, they learned that men were hooked more on physical and visual aspects of sex, unlike women, who were more into the emotional side of sex.

We did everything together, which made the bond stronger between us. We ate together, watched movies together, and even slept together in my king-size bed. The whole time, I never showed sexual interest in any of them, except Bless. At night, while we were all in the bed, I'd wake up and start fucking the shit out of Bless.

The other girls would wake up and watch. I wouldn't let them touch me or themselves. I'd read somewhere that by doing that, it automatically made them want to seduce me, and they tried. Every time one of them thought I was going to give them some dick, I'd completely ignore them. That drove them crazy and made them want me that much more.

Even though I had isolated them from the outside world, every now and then, I would isolate one from the pack. I'd either get her slightly drunk or give her a hit of ecstasy to loosen her up. Then I would question her about her past. I'd go as far as her childhood and end up stirring up emotions that brought tears to her eyes.

All of them had feelings of abandonment. That was their greatest fear. The fear I would leave them. I comforted them, and then stirred up more emotions, again bringing tears to their eyes. When I was done with all of them, I knew what made them happy, sad, angry and tearful. I realized then, I was officially in their heads.

After several weeks of constant training, I decided to take them to a club out of state to see if they were ready. We went to this high-class baller club in Hartford, Connecticut. I told them to find the biggest baller.

They went to work, weaving through the crowd. I watched them from my V.I.P. table. They smiled at some, flirted with others and danced with a few. When they finally made their way back to the V.I.P. section, they all gave me the same answer. It was a older black man in his mid-forties, dark complexion, with light-brown contacts lenses. To the untrained eye, he looked normal.

"Tell me, Tonia, why do you think he's the biggest baller in the club?" I asked.

"I don't think I know."

"Give me one reason why."

"His shoes are Luigi Borelli, monk strap calfskin. They're worth a couple of thousand."

"How do you know they're Luigi Borelli's?"

"By the L.B on the Strap."

"Lasandra, it's your turn."

"He's drinking a 1985 Sassicaia Tuscany worth a $1,000 a bottle, and there are six bottles at his table."

"Good, real good. Akura, you're next."

"When I got close to him, I could smell Giorgio Armani's 'Prive'. That's Armani's private collection. He only lets his close friends get some. I doubt he knows Armani, so I figure whoever is selling it to him is charging him out the ass for it. $5,000 to $10,000 a bottle."

"I like that. You could smell the money on him. You a beast, for real." I gave Akura a wink, and she blushed.

"Tiffany, talk to me, girl. What makes you think he's the biggest baller in the club?"

"I just didn't look at him, I also looked at the people he was with."

"And?"

"The girls he's with are wearing jewelry from the Pasha de Cartier collection. All of them combined got over $200,000 on, easy."

"Bless, you have anything you want to add?"

"His watch is a Blancpain Villeret Equation Marchante worth about $130,000. Also, I asked the bartender who he was, and he said his name is Cider. He's from Nigeria, and he moves dope."

My Queens were right. The dude didn't have on any diamonds, big heavy chains, or anything screaming, look at me. Instead, he had on the type of shit that if you didn't know the name, you'd dismiss it as cheap. So, having my Queens go through those super-rich catalogs paid off. Yeah, they were almost ready.

Chapter 18

A couple of days before my birthday, the girls prepared an extravagant dinner. The long, rectangular, smoked glass table was adorned with candles, expensive wines and enough food to feed a small village. I sat at the head of the table in an egg shell white, silk Armani suit. Around my neck hung a custom-made Gorilla medallion, encrusted in diamonds. As I sat there, I looked at my Queens, one by one. I was proud of each one of them, like an artist would be of his paintings he considered masterpieces. My Gorilla Queens were my creation, sculpted by my words and ready to do whatever I said. That night, I think, was my first taste of the God complex. I became addicted. My Queens sat attentively, waiting for me to say something.

"Everything alright, Daddy?" Bless asked.

"Yeah, everything is cool. I'm just taking it all in."

"Do you like what you see?"

"Without question."

They all smiled.

After a few more minutes of comfortable silence, I stood up with my wine glass. "Listen up, my beautiful bitches." Again, they smiled. "I want to tell you how proud I am of y'all. Bless couldn't have selected a better group of females to become my Queens." I lifted my glass to Bless, and she did the same in return, mouthing the words, "Thank you."

"This last month or so we've been together has been perfect. So I want y'all to give yourselves a round of applause."

"We love you too, Daddy," Tonia said.

"Of course, you do," I said, giving her a wink. "I think y'all are ready to put in work for Daddy."

"You damn right we are!" Lasandra said.

"That's what I want to hear. Now pay attention. Ballers that got money want it all: the finest cars, jewelry, clothes and women, etc. After a while, they tend to get comfortable and let down their guard."

"And that's where we come in," Bless cut in.

"That's right." I said, as I slowly walked around the table. "You all will enter their lives, offering excitement and pleasure that can't be resisted. Every girl that came before you will pale in comparison to you. Pleasure comes to those, when they are taken from the safety of their world and thrown into unfamiliar territory. Everybody wants to be overwhelmed, and your targets won't be any different. You'll do the things the other girls won't. At the same time, they'll let you in their hearts, minds and pockets."

"We'll leave them drunk off these pussies for you, Daddy." Lasandra said.

"And when you get them like that, you'll move in and plant things in their minds and extract information they ordinarily wouldn't tell."

"When do we get started?" Tiffany asked?

"Sooner than you think. Another thing y'all need to understand is that you don't want to come straight out giving them some pussy. They'll share you with their crew like dog meat. You're not chicken heads, you're Gorilla Queens, remember that. Make them treat you as such. Sounds easy, don't it? Don't get it fucked up, men can get real evil when they think somebody is trying to steal their money.

"To them, money is power, and without power, they are nothing. They'll kill for that power; that includes killing you. So your game has to be tight. I mean, you have to be on some best female actress of the year shit. But don't overdo it. Dudes catch on to that shit quick."

I finished circling the table and took my seat once again.

"With what you taught us Daddy, ain't no muthafucka out there gonna be able to resist us." Bless said that.

"And you know this, girl." Tonia said, trying to roll her neck like a black girl. Everyone laughed.

"May I have everyone's attention? I'd like to make a toast." Tiffany said, standing up, tapping the side of her glass with a spoon. "I want to say, on behalf of your Queens, thank you for turning us ugly ducklings into beautiful swans."

"Here! Here!" everyone said in unison.

"Thank you, Tiff, but y'all were never ugly ducklings. Y'all were born Queens. You just had to find your King, that's all. So let me make a toast." I said, raising my glass. "To new beginnings."

"To new beginnings!" they repeated.

"Gorilla forever, my Queens."

"Gorilla forever, Daddy!" they cheered.

"Now, eat up. The night is just getting started. We still have to go over your targets.

After dinner, we took a couple of bottles of Dom P and went into the living room to relax by the cobblestone fireplace. I sat on the love seat, with Bless's head on my lap.

"I'm going to tell you a little bit about your targets. Bless will have all the information you will need later on in the week. Tonia, you're first. You have Sean Crass from Bolten Village. He pushes dope and has that whole projects on lock."

"I think I heard of him. He's white, ain't he?"

"Yeah, he's worth over a mil, easy. We need that money, shorty, you feel me?"

"Yes, Daddy."

"The stash house is somewhere in the projects. Find out more."

"Okay."

"Tiff, you got Javier. He's into the coke game. I heard that he cops 5-10 at a time. The Gorillas need that. I need you to find out when and how he re-ups. Bless is going to give you some info on custom cars. He's into racing cars down at the drag strip in Chicopee. He also owns five custom car shops. Javier should be easy because he's one of those sucka-for-love ass chumps. He's into eating pussy like a muthafucka."

"Oooh, la-la." Tiffany responded.

"Make sure you do your homework before you jump out there."

"I will, Daddy."

"Lasandra, you got Cool C. He's down with the crew Black House. They fuck with counterfeit dough, strictly. Even though they deal in fake money, the real money has to be somewhere."

She said, "Okay, as you wish, it shall be done."

Akura you have Ming, out from Rhode Island. He lives in Amherst. Ming only fucks with Chinese girls."

"He sells liquid dope, right?" she asked.

I looked at her and said, "How do you know that?"

"I know some people that deal with him."

"So I don't have to tell you how hard it is to get on the inside of a Chinese gang. Especially the Kenji Dragons. They're known for killing D.A's, police and judges. So take your time and don't rush. Ming likes to gamble."

"Like most Chinese guys with money." Akura said.

"Do you know how to play poker?"

"Yeah."

Good, because he owns a high-stakes gambling house in the boulders. It's a Chinese-only establishment. You have a problem setting up one of your own?"

"I'll do anything for you, Daddy?"

"That's what's up. Bless, you got Tito. You already know what to do. Now, for the goodies. Waiting outside in about three hours will be a limo to take ya'll shopping in New York. To play the game, you have to look the part. Bless will give each of you $5,000 to spend. We want sexy, not slutty. When you get back, you'll pick up your cars from Jinto's and the keys to your apartments."

"We won't be living with you, Daddy?" Lasandra asked.

"Of course, you are, but you won't be bringing your targets here, will you?"

"No," she replied like a little kid.

I stood up, but Bless motioned for me to be still.

"Yall bitches get over here and kiss his dick." she instructed.

Bless pulled my dick out and held it so they could kiss the tip. Each Queen crawled over on her knees and kissed my dick like they were told.

"See, Daddy, I told you I would keep these bitches in check for you."

Chapter 19

When night fell upon Chestnut Park, it was just as beautiful as the day was. Stars studded the night sky like diamond dust sprinkled across a black blanket. There was something about a warm summer night in the city that got my blood pumping. It was almost euphoric, in some ways. Being that it was my birthday, it made the night even better.

As I cruised down Sergeant Street on my brand-new Suzuki GSX-R1000, a million things raced through my head. Have you ever notice how you see things differently when you have money? Money allows you to be free, physically and mentally. When your pockets are fucked up, the chains of poverty hold you down. Physically, you're limited. You can't do all the things you want to do. Mentally, you're focused on one thing, getting money. Nothing else seems to matter.

With those two problems lifted off your shoulders, you're able to see further and do more. You're no longer trapped, mentally and physically. You're not affected by the daily struggles that plague most people. Your dreams are no longer dreams, but reality. I heard somewhere that money can't buy you happiness. Whatever dumb muthafucka said that, never been to the ghetto.

Turning onto Chestnut Street, there was barely any room to ride, so I pulled up on the sidewalk. All of Holyoke seemed to be there that night. The streets were lined with the hottest whips, rimmed out with bangin' systems.

The sidewalks were filled with street dudes dressed to kill and bitches looking sexy as fuck. Music pumped from the third floor of the now official Gorilla Family Clubhouse. T-Money, Jessito, Daryl and Country were out in front, amongst the crowd.

"Oh, shit! Check Pharaoh out, yo!" Jessito said, pointing as I drew closer.

"Clear a path, make room, move, yo! Let my man through!" T-Money shouted clearing the path for me.

I popped a wheelie and blew passed everybody. I slowed the bike down and made a U-turn with my front wheel still in the air. Half way back I let my wheel down and pulled up to the front of the club house.

Country said, "Now, that is how you roll up to your birthday party, son!" giving me dap and a thug hug.

"Happy Birthday, yo," Daryl said, giving me some dap.

"Yo, that bike is sick, kid!" T-Money shouted as he walked around the bike.

"You like it?"

"Fuck, yeah, yo!"

If everything goes the way I plan, this is how we are gonna be living, big kid style."

"No doubt, I'm feeling that.

"Yo, Pharaoh, come check the clubhouse out!" Jessito said.

As we pushed our way through the mob, I felt like a superstar, for real. People I didn't know were giving me dap. Girls who never gave me the time of day before were giving me all kinds of hugs and kisses. I think a lot of it had to do with killing Crazy Eddie.

We bypassed the third floor where the party was. We went straight to the fourth floor. I liked what Bless did to my crib so much, I told her to hook up the clubhouse, too. Jessito opened the door and stepped to the side, so I could be the first to step in.

Yo, the shit was crazy. I told Bless to go all-out, but this was some next level shit. The new pine floor shined like a pond on a sunny day. Having all the walls of the four apartments knocked down made the floor plan larger than I thought. Right off the back, a fifteen-foot glass bar stole my attention, with ten piranhas swimming about.

Up behind the bar were two more tanks. In one of them was a white snake on black sand. In the other one was a black snake on white sand. Off to the right of the bar were pool tables. What made them stand out were the colors. It was all black with white balls with black numbers.

Suddenly, someone knocked on the door.

"Who the fuck is that at the back door?" Daryl said, going to open it.

When the door swung open, his eyes got as big as shit. Bless and my Queens walked in.

"Okay, now this is what the fuck I'm talking

about. Who ordered the strippers?" Daryl said.

"Strippers? We are not the strippers, well, unless our Daddy wants us to be. We're Queens." Bless said arrogantly.

"Queens? These bitches ain't no Queens."

"Yo, they're Gorilla Queens, and don't call them bitches again!" I warned.

Each one of my girls came up and gave me a kiss. All of them were looking fine as hell. They had me feeling myself.

"Here Daddy," Bless said, handing me the backpack.

"A'ight yo, check it. I'm going to run down how this shit is going to go. Jessito, you're the Gorilla diplomat until Joey wakes up. That's kinda like being the spokesperson."

"Got it."

"Country, you'll run the coke operations until further notice."

"Bet."

"Daryl, you'll be the family enforcer, for now, you'll need to form your own crew."

"Cool, I like that."

"T-Money, I got something special planned for you. We will talk later. Anyone have any questions?"

"Yeah, what are your Gorilla Queens gonna do?" Country asked.

"You don't worry about them. They're my Queens. That's all you need to know. Now, everyone take one of these."

I reached into my backpack and handed everyone a copy of, 'The Way Of The Gorilla.'

"What's this?" T- Money asked.

"Our foundation, T-Money. I want everyone to read this and know it, front and back."

"Man, you crazy, yo." Daryl said.

"If you want to remain a Gorilla, Daryl, you'll read it. I'm done, for now. Finish showing me this place, so I can start enjoying my birthday."

Country said, "A'ight, a'ight. You can see the rest of this shit later. Let's go see my work downstairs."

He headed to the front door. We followed Country down the stairs, bypassing the party once again. We came to the second floor, and the first thing I noticed was that the doors had been changed.

"Yo, the first thing I did was reinforce the doors." Country banged on the door a couple of times. "They only open from the inside."

"So that means somebody has to be in here at all times?" Jessito asked.

"Yeah, yo, we are set to run twenty-four hours a day, seven days a week."

"How do you know who's at the door?" T-Money asked.

"Right there." Country pointed at two cameras in the corner of the hallway.

Just then some dude opened the door. We filed into the apartment, one by one. All the walls were knocked down, just like upstairs. The spot was practically bare, except for three, long, glass tables and a sitting area with a huge screen TV. On the other side of the loft were six brand-new stoves, lined up next to each other.

"A'ight, tell me about this set up."

"Check it, this spot is for cooking, bagging and counting money. Underneath us are four apartments. Each of the apartments has its own function. One is for pushing weight in coke, one is for pushing weight in crack, and the other one is for all the shit we bust down into pieces. The other apartment I left open just in case we start pushing something else."

"Okay, I like how this shit is looking. Keep going."

"The customers will go to the first floor to get what they want. The doors downstairs are sealed shut. Now, this is the fly shit, right here." Country walked over to one of the throw rugs. He pulled it back to reveal some kinda door.

"What the fuck?" I said, bending over to open it.

"This door goes to the empty apartment right under it. This is how we pass the coke and collect the money. This is the only way out and in the apartments downstairs. The windows and doors are both sealed shut."

"Yo, no bullshit, this shit is tight yo. I couldn't have done it better myself. Cool, we're gonna open up shop Monday. A Queen will drop off two birds."

"Hold up, Pharaoh. I know you got at least five to seven kilos from Dante's." Daryl interrupted.

"I never told you what I got from Dante's, so what the fuck are you talking about?"

"Whatever, yo, I know you came up. How much are you holding out on us?

Daryl was trying to put me on blast in front of the crew.

"How the fuck am I holding out? Matter of fact,

I don't have to explain shit to you, son. If I say two kilos are going to be here Monday, then that's that. Don't question me again. You got shit fucked up. I'm the fuckin' boss, remember that?"

"Yo, who the fuck you talking to like that, kid?"

"You, muthafucka!" I snapped back.

Daryl approached me like he was going to swing on me. Lasandra stepped in front of him and pulled out her .22 caliber pistol. Bless already had her .38 out and down by her side. Akura had her hand in her purse. Tiff and Tonia both stood on either side of Daryl with their .38's pointed at his head.

"Oh, it's like that now? You're hiding behind your girls, huh, punk?"

"Yo, chill. Put the guns down. We're all Gorillas, aren't we?" Country said.

My Queens didn't move, flinch or blink. I knew then if Daryl would've swung, he was a dead man. There was no doubt in my mind after that, my Queens would've killed for me. Daryl took a few steps back and put his hands in the air.

"A'ight Queens, put the guns away, and let's go party."

The girls put their guns away, one by one, and left. Country stayed back with Daryl. "Yo, Country, this muthafucka is going to make me kill him! He get a little money and everything changes."

Country said, "Be Like That Sometimes."

"Fuck that!" Daryl shouted, smashing his Heineken bottle into the wall.

"Yo, what's really up with you?"

"Listen, he's always been on some better-than-me shit. Ever since I've known him, he's always been trying to out-shine me. He ain't no better than me! Fuck Pharaoh!"

"I'm saying, yo, what are you gonna do about it?"

"For real, between you and me, I think the Gorillas will be better off without this dude around, you feel me?"

"Yeah, I feel you, yo."

Chapter 20

Back at the party, shit was jumping like a muthafuka. T-Money went all out in hooking up the clubhouse. He had a stage built with a D.J. booth behind it. Graffiti was on all of the walls, even the ceiling. On the opposite end of the club house were the bar and two tournament pool tables. In the same area were sofas, chairs and stools for relaxing.

"Yo, what do you think, son?" T-Money said, trying to shout over the music.

I shouted, "This shit is tight, yo!"

Bodies were everywhere, with barely any room to dance. Rascal, the local superstar D.J. kept the party alive with the latest beats. Every five minutes, he'd give me a shout out and the crowd would go wild.

"Yo, Pharaoh, I want you to meet a few friends of mine, right quick." Jessito said, leading me over to the bar. "I know you said for Daryl to find guys to enforce shit, but I know some real serious cats that want to get down."

"Cool, where are they?"

"Over here. Yo, this is Task, Guillotine, Dirty

Chuck, Killer, K and Lethal. We all used to go to school together. They heard about the Gorillas and are trying to get down."

"What do y'all do?"

"Bust them thangs," Task spoke up. All of them had that look: baggy jeans, hoodies and Tims.

"A'ight, I'm going to put y'all on probation for thirty days to see how y'all act. Jessito, make sure they get a copy of, 'The Way Of The Gorilla.'"

"A'ight, yo."

Even though they looked like every other thug in the party, they also had something extra… that look. Not just in their dress code, but in their eyes. They were hungry, for real, plus, they were young and wild. That was a deadly combination.

I went back over by the pool tables. I was on my third beer. I decided it would be my last. There were too many crews, and I figured something was bound to jump off. E-Love and his crew were out front. The Latin Crowns were somewhere in the party, acting a fool. The Pine Street crew was there too. Then there was a crew standing over by the kegs I had never seen before. It was hard to see their faces in the dark.

"T-Money, who dem dudes over there by the bar?"

"I don't know."

Then someone accidently bumped into the light switch, I caught sight of Sean Crass coming through the door. I made eye contact with Bless and motioned to the entrance. She caught on fast and whispered something in Tonia's ear. Bless looked back at me and winked.

Sean Crass was one of those ghetto-ass white

dudes. He was a perfect example of what happens to a white boy when raised in a black neighborhood. Everything about him was ghetto, his walk, his talk and even his dress. Sean made a name for himself by pushing pounds of weed out of his mother's house in Bolten Village. He had that on lock until E-Love came in and shut him down with cheaper prices. Since he couldn't make any money off the weed tip, he fell off. Not long after, he caught a rape charge and got sent upstate for five years. It was there he met Ming, the up and coming lieutenant in the Kenji Dragons, a Chinese gang. I guess they formed a tight bond because when Sean got out, Ming fronted him a kilo of dope. It was bad enough to try to buy off the Chinese when you weren't Chinese. To be fronted a kilo was unheard of.

Sean came up at the right time. See, heroin comes and goes like a fad amongst young people. It was all cool and shit until somebody you knew had an overdose. Then it fades out like last year's fashion. Well, the year he was fronted that kilo, heroin was back and popular, more than ever. Teenagers and adults alike indulged in the lethal drug. Since Sean was white, the upper class white kids felt safer buying it from him. Also, being from the ghetto, naturally, his crew embraced the chance to come up. With the perfect connect, a loyal squad and a hunger for money, Sean came up fast.

Within six months, he bought the Bolten Village projects he grew up in and turned them into a heroin Mecca. The projects were filled with dope fiends and dealers. Every major heroin dealer in Holyoke copped from him, including the Latin Crowns.

"Yo, Pharaoh, let me holla at you for a second,"

Country said.

"What's up?"

"Daryl is tripping. He's talking some crazy shit, yo. I played along like I was with it, but yo, I think you need to watch yourself."

"He's just going through some things. He'll get over it."

"I think it's deeper than that."

"Don't sweat it, Country."

"You're the boss. I thought I'd let you know."

I should've listened to Country. If you notice, anytime something fucked up was about to happen, there were always signs. You never notice them until it was too late. Then you be like, damn, I should've seen it coming. Country just gave me a sign, and I didn't pay attention.

"Yo, I got to use the bathroom. I'll holla at ya."

The line to the bathroom was long as shit. I was just about to piss out on the fire escape when a fine, light skinned chick stood in front of me. She had on one of those sexy school girl outfits and her hair in two pigtails. Her red and black plaid mini-skirt was barely covering her juicy, round ass. She wore white thin socks pulled up to her knees with black traditional school girl shoes. The top four buttons of her white shirt were unbuttoned, and to top it off, she wasn't wearing a bra.

"Damn, shorty, you look good as a muthafucka." She turned around and smiled. "And you have a cute smile. What's up? What's your name?"

"Coco."

"Coco huh, tell me, do you taste like Coco?"

Coco smiled again. "I never tasted myself. You'll

have to ask my man that."

"Well, I'm not the type to take another man's word for anything. I'd rather taste you for myself."

"Ooooh, you're good., what's your name?"

"They call me Pharaoh."

"Pharaoh? So you're the birthday boy. I heard about you."

"I hope it was all bad."

"Why?"

"Because you look like you're into bad boys."

Right then, the bathroom door opened, and Coco went in. She turned around and winked as she closed the door. A second later, she opened it. "I thought you were a bad boy."

"I am."

"Then why are you standing out there like a good little boy?"

"Say no more." I slid into the bathroom with her.

"I only got ten minutes, so do what you do."

I stripped off my jacket and my shirt, then I pulled my pants down far enough to get my dick out. I picked her up and sat her on the sink. I put her legs over my shoulder and slid her pussy to the edge of the sink.

When I was about to force my way into her wet pussy, she said, "Hold up, why don't you finish off where you started?" She repositioned my dick to enter her ass. "Come on, fuck me, bad boy!"

Coco wrapped both arms around my neck and hung on for dear life.

"Hold on, yo." I said, kneeling down.

"What?"

For some reason, I don't know if it was from the

mixture of weed and alcohol or just being caught up in the moment but I stuck my tongue in her ass first. I know, I know, but don't act like you've never done it or thought about doing it.

"Damn, you're a nasty boy, for real! Yeah, I like this shit! Oooooh! Don't stop! Don't stop!"

I tongued her asshole for another two minutes before my tongue cramped up. I stood up and put her legs back over my shoulders. Coco positioned my dick at the entrance to her asshole. This time, I didn't waste any time running up in it.

Flop! Flop! Flop! Flop! Flop! Flop!

"Ahhhhhhh! Ahhhnhhh! Ahhhhhhhh!"

I fucked Coco like a crazed maniac with a drunk dick. After punishing it for five minutes straight, her ass became too sweaty and began to slide.

"Bend over the toilet." I said.

She obeyed.

Coco bent over, resting her hands on the back of the toilet. She looked back at me. "Fuck me in the ass, you black, nasty muthafucka!"

And that's exactly what I did.

Flop! Flop! Flop! Flop! Flop! Flop!

"Agggghhhh! Ummmmmmm! I love this shit! That's it, Fuuccccckkkk my ass, nigggaaa!"

I worked her ass like a jackhammer cracking the city pavement. Her head banged off the back of the toilet tank. I didn't care. I barely knew her, plus, I could tell the rough shit was getting her off.

"Ummmm! Aggghhhh! Harrrrrder!"

Coco responded to my anal assault with growls and grunts. Another five minutes passed before Coco started throwing up all over the back of the toilet.

"Don't stop! Don't stop!" she said as she wiped chunks of whatever she was throwing up off of her lips.

I didn't have plans on stopping, as long as she was standing. I was going to keep banging away. Coco brought me closer to busting my nut every time she'd gag. All the muscles in her body would tighten up, including her asshole. Then, when her legs got too weak to hold her up, she turned around and sat on the toilet. To my surprise, she took my shit-covered dick in her mouth. Then to top it all off, she ended up pissing and shittin' at the same time. Coco had a twisted look of gratification as she swallowed my nut while looking me in the eyes.

"Damn, you're a nasty bitch!"

"Happy Birthday, Pharaoh," Coco said, licking my balls.

"Who's your man?"

"Why? He don't have nothing to do with this. He thinks gettin' fucked in the ass is for white girls."

"I tell you what, here's my number. You can call me, and we can do whatever."

"No, I'll tell you what. I'll call you, but only for ass shots. My man takes care of my pussy."

"Bet."

We both washed up and headed back to the party. Things were still jumping, and everyone was centered around the stage. When I got a closer look, I saw it was Guillotine rockin' the mic.

"Yo, Jessito, Guillotine got skills like that?"

"Hell, yeah, yo, Guillotine is the hottest thing to ever come out of West Mass."

By the way the crowd was reacting; I had no

choice but to believe it.

"Yo, Jessito, get the crew together and meet me outside."

A couple minutes later we were out front, taking in the fresh air.

Country said, "What's the deal? I got two bad bitches waiting for me."

"Trust me, Country, they can wait. Follow me."

I led them through the alleyway to the back of the clubhouse. Parked under a street lamp were four GSX-R1000s, identical to mine.

"Here," I said, handing each of them a set of keys. "They're yours."

"Stop playing, Pharaoh." T-Money said, giving me that-I don't believe it-look.

"What are y'all standing there looking stupid for? They're yours."

"Man, I don't know what to say." Jessito said.

"You don't have to say shit. Listen, yo, if I shine, you shine. It's simple as that."

"No doubt. Gorillas forever!'

"Gorillas forever!" I left them to play with their new toys and went around to the front.

"Youngblood."

I turned around and saw Artey.

"Hey, Artey, What's the deal?"

"You didn't think I'd forget your birthday, did you?" Artey said, getting out of his pearl white '69 Lincoln with peanut butter guts and chrome trim.

"You never do."

Artey stole the show everywhere he went. He had this glow about him. Even though today was my day, I didn't mind being outshined by Artey.

"Happy Birthday, Youngblood."

"Thanks, yo."

"So, you got yourself a clubhouse now?" Artey asked, looking across the street.

"Yeah, it's a little something, something."

"Listen, Youngblood, you moved to a whole new level of the game. Things are going to be different now. No longer are you going to be under the radar. Your name is out there now. A lot of people are going to be watching you."

"Like who?"

"Everyone, Youngblood. You have the cops and under covers that are gonna try and extort you. All kinds of hood bitches will come at you with all types of game. Then you're going to have jealous punks plotting against you. Remember this; if your pockets are getting fatter, someone else's pockets are gettin' thinner."

"I feel that."

"Cool."

We sat on the hood of the car, staring back at the crowd across the street. Everything felt perfect. With the warm summer breeze blowing gently, my crew happy as shit, and my pockets about to blow… yeah, life was good.

"Here," Artey said, handing me one of his cigars and a wine glass.

"What are we drinking?"

"Nothing but the best, you can believe that."

Artey snapped his fingers and Pussycat and Baby D got out of the back seat. One poured the wine, and the other lit the cigars.

"Hey, do you want the girls for the night?"

"Nah, I'm straight. I got my own now."

"Alright then, here." Artey reached around his neck and pulled off a platinum chain that he always wore.

"What's this for?"

"It's your birthday present." Artey put the chain around my neck. He took a couple of steps back and admired it. "Yeah, it fits you good, Youngblood."

"Thanks, Artey."

We sat back, sipped wine, and puffed cigars. Artey schooled me some more on the things I needed to look out for. His words were priceless. As long as I had Artey in my corner, I couldn't lose.

Five minutes later, Bless pulled up on my bike and scooted to the back.

"Daddy, are you ready?"

"Yeah, yo, Artey, I got to go. I got to unwrap my other presents, you dig?"

Artey laughed out loud. "I can dig it, Youngblood. Happy Birthday."

We pulled off and left the party in full swing. When I got back to the house, Bless took me to my room. Tonia and Tiffany already had my bath drawn. They bathed me for a minute before leaving. When I was done, Tiffany dried me off. She walked me to my bed. The whole room was filled with candles that gave it a soft glow. I laid on the bed, ass-naked and relaxed.

For the first time, I had time to reflect on all that had happened. From Crazy Eddie to Dante, my Queens, the Gorillas and my man, Joey. Everything played before my eyes as I puffed on some sticky icky. Then, the stereo came on, and I heard Sade's "Sweetest Taboo." One by one, my Queens came in the room, naked.

"Daddy, we have something to show you.

"What's that?"

They all turned around, and tattooed on their lower spines were the letters KPGQ with a crown above it.

"What does KPGQ mean?"

They all said, "King Pharaoh's Gorilla Queens."

"That's what's up for real."

"So, how do you want us? One by one, or all of us at the same time?"

I replied, "We're all in this together." With that said, they all crawled on the bed together and… and… well, you know how I get down. So I'll let your imagination do the rest.

Chapter 21

Five days later, when I pulled in front of the Gorilla clubhouse, Jessito was riding wheelies up and down Chestnut Street, showboating for some bitches.

T-Money was on his bike, kickin' it with some of the newest members of the Gorillas. There was a steady flow of customers going in and out of the building. However, I could tell by the looks of them, they weren't buying weight.

"T-Money, What's the deal, yo?" I said, walking up to give him dap.

"Chillin, yo. You know, the same ole shit, different day, that's all."

"Who the fuck Jessito think he is, Evil Knievel or something?"

"Man, that kid been trippin' on that bike all day."

I watched as Jessito came flying by, standing on his seat, mimicking Jesus on the cross.

"Yo, he's going to kill himself."

"Jessito don't give a fuck."

I shook my head as Jessito came flying back by doing a wheelie.

"Anyway, yo, how's business?"

"Country can give you the exact numbers, but from what I saw, we still ain't moving no weight." T-Money replied.

"Fuck!" I said.

"Chill, yo, shit is gonna start moving soon enough."

"For me, another minute would be too late. We need to start moving that shit now!"

T-Money could see how mad I was and chose not to say anything else.

"Yo, I want you to follow me, right quick."

I turned on my bike and revved the engine a couple of times.

"Where are we headed?"

"Just follow me, yo."

Jessito pulled alongside of us just as we were about to leave and said, "What's up, where are we going?"

"You stay here and look after shit. And stop doing all that wild shit. You're no good to the family dead. Come on, T-Money."

We sped into traffic, weaving in and out of cars until we reached the nicer side of Holyoke. I pulled over to a six story building with 15 apartments in it. This building was one of the ones out of the way.

"Who lives here?" T-Money wondered.

"You." I told him.

"Me?"

"Yeah, yo, this is one of the buildings my Aunt Jo deeded to me."

"You didn't mention this building."

"I had my reasons. Everything is not for everybody.

"I hear that."

"Remember when I told you I had something special planned for you?"

"Yeah, but I didn't think it was a building."

"This is only part of it. You and I both know that you're no killer or hustler. Your thing is computers."

T-Money gritted at me. "So what are you trying to say?"

"Ayo, you my muthafuckin' man, remember that. It's just that I think you can contribute more to the Gorillas in ways the rest of us can't. But check it, I can show you more than I can tell you."

T-Money followed me into the building and up to the top floor.

"Go 'head, yo, check it out. Tell me what you think."

"T-Money opened the door and walked into the vacant apartment. He looked around, then back at me, and threw his hands up.

"Besides this old ass table and two chairs, the place is empty."

"I can see that."

"So, what do you mean, tell you what I think?"

"Have a seat."

I pulled out a bag of Lamb's Breath and a Garcia Vega cigar.

"A'ight, this is what I want you to do, and tell me if you think you can do it or not."

"What is it?"

"You know how you hacked into the Holyoke Police Department's main computer and got all that information on Javier, Cool C, Tito, and Sean Crass?"

"Yeah, that shit was simple."

"I want to expand and do something a little bigger."

"Like that."

"I want you to create a database on under covers, police and big-time dealers in Western Mass. I want to know everything about them, and I mean everything."

"You're serious, aren't you?"

"Dead serious, son. I want to know what they know. I want to know who's watching us and who our competition might be. I want cameras set up all over the city in key spots, and I want tracking devices on cars of our enemies, and the police, too. Do you think you can put that together?"

"Yo, Pharaoh, hold on for a second. The shit you're asking me to do is simple. I can do the shit in my sleep. The thing is what you're asking me to do requires some heavy equipment. That translates into some heavy dough."

"How much dough?"

"A lot of dough?"

"Give me a number."

"About $50,000, for starters."

"That's it?"

"That's for starters. Then you got to modify and upgrade shit. That $50,000 don't include software, either."

I got up, walked over to a closet and retrieved a duffle bag. I walked back to the table, unzipped it and dumped blocks of cash all over the table.

"Do you think that will be enough?"

T-Money looked at the cash in amazement.

"Yo, how much is it?"

"A little over $100,000 and some change."

"Yeah, I can work this like a muthafucka."

"Yo, listen here," I said, getting his attention. "Everybody has their part to play in the grand scheme of things, and this is your part. From here on, this is all you do."

"What's that?"

"Gathering info. You'll be the Gorilla's version of the C.I.A. The top two floors of the building are yours to do whatever you want.

The other apartments belong to my Queens. I want you to lace their apartments with cameras in every room. I don't want them to know about it either. Also, I want the clubhouse bugged and laced with cameras too."

"Anything else?"

"Yeah, nobody can know about this place or what you do for the family. You'll take an apartment in the building too, just so it don't look suspicious. The database you create will be the brains of the Gorillas. The more information you gather, the more powerful we become. In the future, the streets will become only one aspect of the business. Trust me when I say this, I got my sights on much bigger things, and that database has a lot to do with it."

T-Money sat back, and took several puffs off the cigar and released the weed smoke through his nose. He looked at me, then at the stacks of cash on the table.

"How the fuck do you come up with shit like this? You're a mad scientist when it comes to this street shit. I wonder if I looked inside your head, what I would see."

T-Money passed the Garcia.

I sat back in the chair and smiled. "The future, yo, the muthafuckin' future."

Chapter 22

Lying in bed with Bless that night, I could tell something had been bothering her for the last few days.

"What's up with you?"

"Nothing," she replied.

I snatched her by her hair. "Don't lie to me."

"Do you love that bitch more than me?"

I let her go. "What bitch? Who the fuck are you talking about?"

"That bitch, Coco from the Flats you've been fuckin' with lately."

"I don't love bitches, I fuck'em, that's all."

"You don't need to fuck that stank bitch or any other bitch, for that matter. You got me and the girls that will do anything you say, I mean anything."

Bless straddled my waist. Her eyes were red and slightly puffy.

"What's up, B? Tell Daddy what's on your mind."

"I'm saying, Daddy, I don't trust that bitch."

"Why?"

"I don't know, I don't trust that bitch, for some reason."

"You jealous, B?"

"I'll never be jealous of that bitch! I'm a fuckin' Queen. I'll kill that bitch!"

"Calm down, chill out, shorty. Why are you always trying to kill something?" I said, smiling back at her.

I loved it when she got mad. Her bottom lip poked out, and her eyes got real chinky. Damn, Bless was fine.

"Where are we at?" she asked.

"What?"

"I'm saying, where do we stand, you know, me and you?"

"We stand to make a lot of money if everything goes right."

"I'm not talking about that, stupid!" Bless playfully punched me in my chest. "Daddy, I'm serious. What's up with me and you?"

"For real, I don't know what you're talking about."

"Stop playing, you know what I mean. You just want me to say it, punk."

She punched me again, but this time her oversize robe slipped off one shoulder exposing her succulent nipples, while her hair fell seductively in front of her face, covering one eye.

"Then say it."

"I'm the only bitch you need. Fuck all them non-Gorilla bitches you stick your dick in. They don't know you like I do."

"Is that right?"

"Yessss, that's right. I know how you like your dick sucked at least five times a day, and how you like it when I fall asleep with it in my mouth. I know how you like your Garcia's rolled, I know what you like to eat, your favorite color, how to clean your gun, I know you like Tonia's titties over mine, and I'm cool with that. I also know..."

She paused.

"What else do you know?"

"I know I love you more than anything in the world."

"Yeah, well show me how much you love daddy."

Bless opened her robe completely and let it fall off her smooth, caramel shoulders. She reached over to the end table, picked up a pencil, and wrapped her hair up, Chinese style. Her hypnotizing nipples wiggled before my eyes as she inserted my shaft into her wet pussy.

For real, I think we made love that night. I'm not sure because I never made love before. Normally, we go at it like wild animals, you know punching, slapping, biting, and a little bit of choking. Not that night though. That night, shit was beautiful, and beautiful isn't a word I associate with sex.

Chapter 23

When August first rolled around, the spot had been opened a month. The coke still wasn't moving as fast as I wanted, and the money supply was getting low. I ended up getting $350,000 for Dante's jewelry. Most of that went to buying bikes, buying the girls their cars, and giving everyone $10,000 a piece. Not to mention the money for Joey's ongoing medical bills. We still had 17 kilos left, and since we weren't known for pushing weight, it looked like we were going to be stuck with it.

"Yo, why the fuck aren't we moving any weight in coke!"

I hurled my shot glass into the wall, shattering it into a thousand pieces.

Everybody was seated around the meeting table. Since Country was in charge of the coke spot, he felt the need to speak up.

"Son, you got to understand, we're not the only ones with coke. Javier got the flats sewed up, and Tito got the rest on lock. Then, all of the smaller crews are going to New York to cop a brick here and a brick there. The truth is, we aren't known for pushing weight, so nobody is gonna take us seriously." Country explained.

"You don't think I fuckin' know that!?" I spat.

"Chill, son, give it some time. If anything, we are killing them on the nickel and dimes."

"If that is the case, Country, we don't need the clubhouse, we can go back to hand-to-hand in the park!"

"So what the fuck you suggest we do?" Daryl spoke up.

That was exactly what I was waiting for.

"We? Nah son, you! You're the one I put in charge of dealing with the small crews, right? I gave you all the guns and shit you needed, and you haven't done shit with it! What the fuck, you got all that shit for show?"

"Ayo, you need to check yourself, son."

"Nah yo, you need to check yourself and get out there and handle your fuckin' business, or do you need me to do it?"

Everybody looked at Daryl. They knew what I said was right. Even Daryl knew it. That was why I was waiting for him to jump out there, so I could put his ass in the spotlight.

Daryl snarled, then relented. "What do you want me to do, Boss?"

I smiled at him as I took my seat at the head of the table again. Bless came and passed me a lit cigar.

"I want you to visit the Pine Street crew, the Dominicans on Main Street, them cats on Appleton across from the McDonald's, and every fuckin' crew that don't cop off of us. By the end of the week, I want them buying weight off us, or their people will be buying coffins for them. Whatever money you get, you keep.

All the coke you find, flush it. Can you handle that?"

"You're the boss. If that's what the boss wants, that's what the boss gets." Daryl rose from his seat and saluted as he stepped off with an attitude.

"Jessito," I said, drawing everybody's attention back to me. "I want you to deliver a message to Tito and Javier. I want you to tell them that King Pharaoh said it's time for them to retire. Tell them I said it is in their best interests to buy a boat and sail the Caribbean."

"Do you think they're gonna go for that?" Jessito asked.

"Fuck no, they aren't going for it. I don't want them to either. I want to go to war with them."

Everybody started looking at each other for a second and then, at the same time, they all looked at me.

"War?" T-Money said timidly.

"Yeah, what the fuck you think, that we were going to take over these streets without a fight? You think dudes are just gonna lay down and let us take food out of their mouths?"

"No, but I didn't think we would go picking the fight, either."

"T-Money, listen, yo, one way or another, we were eventually going to war with them. You may not want to admit it, but you know it's true. So if that's what's going to happen, why wait? Why not beef on our terms?"

"Hold up. I don't mean to sound like a bitch, but we can't go to war with two crews at once. For real, we may have more guns than them, but I know for a fact we don't got enough Gorillas."

"You're right, we don't have enough to go toe-to-

toe with them on the street. That's why were gonna use guerilla tactics. We're gonna pick a fight with them, but that's only to distract them from what's really going on."

"And that is?"

Bless walked over and stood behind me. "Me and the Queens are getting close to Tito, Javier, Cool C, and Sean. And, well, all I can say is, pillow talk is a muthafucka."

Chapter 24

No more than a few days after I hit T-Money with the $100,000, he gave me a call.

"What up, King Pharaoh?"

"Shit. What's up with you?"

"Just calling to give an update on what I been doing."

"And that is?"

"First, let me tell you I was able to get all the shit you wanted and then some."

"That's what's up."

"I would go into detail about what I got, but you wouldn't have a clue what I'm talkin' about. All you need to know is I got the top-of-the line shit." T-Money proclaimed.

"You got the tracking devices?"

"Yeah, and they're going to be activated tomorrow."

"You got all the cameras set up, already?"

"Son, like I said, I got everything. There's nothing that's going to happen without you seeing it."

"How do I see it, then?"

T-Money went and told me that he hacked into my satellite and reprogrammed it to receive a low-frequency feed from a transmitter on top of my building. Each Queen's apartment had its own channels; so did the clubhouse and a few other spots I had T-Money lace with cameras.

"Each camera has a motion beam. Anytime a person is in the room, the camera will activate automatically. If you have one person in the bathroom and another in the bedroom, the screen will split to show both."

"Just like that?"

"Yeah, yo."

"You a muthafuckin' beast, yo."

"Tell me something I don't know," T-Money said. "Yo, I got to let you go. I got more shit I got to hook up. When are you gonna come through and check out the Bat Cave?"

"When I get time, I'll be through there."

"A'ight, yo, I'm out."

"Peace."

Soon as I hung up, I started surfing the channels T-Money re-programed for me. Tonia's was the first one to pop up, and I was lucky enough to catch her in action.

Sean Crass was in Tonia's room with her.

"I was going to surprise you over dinner, but I can't wait to show you."

"What is it? I don't need any jewelry. My Daddy will buy me all the diamonds I want."

"Damn, girl, give a brother a break," Sean complained, taking off his jacket and his shirt, then said, "See?"

This clown went and tattooed Tonia's name on his arm.

"And I'm going to let you erase all the girls' numbers out of my phone."

Tonia got up and walked over to the sofa. She leaned over and inspected the tattoo. Then she stood up and pulled her shirt over her head, letting her supple tits fall out. Sean's eyes locked in on her thick, brown nipples. Tonia then pulled her mini-skirt down over her hips and let them fall to the floor.

"So, what does it mean?" Tonia asked him.

"Shit, it means you're my girl, now."

"Are you asking me or telling me?" Tonia asked, moving closer to Sean.

"I… I mean, if it's all right with you."

"What about them other bitches?"

"Fuck them other bitches. You don't see their names on my arm do you?"

"It better stay that way too." Tonia stood directly in front of Sean, ass-naked. "Well, are you gonna fuck me with your eyes or your dick?"

As Sean fumbled with his zipper, I sat back and watched in amazement how Tonia controlled every aspect of the situation like I taught her. There he was, Sean, Holyoke's biggest dope dealer, strung out on one of my Queens. In the streets, he played the tough-guy role, but behind closed door, he was a cold bitch.

"Damn, you fine as shit." he marveled.

"Tell me what you want to do to me." she purred.

"Whatever you want me to do to you."

Tonia giggled. "So you saying that it is all about me?"

"Of course, it's always been about you."

Even though I was a few miles away, I could still feel the sexual tension in Tonia's apartment. She was close enough to touch, but she had Sean trained so good, he waited for permission to touch her. She teased him by licking her lips and sucking on her nipples.

"You got a condom?"

"Yeah."

"Good, because I feel like going for a ride."

After he put on the condom, Tonia mounted Sean's dick and started fuckin' the shit out of him. She really put that pussy on him something furious. Her thrusts were so hard, the sofa sounded like claps of thunder.

"Ahhhhhhh! Sean, yeah!"

FLOP! FLOP! FLOP! FLOP! FLOP! FLOP!

Damn, Tonia rode Sean's dick better than the chicks on the porn flicks we watched. She made all of the right faces and moaned exactly like she was told to. Her tits slapped him in the face while she pulled his hair.

"Aggghhhh! Damn, girl, take it easy."

"Shut up! I'm about to cum!" Tonia began throwing her head around and rolled her eyes up in her head until all you could see were the whites. She abused him for a few more minutes before she stood up and said, "Open your mouth!" Sean obeyed.

Tonia positioned her pussy directly in front of Sean's face. She roughly massaged her clit until jets of cum squirted out, hitting Sean in the eyes and dripping down his cheeks. When the last of Tonia's cum splashed across his face, Tonia collapsed on his lap. After watching that, I knew it wouldn't be long before we'd have everything Sean owned.

Next, I checked on Tiff's apartment. Her and Javier were sitting on the couch eating Chinese take-out. Javier was doing most of the talking, while Tiff was pretending to be interested. I could tell she was bored by the way she played with her food with her chopsticks. Javier didn't have a clue, and before he caught on, I gave Tiff a call.

"What's up with you, shorty?"

"Hey, Daddy." She looked at Javier and said, "It's my Daddy,"

Tiffany got up and went into her bedroom, closing the door behind her.

"What's up, Daddy?" I could hear the excitement return in her voice.

"I was just calling to check up on you. You sound like you're bored,"

"How did you know?"

"Even when I'm not with you, I'm with you."

"Okay, then if you're with me, what am I doing right now?" Tiff slid her hands down her pants.

"You're laying on your bed, playing with your pussy."

"Oh, my God!" Tiff giggled as she looked around the room.

"Now, tell me why you're bored."

"Javier is here, and all he's talking about are his cars. I'm trying to act interested, but I'm falling asleep."

"You got to take control of the situation. Use his love for cars against him. You give him some pussy, yet?"

"No, I was waiting for you to give me the okay."

"Go ahead, hit him off, and fuck the shit out of

him. Maybe then he'll shut the fuck up about his fuckin' cars."

"I don't know if I can really get into it, Daddy. I'm not attracted to him. He looks like Ricky Martin. Nothing about him gets me excited."

"It's not about you. It's about becoming whoever he wants you to be. You got to play the role of the Siren. Think of it as a game, and if you're able to seduce him into doing anything you want, you win."

"Okay, Daddy."

"And besides, there will never be another man that'll be able to do for you what I can."

"I know, Daddy. Nobody understands me like you do," Tiff moaned while sliding her fingers deeper into her panties.

"I know what you like." I said.

"Tell me what I like, Daddy."

"You like it when I show you off in public, don't you?"

"Yesssss."

"You like it when I tell you to suck my dick in front of people you don't know, don't you?"

"Yessssssss, Daddy."

"I tell you what, you go back and handle your business with Javier. When you're done, I'll strip you naked, put a leash on your neck, and walk you around until you shit for me."

"Mmm…" Tiffany viciously massaged her clit. As she neared her climax, she arched her back off the bed. "Ummmmmmmm!"

"You better not cum until I say so."

"Hmmmmm, Yeh, Yeh, Yessssss, Daddy!"

"Hold it, Hold it."

Tiffany used every muscle in her body to fight back her orgasm. The way she contorted her face had me squeezing my dick.

"I can't, I… I… I can't hold it no more, Daddy!"

"Bark for me, Tiff."

"Arf, arf, arf, arf, arf, arf."

"Now, ask me for permission to cum."

"Mm, Mm, May I… cum?" Tiff moaned, still rubbing wildly at her clit and fighting back her orgasm, at the same time. "Please, Daddy!"

"Go 'head."

Tiffany's cum shot out of her like a cannonball and splattered on a chair three feet away. She threw her head from side to side as the last of her gooey nut seeped out on to the bed sheets. Her orgasm was so strong, she had to take a second to catch her breath.

"I betcha your curls are sticking to your sweaty neck, and you're feeling like you just gave birth.

"Yesssss," Tiffany hissed with her eyes closed.

"How do I know that?"

"Because even when you're not here, you're here."

"That's my girl."

"Thank you, Daddy, I needed that."

"Now, go handle your business."

"Okay, Daddy." Tiffany got up from the bed, went to the bathroom and strA'ightened herself up. When she passed by her cum splattered chair, she used the cum as ink and wrote I love Daddy with a smiley face on the mirror. "I'll see you in an hour."

I checked Akura's channel, and nobody was home. The next few channels were Lasandra's crib. Remember when I told my Queens that one of the quickest ways to a man's pocket was through his dick? Well, Lasandra found a quicker way. She had Cool C on his stomach, ass in the air, tonguing the shit out of his asshole. She had Cool C moaning like a cold bitch. That made it hard to beat my dick to it, so I went to Bless's channel and caught Tito coming through the door.

Tito wasn't young, like my other Queens' targets. He was 51 years old. A short, fat slob with wavy gray hair. Let him tell it, he was still a Latin American heart throb. He came from Colombia and had been selling coke in Holyoke for what seemed like forever.

Tito had a daughter a few years younger than Bless, getting ready to graduate from private school. His wife Maria was a church fanatic and never went anywhere without the Bible. They both were members of the Betterment of Latinos in America Society. They donated money to the local fire department, and when nobody was looking, Tito slid stuffed envelopes full of money into the hands of the Holyoke Police.

Tito was deeply rooted in the streets. I remembered hearing his name when I was coming up. He had more coke spots in Holyoke than McDonald's had restaurants in our town. Once, I heard one of his runners say, "Tito got so much coke that he can make it blizzard on the block for three days straight!" That was five years ago, imagine what he was working with now.

Bless was able to get close to Tito, courtesy of one of the tracking devices T-Money had planted on his car. We tracked Tito's movements until we were able to figure out his pattern. After that, Bless got a job at one of the Colombian bars that Tito frequented. Since Tito had a thing for young girls, Bless had him chasing her in no time.

Not long after they met, Tito started making regular visits to Bless's apartment. He showered her with gifts and took her to expensive restaurants. She had the old fool eating out of her hands.

"Nola, Jouen."

"Role, Papi Chulo."

"I see you been practicing your Spanish."

"Si Papi."

Bless's Spanish had my dick throbbin'. Tiffany had been working with her, but I didn't think she would catch on so fast or speak it so good.

"I bought you a little something." Tito handed Bless an Adam and Eve bag. "Why don't you go put it on for Papi, Yes?"

Bless looked in the bag, then smiled. "Papi wants to roll play?"

"Papi wants you to take care of him. I think I'm sick, and I need a nurse.

"Then why don't you lay down on the sofa?"

Tito stripped down to his coffee bean printed boxers and stretched out on the sofa. The TV screen split and showed Tito in the living room and Bless in the bedroom, trying to squeeze into a tight, leather nurse's outfit. Of course, it was way too small, and the bottom half of her plump ass cheeks were exposed. The top was also too small and she had to leave the top four buttons undone.

Tito practically drooled when Bless came back into the living room. She began performing imaginary nurse duties on him. Every chance he got, he grabbed her pussy or stuck a finger up her ass. Bless would let him probe her for a minute or two before slapping his hands away.

"You're such a dirty old pervert."

Bless even used the stethoscope he had in the bag and checked his heart with it. When she bent over him, one of her tits fell out, and Tito sucked it greedily like a baby.

They went on with the games for about an hour. Tito loved every bit of it. When Bless said it was time for his medicine, Tito's face lit up. Bless climbed up on the sofa and pulled her skirt up over her hips. She squatted over his chest and started straining so hard, beads of sweat covered her forehead. Bless made noises as if she was in labor, and that was enough to have me jerking the shit out of my dick.

"Come on, give Papi his medicine."

"Unnnnnn! Unnnnnn!" Bless's face became twisted the harder she strained. "Unnnnnn!"

"That's it, that's it, here it comes."

Gradually her sphincter began to wink. Bless then braced herself by holding on to her knees. Tito jerked his dick like a mad man as he watched Bless's feces coil up on his chest like a sleeping snake.

I never shitted on a chick, but after seeing Bless do it, I was definitely going to be shittin' on my Queens. Yeah, so what, I'm a freak. If you haven't put this book down by now, you're a freak too.

Chapter 25

It was around 11:30 at night. Three all blacked out full-size Yukon Denali trucks prowled the streets of Holyoke, each one packed with fully strapped, masked up Gorillas. Daryl was in the driver's seat of the lead truck. Country was in the passenger's seat, smoking a blunt.

"Yo son, you see how that chump tried to play me in front of the crew the other day?" Daryl growled as he took a swig of E&J.

"Yeah, that was crazy. He should've pulled you to the side, but you know Pharaoh, always a showboat." Country replied.

"No bullshit, yo, I wish I had picked up the gun and blew Crazy Eddie's brains the fuck out. For real, that shit was about nothing."

"That's easier said than done."

"So what the fuck are you saying?"

"Talk is cheap, yo. Anybody can say what they should've done, you feel me? Actions will always speak louder than words."

"Fuck!" Daryl hissed at Country, "You act like

you're taking his side. Now that is crazy son." Daryl pulled over, and the other trucks pulled over behind him. "I thought me and you was me and you."

"Without question, me and you is me and you. Yo, you talk all this shit about Pharaoh, but he got us out the park, got us cribs, cars, and he's putting money in our pockets. What the fuck are you doing? You want the streets to respect you, for what? Respect is earned, son."

"Word, that's how you feel?" Daryl pulled out his Mac-11 and checked the clip.

"It is what it is. You think you got what it takes to be a boss?" Country challenged him.

"Fuck, yeah. If this clown can do it, I know I can do it." Daryl screwed the silencer onto his Mac-11. The rest of the Gorillas in the truck did the same thing.

"Then you got to go hard and make the streets respect you. And the way you get respect is puttin' in work and puttin' money in a cat's pockets. Right now nobody knows who you are. When anybody mentions the Gorillas, King Pharaoh is the only name they know. We live in his shadows. Me, I'm cool with that. You, on the other hand, are a different story. One thing you got to remember is there can only be one king. So, what are you gonna do?"

Daryl looked at Country and smirked. "I'm gonna go get my respect."

Daryl climbed out of the truck and cocked his Mac-11. The Gorillas in the other trucks got out and did the same. They were in front of a heavy crack spot run by a bunch of dudes from New York.

Daryl told all the Gorillas to stay back as he

crossed the street, maskless. Daryl was going to make a name for himself, get the respect he felt he deserved. If he was going to be king, he couldn't be stuck in the shadows anymore.

By himself, Daryl laid everybody down and robbed them of everything. From there, he visited six other spots that night and did the same thing. Daryl went at any and everybody. Gangs, street crews, drug organizations, cops, under covers, and snitches.

Single-handedly, Daryl had turned the streets into a blood bath. Weeks after, people were still afraid to come out. Police rode around four deep, fully suited in S.W.A.T gear. All the street crews that were copping from New York beat a path to the Gorilla clubhouse to cop coke.

I couldn't complain. He did what I asked him to do, but because of it, we made more enemies than any other street crew. If I had known what was in Daryl's head at the time I told him to handle his business, I wouldn't have said shit to him, but because I did, I created a monster.

Chapter 26

The backlash from Daryl's week long rampage would be worse than I thought. I knew things would be crazy for a while. A couple crews were still bucking, not to mention a couple Gorillas got shot in the process, but Daryl made sure that for every one Gorilla that was shot, he shot ten of theirs.

We weren't known as that punk ass crew in the park that sold pieces, anymore. The Gorilla name was ringing bells as far away as New York, Boston, and everywhere in-between.

By Daryl making a name for himself, he made an even bigger name for the Gorillas. That was a good thing on the streets, but the bigger you get, the bigger your enemies become. Like I said, I knew things would get crazy, but not this crazy.

"Yo, everybody, Diane Fletcher is about to do an interview with Senator Holten about the streets of Holyoke," Jessito announced. "The rumor is he's gonna announce some type of campaign to take back the streets of Holyoke."

"Take back the streets from who?" T-Money asked.

"Us, who do you think?" Daryl replied.

Everybody moved in front of the big screen TV as Jessito turned to Channel 40.

"Hello, my name is Diane Fletcher for Channel 40's 'Hard Talk Live.' Joining us today is Senator Holten of Massachusetts to address the drastic rise in the murder rate in the city of Holyoke. Before we begin our interview with the Senator, here are some crucial facts and figures."

Diane went on to say that in the last 20 years, Holyoke's crime rate had steadily risen, since 1983, the crime rate had shot up 40.8% and was still climbing. Some of that could be attributed to the lack of available jobs, especially since the paper mills closed along the canals, taking with it over 50% of the city's jobs. According to City Hall, the crime rate didn't start rising until the state implemented it's faulty welfare system. Instead of helping those already in the city, it attracted those from other cities and states, mostly low-income families trying to take advantage of the benefits.

At that point, officials say crime began to flourish. Drug-related crimes increased ten-fold with the introduction of crack on the streets. Burglaries rose considerably as crack addicts stole to feed their addiction. At the same time, street violence rose 38% from 1990-2000. At one point, the newspapers were comparing Holyoke to the gangland era of Al Capone.

"Damn, I didn't know Holyoke was that fucked-up back in the day." Jessito said,

"What do you mean? Shit is still fucked up." I said.

"Yo, yo, it's back on." T-Money said, snapping his fingers.

"Good evening, I'm Diane Fletcher, and if you're just joining us, the topic is Holyoke's alarming crime rate. With us today to discuss the problem and hopefully a solution, is Senator Holten."

Holten was a tall, lanky Caucasian, who was slightly balding. His nose was pointy, face a tad wrinkly and he had ivory white teeth. Like most politicians, he had a way with words and people.

Senator Holten rose pretty fast up the political ladder. People would argue it was because his family was wealthy and powerful, but the truth was he was good at what he did. First, as the D.A. then, the Mayor of Holyoke and finally, senator of Massachusetts in his second term. He was known for his take-no-prisoners attitude when it came to crime. Something told me I wouldn't like this interview.

"Good evening, Senator Holten. Thank you for joining us."

"Good evening, Diane, and thank you for having me."

"Senator, I want to get straight to the point. We have a problem, and it's only getting bigger. The streets of Holyoke have fallen victim to a drug epidemic sweeping across America. Addicts are getting younger and younger, even babies are born addicted to crack. The numbers of drug related murders have soared. Yes, we have the numbers here." Diane riffled through some paper. "It says here that in the last three weeks, there were 28 drug-related murders."

Everybody looked at Daryl, and he just sat back and smirked.

"Yes, Diane, the numbers are troubling. Just last

night, a body was found in a Northampton Street apartment. Apparently, it had been there for over a month. The victim was a known cocaine dealer from Chicago."

I found out about Dante from my Aunt Joanne. She told me some detectives came and questioned her. By then, Joanne didn't give a fuck about Dante. Once the money started rolling in from all the properties, she forgot all about him. Funny how money changes a situation.

"As a native of Massachusetts, born in Holyoke, Senator, please tell us your views on the situation."

"Well, I'm disappointed, Diane. I've seen this beautiful city of ours descend into chaos. Playgrounds where our kids used to play are now distribution points for illegal drugs. This needs to stop now."

"I agree with you, Senator, but it's a lot easier said than done."

"That's true."

"Senator, where's the taxpayer's money going? None of it appears to be spent saving our city. I've seen the police driving around in brand new cars, but what good is that doing for the people of West Mass? I think it is safe to say the people want their streets back."

"And you'll get them back, Diane. Right now, my office is coordinating with the mayor to form a state task force, consisting of state, federal, and local agents. Together, we'll gather every resource in our power to put a stop to this madness."

"What makes this task force any different from the other ones over the years?"

"I'm involved, and that makes it personal." The camera zoomed in on Senator Holten's face. "This is going out to all drug dealers in Holyoke and beyond. Take heed. We are coming for you. We'll spare no expense to get you. I don't care if you're the lowest person on the totem pole. You'll be treated as a kingpin and prosecuted as such. Those of you watching who sell drugs, go tell your buddies this, Senator Holten says, get off his streets or else!'"

"And that's all the time we have. Senator Holten, it's been a pleasure. Thank you for coming."

"Thank you, Diana."

"This is Diana Fletcher for 'Hard Talk'. Good night."

Everybody sat in silence. I think Senator Holten's little speech scared my crew. I had to think of something to say to ease their minds.

"Ayo, what the fuck is up with y'all? What the fuck is with all the silence? I know y'all didn't take that shit the Senator said serious. Yo, that chump was talking out of his ass. Do anybody know why he did it?'

"Because he meant that shit!" Jessito said.

"Fuck no. The reason he's talking shit is because his ratings are low. This is nothing more than a publicity stunt. He's doing the same thing we're doing."

"What's that?"

"Starting a war, Jessito."

"A war, with who?"

"With us. He said he wanted his streets back. Fuck him. These are our streets. We grew up here, live here, and will probably die here. All he wants to do is make some TV arrest, then go home to his plush mansion in the Highlands. He doesn't really want it with us. He doesn't want to enter the jungle where the Gorillas roam." I stood up and started pacing, back and forth. "You know why I'm not afraid of his bitch ass? It's because he puts his pants on the same way I put my pants on. He bleeds just like I bleed. He's no more of a man than I am. I don't fear no man, because I'm a muthafuckin Gorilla!"

"No muthafuckin' doubt!" Daryl said, standing up to give some dap.

"Now, that's that shit I'm trying to hear, yo!"

"Word, kid." Country said, standing up, also giving me some dap.

"Spoken like a true king."

"Gorillas forever!" I shouted.

"Gorillas forever!" They all repeated.

Chapter 27

Things started to pick up as the weeks went by. We were still dealing with the beef Daryl started with everybody, but all in all, shit was starting to calm down.

Shit wasn't moving as fast as I wanted to, but because of Daryl, we were moving way more weight in coke than before. Besides that, Country handled the coke shop. Bless and the girls were steadily gathering information from their targets. Jessito was going around to the smaller towns that surrounded the city, recruiting more Gorillas. T-Money was doing the computer thing, and Joey was still in a coma.

With everybody busy, it left me with some extra time on my hands. When Coco called, I knew exactly how to spend that time.

"What up girl?"

"Shit. What's up with you?" Coco replied.

"I'm laid back. Where you at? I hear a lot of people?"

"I'm at my man's store, in the Holyoke Mall. Me and my sister run it."

"Word, so what do you want?"

"Damn, it's like that now?"

"Coco, me and you are about one thing, so cut the bullshit and just say where and when."

"I like that. How about meet me here at After Dark. It's across from the Champs Sports store. If you get here quick enough, I'll let you fuck my sister, Chocolate."

"Have her already unwrapped. I'm on my way."

Fifteen minutes later, I pulled up on my Ducati. Fall weather was setting in, and I figured I'd get a few more rides out of my bike before I put it up.

To tell you the truth, I was expecting to see a ghetto-ass store. You know, the kind that sold knock-offs from China. Instead, to my surprise, it turned out to be some high class shit. It had a Victoria's Secret feel to it, but it was more seductive than classy. Whoever Coco's man was, he had to have dough to own a high-end lingerie shop, especially in the Holyoke Mall. As I entered the store, I knew I had to find out who was Coco's man.

I spotted Coco in a flaming pink, lacy robe. It dropped to the bottom of her ass and every time she bent over, you could clearly see her pussy print. When she approached me, she had one of the sexiest walks I've ever seen. The way her titties wiggled with each step she took, I could tell she didn't have a bra on.

There was something about her that kept me coming back. Maybe it was her round ass, cute face, or better yet, her slutty-ass personality. Yeah, that was it. It tripped me out how a chick so cute could be so nasty.

"Welcome to After Dark. May I help you?"

"Yes, I'm looking for something about 5'5, light skinned with a fat ass."

"Come with me. I may have what you're looking for. It's in the back."

Coco smiled and led me to the back of the store where the dressing rooms were. In the back were eight dressing rooms, two sofas and a bunch of mirrors. Six of the dressing rooms were occupied. The sofas were full with girls waiting for their friends trying on clothes. Coco ignored all of them and led me into an empty stall.

"Damn, baby, you got a girl aching for this dick." Coco sat on a small bench and undid my pants in a hurry. When she finally got it out, she licked her lips and started talking to it. "Hello, there, Mr. Dick. Long time, no suck or fuck. My ass missed the hell out of you. So I want you to do me a favor and bury that mushroom head as far as it will go up my ass." She kissed it with tiny pecks and licked the tip several times.

Coco was truly fiending for the dick because she was letting out farts like a true fiend would. Damn, she was a nasty muthafucka. "Deep throat it!" I demanded.

"Make me."

I grabbed the back of her neck, yanked her head back and forced my dick down her throat.

"Is there any room for me in here?"

"Pharaoh, mmmppphh, meet my sister, Chocolate, mmmppppph!"

Chocolate slid in and stood on the other side of me. She was slightly taller than her sister, but they damn near looked identical.

"So this is the guy you're always talking about?"

"Uh-huh. Pharaoh, me and my sister share everything."

"Is that right? You a nasty bitch too?"

"I'll let you be the judge of that."

Chocolate fell to her knees behind me and pulled my pants down to my ankles. She parted my cheeks and drilled her tongue into my asshole.

"Yeah, you a nasty bitch too."

After my dick was nice and hard, Coco stood up, turned around and bent over.

"Do what you do, muthafucka." she said, winking back over her shoulder.

I pulled out my gun and sat it in the corner then I let out a big glob of spit right on her brown eye. Slowly, I worked my dick into her ass. She purred like she always did. Chocolate repositioned herself under both me and Coco.

"Come on, muthafucka, don't hold back now. Do what you do!"

"You want it hard, don't you, you a nasty bitch?"

"I want to feel that fuckin' dick up in my stomach!"

"Like this!" and I thrusted up in her with all my might.

"Agggghhhh! Yessss, like that, Mmmmm, again, damn it, do it again!"

I granted her wish and began to plow deep into her ass.

"Yesss, like that! Ahhhh, harderrrrr!"

My thrusts grew more aggressive, as I watched Coco's ass forcefully swallow my dick. Her plump asscheeks rippled, which only intensified my anal assault. Listening to her whorish moans made me fuck her even harder.

FLOP! FLOP! FLOP! FLOP! FLOP! FLOP!

The clerk at the counter attempted to drown out our animalistic noises by turning up the stereo, but it didn't work. One of the clerks came and knocked on the door, but we ignored her.

With Chocolate's tongue going back and forth between my balls and Coco's clit, it brought me closer to my climax than I wanted. Since I was about to explode, I gave it my all, doubling my speed like a jackhammer. It got to the point that we had the whole stall shaking. Eventually, the cheap ass lock on the door unlatched, and the door flung open, for all to see.

Shit, you know I didn't give a fuck. I was on my Sean Michaels shit. Some customers left in shock, while others stayed and watched until Chocolate closed the door. It felt like I was blowing Coco's back out forever.

"Fuck, this dick is killing me!"

FLOP! FLOP! FLOP! FLOP! FLOP! FLOP!

The combination of my anal attack and Chocolate's tongue action took a toll on Coco. First, her legs started to tremble and then she lost her grip. Finally, when her eyes rolled up in the back of her head, I knew she was at the point of no return.

"Oh, God! Oh, God! Oh, God!"

FLOP! FLOP! FLOP! FLOP! FLOP! FLOP!

"Unnnnnnnn!"

Coco came so violently that she collapsed to the floor, sweating like a pig. Her sweet nectar continued to pour from the folds of her pussy. When she regained the energy to move again, she used my legs as poles to pull herself up. She took my dick into her mouth and cleaned her shit off.

"Thank you, Mr. Thick Dick."

"Damn, if that dick got my sister like that, I gots to have some."

"Girl, I told you he had that bomb shit." Coco got up and straightened herself out the best she could. "I got to get back to work. Have fun with my sister."

Coco waved bye and left, closing the door behind her. Chocolate removed her thong and looked at me with puppy dog eyes.

"Please, take it easy, I'm not broken in yet. I don't think I can take that dick like my sister."

"Turn around." she did as I said. My heart raced too fast to take it easy. If she hadn't been broken in yet, she sure enough was about to be.

"Bend over and hold on."

"Remember, I said take it easy."

I paid no attention to her pleas. Without hesitation, I buried my black snake into her black hole. Her eyes opened wide. I think it was then she realized nothing about this was going to be easy. Chocolate tried to wrestle away, but I had a hold of her hips, and it stopped her from going anywhere.

"Aaaagggghhhhh!"

FLOP! FLOP! FLOP! FLOP! FLOP!

I picked up where I left off with Coco, with the same violence in every thrust. I was trying to bury my dick so far up in Chocolate, if she opened her mouth, you'd be able to see my dickhead.

"Look at me!"

I wanted to see the expression on her face.

"Bitch, I said look at me!"

Chocolate slowly turned her head back. The look in her eyes was a mixture of pain and fear. Then, when

I saw the tears form in her eyes, the savage in me came out.

"Aggggggggghhhhhhh! Owwwwwww! Owwwwww!"

"That's it, bitch, let it out, or I'm gonna fuck it out of you, I smacked her ass a few times before I positioned her flat against the mirror. Chocolate went up on her tiptoes to lessen the pain, but it didn't work. Next, she tried climbing the wall in desperation each time I rammed my dick up in her.

"Stop it! Stop it! Stop it!" she begged.

"Fuck no! Shut the fuck up!"

I yanked her hair so she was looking up at the ceiling. That was when I saw the first tear roll down her cheek. I licked it up and that salty teardrop might as well have been pure adrenaline. After that, I lost control.

I began thrusting so hard her feet were coming off the ground. A couple of minutes after that, I got some more tears. I couldn't tell if it was from pleasure or pain. Really, I didn't give a fuck. The tears said that she was officially broken in.

When I pulled out, she collapsed like my dick was the only thing that held her up. I nutted all over her face. I used her thong to clean my dick off and left her there on the floor, sniffling. Coming out of the stall, I noticed some girls I knew.

"Damn, Pharaoh, you need to let a girl get some of that cock, for real. I know I can take it better than that bitch."

I looked the tall, slim redhead up and down. "Yeah, I know you can take this dick, Tina. They say white chick's asses run deep."

"The only way to know is to find out."

"Maybe some other time."

She and the girls with her, JadaMonet and Kasha, were freaks, for real, but they got their own story.

Coco approached me just as I was about to exit the store.

"I know you wasn't going to leave out without saying bye to me. Especially after the way you put that dick in me."

"I'm not trying to get in the way while you makin' that money. I respect the hustle."

"You know what?"

"What?"

"Maybe I should give you a taste of this pussy. Maybe you'll act right."

"If you give me a shot of that pussy you might just leave your man."

"Oh, you think so?"

"I've been known to wreck a few relationships."

"You keep dickin' me down the way you do, I just might leave my man. So, how was my sister?"

"Officially broken in."

"Listen to you. I think I'm too good to you, letting you fuck my sister and all."

"Yeah, whatever. Turn around and let me see that ass one more time before I go."

Coco turned around and arched her back. I smacked it hard enough that a couple of heads turned to look. Then I groped it roughly before letting go.

"Oooooh, don't get me started again."

"Peace, yo."

"Bye, bye, Pharaoh."

Chapter 28

As I stepped out into the mall's foot traffic, thoughts of Cocoa lingered in my mind. It was like she knew exactly what I wanted without me having to say anything. While I was too busy thinking about Coco, I failed to see some dudes running up on me.

"You punk-ass muthafucka!"

That was all I heard before I caught a solid punch to the jaw. I stumbled into Kid's Footlocker, falling over a shoe display stand. Before I could get back to my feet, someone else jumped me from behind. One stomped on my head while the other one was kicking me in the ribs.

"Fuck this shit. Buss that muthafucka in the head, yo!" one of them said.

The one with the Pepsi blue Timberlands pulled out what looked like a .22. I thought it was all over until I saw Coco trying to grab dude's gun.

"Bitch, get the fuck off of me!"

Coco distracted him long enough for me to get to my feet. Still a little dizzy, I pulled out my Desert Eagle.

BOOM! BOOM! BOOM! BOOM!

My Desert Eagle exploded like a cannon, making everybody in a hundred-foot radius run or hit the floor. I stumbled out of the store, holding my ribs and spitting up blood. Luckily, I was at the entrance where I parked my bike.

POP! POP! POP! POP! POP! POP! POP!

Bullets whizzed by my head, shattering the glass of the store across from Kid's Footlocker. I ran behind an island of telephones for a shield. I tried my best to catch my breath at the same time, I wiped the sweat from my eyes. I had to think fast. Running for the door would've gotten me shot in the back. That was what they wanted me to do, I knew it. So, I dropped to my knees and rolled out on my stomach and fired shots. They weren't expecting that move as one slug each slammed into their chests. Fuck waiting for them to fall, I got up and dashed for the door.

Soon as I made it outside, a shit-colored Suburban skidded to a stop, right in front of me. Out of the front passenger's seat jumped a wild-ass Jamaican with an Uzi automatic. Two more jumped out of the back with Uzi's too. Before they took aim, I started running along the wall. It felt like a shit-load of bullets trailed me as I ran, covering my face with my arms. I was only a half a step in front of them the whole time. I dove into a bunch of bushes and started crawling my ass off. They continued to fire where I dove, but I was nowhere near there.

Finally, the driver started honking the horn. My would-be killers ran back and piled back into the truck. I emerged from the bushes, contemplating running up on the truck and letting everybody have it. For some reason, I decided against it. I took aim at the gas tank, with the fifth shot, the Suburban exploded and rocketed into the air into a giant fireball.

The force from the blast knocked me back 15 feet. Although dazed after I hit my head, hearing sirens approaching made me jump up. My adrenaline had me so amped, I couldn't focus. People were running in every direction. My head was killing me, my ribs ached, and all I could taste was blood in my mouth. All that made finding my bike impossible. As I jogged aimlessly through the parking lot, faintly I heard someone calling my name.

"Pharaoh! Pharaoh!"

My eyes searched through the sea of cars, trying to find the voice. Suddenly, an emerald-green Jaguar pulled up next to me.

"Get in." It was Tina.

I did and we sped out of the parking lot. I heard police sirens passing us and fading in the distance. My visit to the mall to get some pussy turned into a Wild West shootout. I was sprawled across the backseat with my head on JadaMonet's lap.

"There's never a dull moment with you, huh?" JadaMonet said, wiping the sweat off my forehead with a napkin.

"Not if I can help it."

Chapter 29

Ain't that a bitch. Somebody tried to kill me for real. I knew it wasn't no street beef either. It was more like an assassination attempt. The events of that day left me laid up with a severe concussion. Three of my ribs were broken, my jaw was swollen and I had a bruised left shoulder. I couldn't complain though, it was better than being shot the fuck up. The doctor ordered me to stay off my feet for a while. I was cool with that because it gave me some time to collect my thoughts.

Bless and my Queens automatically fell into the role of being my nurses. Bless also controlled the traffic to and from the house. No one could show up without calling first. Anybody that did, Bless gave the order to shoot them on sight. Then she set them up on shifts to make sure I didn't need for nothing. I didn't' mind being pampered. I just hated being laid up while someone out there wanted me dead.

The following week, T-Money found out by hacking into the police central computer, that the Jamaicans in the Suburban were hired hit men out of New York. They were in town a week before the hit. We didn't know who hired them. Whoever did must've had some dough. Coming out of New York, the cheapest a body will cost you was $10,000. There was five of them, so they had to of gotten no less then $50,000.

It couldn't have been a petty ass corner hustler. I ruled out stickup kids, because this wasn't their style. Damn, who wanted me dead? That was all I thought about as I laid up in bed, recuperating. Don't get me wrong, I knew shit like this came with the game. I just hated not knowing who wanted me dead, and as the days passed that shit started to eat me up.

"Who do you think it was Daddy?"

"I don't know Bless. I don't have the slightest clue."

"What about that bitch Coco?"

"It wouldn't make sense if it was her, why would she save my life? Yo, don't let your feelings think for you."

Bless was silent for a minute, before she mumbled. "I don't trust that bitch."

"You know what, I'm tired of this jealousy shit with you. Get the fuck out of my face and go make me some grape Kool-aid."

I could see the tears forming in her eyes. I didn't care though. The bitch was getting on my nerves.

Right then my cell rang.

"Who is this?" I answered with an attitude.

"What up, this must be King Pharaoh."

"Who the fuck is this?"

"I see you're still alive. What, do you have a four leaf clover stuck up your ass or something? Anyway, we didn't get you this time, but next time you won't be so lucky."

"You fucked up, yo. There won't be a next time."

"Oh, there's always a next time."

The line went dead.

How that muthafucka got my private phone number fucked with me long after the line went dead. The only thing I figured out about the caller was he had a hint of a Caribbean accent.

I can't explain in words how mad I was. It drove me crazy that no one knew who was trying to kill me. Each day that passed with no clues, only made things worse. I actually felt myself slipping into the darkness. I had to do something to save myself, and quick.

What I wanted to do was send my Gorillas at any and everybody that wasn't copping from us. I wanted them all dead. One of them had something to do with it, the rest would just be casualties of revenge. But the only thing that saved me, better yet saved them, was the last ounce of sanity that I had left. And with it, I remembered something Artey taught me. He said one of the traits of a good leader is their ability to make decisions, during an emotional situation, without making it personal.

I wasn't thinking clearly and because the madness within me grew, I knew I wouldn't be thinking clearly for a while. Another thing, I couldn't let the Gorillas see me like this, especially Daryl. He'd see it as a sign of weakness. Without question, he would've tried me and I'd have to kill him. Somehow I had to release this madness I had built up inside of me, and I had to do it fast. If not, everybody would start questioning my absence. But I didn't have a clue how to do it.

Then one night Bless came in my room followed by the rest of my Queens.

For a second, I thought they were going to tell me they were sick of my shit and that they were leaving me. The truth was, I was treating them like shit, and they had every right to leave me. But fuck that! I told them in the beginning that when you were with me it was for life.

As they stood quietly at the foot of the bed, under the covers I had my finger on the trigger of a Mac-11 automatic. The first bitch that said anything about leaving me, I was going to shoot her right on the spot.

"Give us your pain, Daddy."

It took a while for what she said to register with me. When it did, I realized they knew what I was going through. Somehow some way, they understood. They understood, I had to release the madness.

"Give us your pain," she repeated.

"How?"

"Anyway you want to," Tonia answered.

It so happened, that day I popped two hits of double white blodder acid, a hit of X, and I smoked a Garcia cigar full of mushrooms and weed. Then there was the morphine strength pain pills I was popping like Skittles. Yeah, I was out of my mind.

I threw the covers back and climbed out of the bed. My first step sent me stumbling into the dresser. My Queens all tried to help me up but I shoved them away.

"So you want my pain, huh?" I said halfway out my mind, while drooling through a sadistic grin. "So who's first?"

"Me," Bless said with uncertainty.

"Strip! All of you!" I growled.

They did.

"Get up against the wall and turn around."

Bless did as I asked. "Spread your legs!"

Once Bless was spread eagle against the wall, she peered over her shoulder.

"Give me your pain, Daddy."

I hesitated for a second, but that was it…

"Ahhhhhhhhhhh! Oh God! Oh God! Ahhhhh!" Bless screamed.

She collapsed hard on the floor into the fetal position. Tears poured from her eyes. The look of pain on her face was selfishly gratifying to me. She laid there for a few seconds more before rolling on to all fours. She planted one foot underneath her and pushed herself up. It took a few more seconds but once again Bless was spread eagle, and once again she said, but in a weaker voice. .

"Give… me your… pain… Da… Daddy.

This time I kicked her so hard in her pussy, she threw up chunks of food. Seeing it was going to be a while before she got up again, I turned my attention to Lasandra. She looked at me and said the same thing as Bless. But before she could finish I grabbed her by her hair and repeatedly slammed her face first into the wall. I had put so much force behind it that I ended up putting her face through the sheet rock. When I let go she slumped to the floor.

Next was Tiffany. She was scared to death. But she didn't run. She nervously passed me my cane and uttered the same words that Bless and Lasandra did. I took the cane and beat her. I didn't care where I hit her either. It felt like I was beating her forever. Her beastly screams and howls only made me beat her harder. Then when I broke my cane across her back, I started kicking her in her stomach until she shitted on herself. From there I mushed her face in it.

With Tonia, I snapped all the way out. I found some rope and threw it over the exposed beam in the ceiling. I wrapped the rope around her neck and pulled until she dangled five feet from the floor. I waited until she was blood red in the face before I let her fall to the floor. Then when she had caught her breath, I did again and again.

I took turns with each of them over and over until I passed out from sheer exhaustion. When I woke up, my Queens were at my side. They were beat, bruised, and battered but they were still there for me to do anything I needed them to. That also included beating them again if need be.

But that wasn't the case I was good. The madness was gone but not forgotten. Now I had a clear mind and could make the right decisions that needed to be made. And surprisingly my decision remained the same. I was going to kill all those muthafuckas!

Chapter 30

After a month, I couldn't take being laid up anymore. Although my girls provided me with plenty of entertainment, I couldn't just lie around doing nothing while somebody out there was trying to kill me.

Plus, the streets were crazy. Shootouts and drive-bys became the norm. All the crews Daryl had targeted were trying to retaliate. So that just made him go even harder. Regardless if I liked it or not, Daryl was the reason the Gorilla name was so heavy in the streets. I wondered if he was going to let that shit go to his head. Anyway, it was time to take over and put the fear of God in muthafuckas.

First I met with my Queens. I wanted an update on the targets.

"Bless you go first."

"Okay Daddy, Tito has a direct plug to the big boys in Colombia. Some one in his family is very well connected. They drop off 50 - 100 at a time with no money up front, sometimes more. They keep it in the apartment in the Cherry Hill complex. Every two weeks they come and pick up the money. The Cherry

Hill apartment isn't heavily guarded. The thing is you're not getting in there unless Tito calls, it is the only way he will open the door."

"So what's the best way to get at him?"

"At his house in Easthampton. That shit is way out in east-bum fuck. His wife and his daughter are the only ones that be there. He doesn't bring his work home with him, not even his gun."

"That's what's up, Bless. Come and give Daddy's dick a kiss. For the rest of y'all, that's the way I want shit done."

"Yes, Daddy," they said in unison.

"Tonia, you're up next. What's up with Sean?"

"Both of his stash houses are right next to each other." Tonia began. "One of them holds all the dope, the other holds all the cash. Someone from the Kenji Dragons comes and picks up the cash and then another person drops off the dope. They never run out, ever."

"How much dope do they drop off?"

"When Ming hits Sean off, he also hits him off for everybody else in West Mass that deals with the Kenji Dragons. They have to pick up from Sean, and he cuts the shit out of it before he passes it off. That's where he makes most of his money. Then he has all of his dope blocks around Holyoke and Springfield."

"So what does Ming drop off?"

"Five kilos of pure dope."

"Yeah," I said, shaking my head with satisfaction. "Now, that's what the fuck I'm talking about. What's the best way to get him?"

"I'm supposed to be meeting Ronnie at the stash house tonight. I had to start fuckin' him, because, although Sean maybe the boss, Ronnie is his right-hand man, and he's in charge of the stash-house. He gets off fuckin' the boss's girl, and he don't know when to shut up." She looked innocent and said, "Did I do good, Daddy?"

"Fuck, yeah, you did good."

"Can I kiss your dick, too?"

"Of course, you can."

Out of the corner of my eye, I caught Tonia snickering at Bless. They didn't think I noticed them two had been beefing on the low.

"Daddy, can I go next?"

"What you got for me, Tiff?"

"I finally got Javier to take me to his house in Amherst," Tiff explained, "he never takes anybody there. That's where he keeps everything at, the money and the coke. Matter of fact, we fucked in his walk-in safe on $400,000 and ten kilos of coke."

"That's all he has?" Tonia asked as she rolled her eyes at Tiffany.

Tiffany caught it and gritted on Tonia. "No, that's not all. If you'd let me finish." Tiff rolled her eyes at Tonia, and then looked back at me. "Every hundred thousand Javier makes, he takes it and buys gold bullion."

"Bricks of gold?"

"Yes, Daddy."

"And how many bricks of gold does our boy Javier got, and where does he hide it?"

"He got 3,500 and he melted it down. And get this, he melted them into car rims that he stores at his warehouse in Chicopee."

"Word?"

"Yes, Daddy. Did I do good?"

"You muthafuckin' right, and don't even ask me. Just get over here and kiss my dick."

"Arf! Arf! Arf!" Tiffany barked as she crawled over to kiss my dick.

"Lasandra, it's your turn. Tell me something good about Cool C."

Lasandra got up, went over and pushed play on the video player.

"I hooked up with T-Money and asked him to lace me up with a hidden camera and mic."

Lasandra went hard for real and got hours and hours of shit on tape about Cool C. When it was over, we knew where Cool C printed his counterfeit money, where he stashed the plates, and where he stashed the real money when it was made.

"Daddy, as you can see, he just printed up twenty million in counterfeit." Lasandra passed me a stack of Cool C's bogus dollars. If I didn't know any better, I'd say the shit was real.

"Listen, fuck the money," I stated. "I want the plates and the printing machine. So this is what you do. Just keep an eye on those plates. I want you to know where they are at all times. I have to find a good spot to put the machine first before we take it."

"Did I do good, Daddy?"

"Without question. Now, come and get some."

After Lasandra kissed my dick, she stood and looked me in the eyes. I knew what she wanted so I smacked the shit out of her. She hit the floor and looked back up at me with a smile. "Thank you, Daddy."

"A'ight, this is how this shit is gonna go down." I

ordered.

"Tiffany, you tell Javier you want to make him dinner. Since we know where the gold is, we're just gonna kill him and get him out of the way."

"Do you want me to kill him?" Tiff said with uncertainty.

"You ready for that?"

"I'll do whatever you tell me to do, Daddy."

"I'll do it if she can't." Tonia cut in.

I shifted my eyes to Tonia. She was starting to get out of hand, and she knew it too.

She said, "Sorry, Daddy."

"Tiff, I'm going to send Daryl to handle that. Bless, you take a couple Gorillas to Tito's house and duct tape his wife and daughter up. When he gets there, you have the same thing done to him. Don't do nothing to him. I have something special planned for him."

"Okay."

"Tonia, you make sure that you're in one of the stash houses when we get there. We need you to give us the inside scoop, so we don't walk into no shit. I want to hit them all tonight."

"Lasandra, you and Akura will meet at the elementary school next to Bolten Village with Task and his crew."

"Okay, Daddy." they both replied.

"Now, you bitches go and get ready. Tonight is going to be a big night for the Gorillas. The future of the Gorillas depends on it. Gorillas forever, my Queens."

"Gorillas forever." they all replied.

"Akura, let me talk to you."

"What's up, Daddy?"

"What's up with you? You've missed meetings, and you don't have nothing good on Ming."

"I'm sorry, Daddy, just give me some time. His girl is always around."

"So what are you telling me, you can't do it?"

"I can do it, just give me a little more time."

"A'ight, you got a month."

I watched as my Asian Queen walked out the door.

"Yo, tell me what you got on Ming."

"I had to go deep for this dude. I couldn't find anything on him fuckin' with the local law enforcement. I had to hack into the Boston FBI database. It doesn't have much on Ming, but it does have a lot on the Kenji Dragons." T-Money said.

"Like what?"

"The Kenji Dragons originate out of Shanghai, China. They control 75% of the heroin coming out of China. They make their heroin paste in a small town in Southeast China called Hetian, just off the Ting River. Then it's moved to Xiangang by plane."

"Where?"

"Xiangang is the Chinese name for Hong Kong."

"I forgot you speak that shit."

"The Kenji Dragons own their own shipping business. They have fifty cargo ships and twenty-five cargo planes. In Hong Kong, the cargo ships pick up 10,000 tons of heroin paste and deliver it to Singapore to be refined. Well, not quite in Singapore, but in a small place called KupKup, along the coast. Buyers fly in every quarter to Kuala Lumpur to make purchases in person. The Kenji Dragons take care of all deliveries world-wide and they guarantee it."

"Is there anything else in that file that we can use?"

"Yeah, for about five years now, the feds have had an agent in the Kenji Dragon Organization."

"Do you have a name?"

"Shit, I have his deep cover name, his real name and a picture of the snitch."

"Make me a copy. I have a feeling that information will come in handy later on down the line."

"Already done."

"For real? What do you think, kid?"

"I think Ming will make a better friend than enemy."

"That was exactly what I was thinking. Where does Ming fall in with the Kenji Dragons?"

"Ming's one of the sons of the opium emperor. He was just promoted and is in charge of the entire east coast of the United States."

"If we take Sean out, the dope market will be up for grabs. I guess, after tonight, we'll officially be in the dope game."

"You don't think the Kenji Dragons are going to beef about us killing Sean?"

"Without question, they're gonna try and kill all of us, but if we can move five or more kilos of pure dope, I don't think they're gonna have a problem with it."

"Can we move five plus keys of dope?"

"If we kill Sean, we don't have a choice, now do we?"

Chapter 31

A few hours later, I called a meeting with the Gorillas at the clubhouse. T-Money was on the phone, like before.

"You figure out who tried to kill you, yet?"

"No, and I don't give a fuck about that right now?"

"So you don't have nobody for me to go after? That's too bad because I was really starting to like this enforcer shit." Daryl replied.

"I bet you are, but don't trip, I got a job for you and your crew."

"A'ight, everybody listen up. We're going to war tonight."

"With who?" Country asked.

"Everybody!"

The crew looked at me like I was crazy.

"Yeah, you heard me right."

"Daryl, how many crews are still bucking?"

"There are maybe two or three more, but that's it. Them chumps aren't no threat. Why, what's up?"

"If they aren't pushing our coke, they are a problem, and I want them dealt with. Jessito is going to drop you off a case of grenades, and I want you to blow them the fuck up."

"Word?"

"You heard me, yo. After tonight, muthafuckas are gonna know that there are serious consequences when you don't cop from the Gorillas. Split your crew up so you can hit them all at the same time. I want you to start bombing at 6:15 p.m., not a second later."

"Why?"

"To distract the police. Task, you and the rest of y'all are going to hook up with Vashon."

"That's the nut that killed his stepfather when he was 15?" Task inquired.

"Yeah, that's him. I made him a Gorilla. Not many people know this, but he's been doing hits since he was 17. The boy is vicious."

"Whatever." Daryl mumbled.

I ignored him. "Task, y'all are gonna take out the Pine St. crew for good. I want all them dead, you hear me?"

"Yeah, I got it. Why we hittin' them, though? They get a little money, but they aren't nothin' major."

"T-Money tell 'em why."

"Pine Street was one of the biggest money-making spots in Holyoke. Before Butter got slumped, it was pulling in anywhere from $500,000 to a million dollars a month. Now that it's open territory, whoever locks it down will become instantly rich. Them Pine St. cats don't have the brains to get it back to where it used to be."

"The thing is, if we don't take it, somebody else will." I stated.

"Yo, Jessito, what did Tito and Javier say to my offer?"

"Tito said 'fuck you, you monkies.' Javier said he'll leave when he's ready, and that won't be no time soon."

"That's exactly what I wanted to hear. After tonight, everybody and their momma will know who the fuck the Gorillas are. T-Money got the details for what y'all are supposed to do. I'm going to step out for a minute. T-Money, give me a call when everybody is in place."

"A'ight, yo."

"Gorillas forever!" I shouted.

"Gorillas forever!" they all chanted.

Chapter 32

Instead of going to the roof top like I normally did to collect my thoughts, I decided to go for a drive. At the same auction I bought the girls BMW's. I also purchased a new Lexus GS. I had it sent to the shop to have it tricked out. It was painted a thunder cloud gray and re-upholstered in gothic black leather with suede trim by Armani. I only drove it once, and that was when I first got it. So, I felt safe driving alone because nobody had seen me in it.

Heading out with no destination in mind, I just wanted to cruise. My mind was on what was about to go down. Man, just this summer I was a nobody pushing crack in the park. Now people had to die so I could live. In this game, there was no other way. I was starving for that money, and I planned to keep on eating.

Everything seemed normal as I crept from neighborhood to neighborhood.

Suddenly, a ball bounced in front of my car. I slammed on my brakes and came to a dead stop. When I looked up, a little Puerto Rican kid ran out in the middle of the street and picked up the ball. Our eyes locked for a second, before he gave me the middle finger. I smiled. That was a future Gorilla, I thought, as I pulled off. Stop sign to stop sign, street corner to street corner, the scene was the same. This was my life and these were my streets.

In less than an hour, I was going to change the game in Holyoke. It would be similar to the stock market crash in 1929, the only difference being this would be a coke and heroin crash. By taking out all the major players, I'd be creating a drought. After a week of panic, I'd supply the streets. Everybody would have no choice but to come and see us, everybody.

Relaxing to the soft sounds of Sade, my phone rang.

It was T-Money.

"What's the deal?"

"We're ready, yo. Daryl and his crew are about to set it off in about ten minutes. I also had a Gorilla park a car in the Holyoke Police Department parking garage, packed with explosives. You never know when you'll need a distraction."

"That was good thinking, son. Yo, call Jessito and tell him to meet me at the corner of Walnut and Chestnut."

"A'ight, peace."

"Peace."

After scooping up Jessito, we headed to Pine Street. We didn't say a word to each other. We didn't have to, we knew what the other was thinking. One or two things were going to happen, we were going to get rich or die trying like a muthfucka.

I pulled the GS over on Dwight Street, across

from the post office. We had a clear view of the liquor store and the building the Pine St. crew was in. Although winter was setting in, everybody was out like it was still summer. That was good because I wanted an audience.

    Minutes later, a money-green '79 Impala pulled up behind us. It was Vashon. Like I told the crew, I made him a Gorilla a couple of weeks ago. His father was a CIA "Janitor," if you know what I mean. He died in the line of duty. Up until that point, he taught Vashon everything he knew, I mean everything.

    Vashon caught his first body in the tenth grade. He came home from school and found his mother crying with a swollen eye. Danny, her abusive boyfriend, had been pounding on her all day. Vashon calmly got his father's sawed-off shot gun and almost blew Danny's head clean off his shoulders.

    Vashon beat the charges, but he was ordered to see a psychiatrist. The judge told him it was not normal to have no remorse after killing another human being. Since then, Vashon has accumulated about 48 bodies, and those are just the ones I knew about. I thought he would be a good asset to the Gorillas because it was better to have him as a member before someone hired him to kill me.

    Vashon climbed into my backseat, wearing an all-black jean outfit. He reminded me of a taller version of Tyrese Gibson, the singer. He wore the same dark fudge complexion, with razor-sharp facial features with an intimidating aura.

    "What's up, fellas?" Vashon asked.

    "What's up?" we replied.

"Everything is set."

"Tell me the plan."

"I got two Gorillas on the fire escape out back and one in the alley. That is just in case they try to escape from the street, I got Task and his crew spread out."

"Where?"

"Task is on the pay phone in front of the liquor store. He's packing a Mac-11 automatic. Dirty Chuck and Lethal got AK's laying across the front seat. Blaze, Guillotine, and Killer K are on the corner, shootin' dice. They all got the 9mm with extended clips and silencers."

"Set it off, then."

Vashon reached into his jacket, pulled out a cell phone, dialed some numbers and hung up. "I just called Vicious. She's upstairs with them right now, fucking their brains out."

"By herself?" Jessito said, reading my mind.

Vashon said, "They don't call her Vicious for nothing. Look, there she is in the window."

Vashon then flicked his flashlight at a group of kids standing on the corner. They went inside an abandoned car and emerged with bats, then they ran up on the Pine St. crew's cars in front of the building and started smashing the windows out. Vicious shouted at the kids, and pretty soon the third floor window was full of heads. Then they disappeared.

"You ready, kid?" I said, looking over at Jessito.

"Let's do it."

We both reached under the seat and pulled out our .40 cals and screwed on the silencers. Then, Jessito grabbed our masks out of the glove compartment.

"What's going on?" Vashon asked.

"What, did you think we were going to just sit here and do nothing."

"Yo, you putting in work wasn't part of the plan, Pharaoh."

I looked at my prodigy. "Jessito, why was Caesar loved so much by his soldiers?"

"Because he didn't play the back. He got his hands dirty just like they did. Matter of fact, he would be the one to lead the charge."

I saw a small smile spread across Vashon's face.

"I knew I liked you for some reason, Pharaoh."

We got out of the car and walked down the street as if it was legal to have guns with silencers. It wasn't until we stepped onto the block that we masked up.

There was a sound of thunder as the Pine St. boys came barreling down the stairs. The front door to the building burst open. About 15 to 20 of them piled onto the street. I didn't wait, I wouldn't give them time to peep what was going down. With two .40s, I charged them, guns blazing. Not all of them were strapped, but there were enough with guns to give us a problem. Dirty Chuck and Blaze were the first to pull out the AKs. The rest followed suit. A wild-ass firefight erupted in the middle of the street.

Some tried to run back into the building, but Vicious's gunfire flushed them back into the street. Although I was gunning at all of them, I specifically, wanted one guy. The unofficial shot caller of the Pine St. crew. Just when I thought he got away, I saw him bolt into the alley.

"Jessito, come with me! Vashon, drag all the bodies out into the middle of the street."

Me and Jessito tore after Leon. The muthafucka was fast, but I was faster. With each step, I closed the distance. His Timberland's weren't tied, his pants sagged, and I heard him gasping for air. Once I saw the 15-foot chain-link fence up ahead, I knew he was done for. He wasn't even halfway up the fence before we reached it.

"Jessito, shoot that piece of shit down!" I commended.

He obeyed.

One shot.

"Arggrhhhh!"

Jessito hit Leon in the leg, and he fell hard. I could've offed him right there, and nobody would've seen shit. But what would be the point in that? The point of the whole thing was to send a message.

So me and Jessito dragged him back to the front of the building. The whole time, he begged for his life.

When we made it back, the entire Pine St. crew was laid out, some dead, some wounded in the middle of the street. I dragged Leon into the middle of them and forced him on his knees.

"If anybody asks who did this, you tell them King Pharaoh the Gorilla did it!"

Then I blew the back of Leon's head out. I saw the disbelief, shock and horror in everyone's eyes. People would talk about that night for years to come. And that was exactly what I wanted.

Chapter 33

We jumped on the highway to East Hampton. Jessito kept me updated with the police scanner and by talking to T-Money.

"Yo, shit is crazy, Pharaoh. T-Money said Daryl handled his business." Jessito said while shaking his head in awe.

"That's what's up." I replied.

"He also said Daryl and his crew are doing drive-bys on cop cars."

I just shook my head. I didn't have time to deal with that shit. I had to stay focused. Now that I think about it, that shit ended up working to our advantage. The more the police were distracted, the more I was able to move.

Tito's house was the last one on a dead-end street. The nearest house was at least a mile up the road. At the end of a red brick driveway sat a huge, white Victorian. Nobody in a million years would think one of Holyoke's most vicious drug dealers lived there. That was probably why he lasted so long on the streets.

The flashy go down fast, Artey once told me.

A Gorilla met us at the door. He led me up the spiral staircase to the master bedroom. Inside the enormous bedroom Tito sat, tied to an armless chair. I hated dealing with old Spanish men. They had this macho pride thing about them I couldn't stand. Taking one look at Tito, I knew he was going to be stubborn.

I pulled up a seat directly in front of Tito. Country must've worked him over pretty good. His eyes were damn near swollen shut, blood leaked from his mouth and his nose was broken. Yet he still sat there like nothing in the world was wrong, that was that macho shit I was talking about.

I waved my hand, and Jessito removed the duct-tape from his mouth.

"Tito, Tito, Tito, I bet you wished you bought that sailboat, now don't you?"

"What kind of man are you, to come into another man's house and touch his family. What we do stays in the streets!"

"Oh, really? What book did you get that shit out of? I wasn't aware that hustlers had a book on the rules of engagement, did you, Jessito?"

"Nope."

"A man's family is sacred!" Tito bellowed.

"No, Tito. That's where you're wrong. In this line of work, a man's family is a liability."

"You young punks fucked the business up! You don't know anything about respect. Back in my country..."

"Fuck your country, and fuck you! I gave you a warning and you called me a monkey!" I shouted.

"This is wrong!"

I took a breath and calmed down for a second.

There was no reason for me to yell, Tito was the one tied up.

I said, "I don't know what you're so worked up about. We're cut from the same cloth."

"You'll never be me!" Tito said, spitting at my feet. "I'd never touch another man's family!"

"Well, that's too bad because I'm about to touch the hell out of yours. Jessito, tell Country to bring his wife in here."

Jessito left, returning seconds later with Country and Maria. Maria was a short, fat, ugly old lady with saggy tits. Country smacked her on her naked ass before pushing her to the floor.

"What the fuck is that in her hand?" I asked.

"A Bible." Country said.

"Oh, my God, Tito, why are they doing this to us? What do they want? Please, just give it to them." Maria cried.

"Country, go ahead and fuck that fat bitch."

"Don't you dare do this. I'll hunt you down and kill your whole family." Tito threatened.

"Hold up, you're threatening me? You're the one bleeding to death, tied to a chair. Maybe you haven't grasped the situation fully. Tito, you're going to die tonight. All we're doing here is seeing if your wife and daughter will be joining you."

Tito looked at me with stone cold eyes. I leaned in and looked directly into them.

"If you don't want to tell me where the coke and money is at now, we'll get on with the show."

Country already had Maria in doggy-style position on the bed. Two more Gorillas waited in line for their turn.

"She's a child of God for Christ-sake!"

"Aren't we all, Tito, aren't we all? Maria, let's make this a little interesting. I want you to pick a chapter out of the Bible and read it to us."

"What... what... chapter?"

"I don't know, I never read the damn thing but I'm sure you can find something suitable for the occasion. Now, if you stop for any reason I'm going to have your daughter brought in here."

"Please, not Silena. She's innocent and she's still a virgin. Whatever you're going to do, do it to me." Maria said, with tears streaming down her face."

"A'ight now that we have an understanding, Country, fuck her in the ass while she attempts to give us the good word."

Country began sodomizing Maria. She yelled and squealed like a wild boar, but she managed to keep reading the Bible. I was perversely turned on and impressed at the same time. I knew then that I was going to hell. Country punished Maria's asshole for ten or more minutes before he pulled out and walked around to her face. He grabbed a handful of hair and forced his dick into her mouth.

"Bitch you better swallow it!" Country shouted.

"Maria, remember our deal." I reminded her pointing to a picture of Silena on the dresser.

Maria reluctantly opened her mouth and Country rammed the length of his dick down her throat until his balls smacked her chin.

"Swallow it and you better not spit it back up!" Country growled as he fucked her face.

"Now tell me this, Tito. How can you who claim

to be a family man allow this to happen to your wife? She's letting us do this to her so we don't touch your daughter. What are you doing to help?"

He didn't reply, he just kept a stone face. Maria, on the other hand grimaced as she swallowed Country's nut.

One of the Gorillas, waiting against the wall, took over from the back. Maria went back to screaming and reading from the Bible. I wondered how long Tito could keep this up. Then it dawned on me that Tito didn't give a fuck about his wife. If he did, he wouldn't have been cheating on her. Shit, he was probably getting off watching his wife get the shit fucked out of her.

"We could do this all night, Tito, but I don't have all night. Jessito, go get his daughter."

"You said you wouldn't touch her!" Tito shouted.

"Listen, if you don't tell me where the coke and dough is at, touching her is the least I'm gonna do."

Jessito came in with Silena. She was beautiful, with long black hair and a tight little frame.

"Country, how many pills did you give her?"

"Four." Country answered.

"What did you give her?" Tito demanded.

"Chill, Tito, it's only X. She'll be fine, or she'll develop an addiction. Then again, who doesn't have an addiction these days?"

I started unbuttoning Silena's jeans and pulling them down to her knees. She didn't put up a fight at all because the X wouldn't let her. After pulling her cotton panties to her knees I parted her lips, and ran my tongue over her clit a few times.

"Hey, Tito, look at me eatin' your daughter's

pussy. Mmmmmm, this shit tastes so young and sweet. I see why you like young girls, Tito. Come on, it doesn't hurt to look. Maybe if I do this."

I pushed two fingers inside Silena. She was already wet. After I fingered her a bit, I stripped her until the only thing she had on was a blindfold. I turned her around and sat her on my lap. As I rubbed her clit, Silena grinded her ass into my dick. Then she laid her head back on my shoulder and opened her legs, allowing me deeper access. It wasn't long before she was moaning and trembling from pulsing orgasms. She was grinding her ass so hard into my dick, I felt like I was going to nut.

Maria clenched the sheets as she swallowed Country's nut. She continued to read from the Bible the best she could. Every chance she got, she shot Tito an evil glare until finally she snapped.

"Stop it! Stop it! Stop it! Tito, please! That's our daughter, our angel. Oh God, pleeease give them what they want, Tito!"

"No, don't give in yet, Tito. I'm having fun with Silena. The same way you had fun with Bless."

Tito looked at me then closed his eyes and shook his head.

"Yeah, I know. The same thing that makes you laugh, makes you cry."

I laid Silena across my lap and started fingering her asshole. A tear trickled down his cheek. He was breaking down. And, sure enough, another five minutes of molesting his daughter was all he could take. What resistance he had left ran down his face with the tears.

"Okay, okay! Stop it!"

"Where's the shit at Tito?"

"You have to promise me one thing, Pharaoh."

"What's that?"

"Let my wife and daughter return to my country, unharmed. Promise me!"

"I promise you I'll let them return to your country."

"In the cellar behind the wine racks. There's a fake wall. It's all there."

"What about the apartment in Cherry Hill?"

Tito dropped his head.

"Apartment 29, the keys are on the table."

"You got all the sense, Tito. You think we don't know that you got to make a call first before the dude inside will open the door?"

I passed Tito the phone and he made the call.

"A'ight, that's a wrap. Jessito, take some Gorillas and hit the cellar. Country, you take the rest of the crew and go to the Cherry Hill apartment."

Everybody left, leaving me alone.

"What now?" Tito mumbled.

"Now it's time to have some fun."

As soon as I said that, Bless came walking in the door with a fine-ass chick.

"Daddy, this is Debbie."

"What's up, Debbie?"

"Hi."

"Hey, Tito, Bless came up with something special for you. You see, it's not enough to kill you. I want to kill that macho pride shit you got." I told him.

Bless cut Tito from the chair. "Get up on the bed,

Papi. I got a big surprise for you, so why don't you strip for me."

"You heard her, Tito, strip."

I pointed the Desert Eagle at Silena's head.

"Don't think I won't kill this bitch."

Tito saw I was serious.

"Hurry the fuck up. I told you I don't have all night."

With the barrel of the gun, I slid it in Selina's pussy. Tito slowly undressed and climbed on the bed.

"Debbie, handle your business." Bless said.

Debbie walked in front of the bed and started doing a seductive dance. She took her shirt and bra off, displaying her voluptuous breasts. Although Tito tried, he couldn't hide his lust for younger women. Even in front of his wife, he couldn't help but stare at Debbie. Once in a while, he would glance at his wife in shame, but slowly his eyes would find his way back to Debbie's half-naked body.

"Do you like what you see, Tito?" Debbie said while throwing her bra on Tito's lap. She turned around, giving Tito her back. "You want to see more? Come on, Tito, tell me you want to see more."

"Si." Tito mumbled shamefully.

Debbie continued to strip until she was in her thong.

Still with her back to him, she said, "Do you still like what you see? How about now?"

Debbie started doing the booty clap. She dropped it to the floor and brought it back up. When she removed her thong and turned back around, Tito almost fainted. Debbie had a dick. Yeah, she was a she-male. She was all woman, other than her dick, which wasn't small either.

Debbie stroked it to life as she walked towards the bed.

"You like what you see now?"

I said, "Doggy-style, Tito."

He looked at me like I was crazy.

"Do it or else."

"Do it, Tito!" Maria screamed. "Do whatever he says! You got us into this!"

Tito shook his head as he assumed the position. His lips quivered, his eye-lids lowered and his whole body trembled.

"This might hurt a bit," Debbie said. "Then again, it might hurt a lot."

Debbie wasted no time in running up in Tito's ass.

"Arrrrrrgggooggghhhh!"

FLOP! FLOP! FLOP! FLOP! FLOP! FLOP!

"That's it, Debbie, fuck that macho pride shit right out of him!" Bless shouted.

Debbie put in some serious work. At least 10 minutes of it, non-stop. Tito was all fucked up. Sweat poured from his wrinkled forehead, his eyes rolled up in his head, and he almost blacked out once or twice.

"Where do you want me to cum, Daddy?" Debbie asked.

"In his mouth."

That was where Debbie dumped her load. I think the sucking of Debbie's dick was what finally broke him. When it was over, Debbie left him crying and holding his ass like a little baby.

"It's not over, Tito. See, I figured out why you like

younger females. I mean, besides the obvious. I think you have an incestuous thing for your daughter. I think when you were fuckin' my Queen, in your head you were fuckin' your daughter."

"So, I tell you what. I'm gonna give you a chance to live out your wildest fantasy. At the same time, I'm going to resurrect you." I got up and walked over to the side of the bed. "Tito, do you believe in life after death?"

"What?"

"Do you think that I can bring you back from the dead?"

"What are you going to do?"

"Really, I'm not going to do anything. You're going to do all the work. Maria, I need you to do something for me." I whispered in her ear and she started crying.

"Please, she's just a baby. She doesn't know what's going on. Please look into your heart."

I whispered some more into her ear. Maria closed her eyes and dropped her head.

"Okay, I'll do it." She broke into tears.

Bless and Debbie handcuffed Tito to the bed, spread-eagle on his back. I tapped Maria on her back. She looked up at me, then slowly climbed onto the bed.

"Maria, what does he want you to do?" Tito begged.

She didn't answer him.

"Maria, look at me!" Tito begged again.

Maria wouldn't look at her husband of 35 years. Climbing on the bed, she took him into her mouth. Against Tito's own will, his erection grew.

"This is what I'm going to do, Tito. I'm going

to resurrect you through your daughter. You'll fuck her, and she'll become pregnant. You'll be born again through her. So, your daughter will become your mother. What do you think?"

"You sick fuck!"

"That's coming from a man that likes to be shitted on." Bless said, spitting in his face.

Silena sat slumped in the chair with her head somewhere in the cosmos. I stood her up and walked her over to the bed.

"I won't do it!" Tito shouted at the top of his lungs.

"Oh, yes, you will do it, or your beautiful daughter will be having my baby. You choose, Tito. Trust me, I don't have a problem blazing your daughter up."

I undid my pants. Silence fell in the room. Finally, Tito came to grips with the situation.

"Oh, God, forgive me."

"Don't worry, Tito, there was a shit-load of incest in the Bible. Plus, given the situation, I think God will understand."

Maria held her husbands erect penis up while Debbie and Bless guided Silena down on it. As Bless pressed down on Silena's shoulders, Silena let out a loud squeal. At the same time, she started digging her nails into her father's chest, drawing blood. Her face told me she was in pain, but the X would melt it into pleasure.

"Ride that dick, bitch!" Bless said, slapping Silena on the ass.

"Ahhhhh!"

Bit by bit, Silena started rocking back and forth. When she got comfortable with it, she started going up and down on it. Faster and faster, Silena rode her father. She looked like a jockey racing for the finish line.

"Yeah, bitch! Fuck your daddy! Faster bitch!" Bless really got off on it. "Ride that dick, ride it!" Bless slapped her on the ass and pulled her hair.

Tito's shaft glistened with his daughter's juices. Then, right before my eyes, it turned to blood. Silena's gasps turned to beastly howls. She didn't stop or slow down, she just kept riding like she was possessed. I could see it in Tito's face that he was trying to hold back, but the way Silena was riding him, there was no way he could hold back much longer. That moment came sooner than I thought. When he came, he let out an agonizing scream.

"AAARRRGGGHHH!"

I let Silena ride him for another few minutes before I pulled her off of him. Bless climbed on the bed pissed all over his face.

"That's one for the road, ole boy." she laughed.

"Come' on, Maria, let's get this over with." I passed her the gun and stood behind her. I then walked her over to the bed. "To be resurrected, you have to die first, Tito."

Maria was shaking so bad she could barely hold the gun. Tito said something in Spanish, and she started crying even more.

"I love you, Maria, do it!"

"God forgive me!" Maria screamed.

BOOM! BOOM!

And it was over.

Chapter 34

After leaving Tito's house, we rendezvoused with the rest of the squad at the elementary school, behind Bolten Village. We changed into black S.W.A.T. uniforms with D.E.A. in big yellow letters on the back. We also switched cars. We had four, dark-blue, cop-style Crown Vics. They came with the red and blue lights in the grill, the cage in the back and a spotlight on the driver's side. We had them fully bulletproofed, with brand new interceptor engines installed.

My cellphone rang.

I answered, "Who's this?"

"T-Money."

"What's the word, kid?"

"Tonia just called me from the bathroom of one of the stash houses. She said most of them are at some party in the same projects."

"How many are guarding the stash houses?"

"Three inside the house with the dope. It's just her and Ronnie in the house with the dough." T-Money explained.

"Where's Sean?"

"At the party, most likely."

"What's the situation with the police?"

"They're still busy with the bombings and the drive-bys Daryl did and the Pine Street shit."

"Keep me updated on their movements."

"A'ight, yo. Hey, Pharaoh, Sean's crew is known for putting in work, for real. Plus, word is they just purchased a shit-load of guns off of Giuseppe. Don't give them a chance to bust first. You got to slump them off the gate."

"I hear you."

"A'ight then peace."

"Peace. Everybody gather around and listen up!" I commanded. "This ain't gonna be easy like Pine Street. I just got word they are strapped heavy. Just because we are going in dressed like cops don't mean shit. Cops get shot at too just like anybody else. So shoot to kill."

"Where are the stash houses at?" Task wondered.

"Towards the back. Bolten Village has a one-way street that runs all the way through it. Girls, I want all the cars pointed to the exit. As far as we know, everybody is at a party. That means if shit jumps off, they could come from anywhere."

"At the entrance to the projects will be a brown Cadillac with five Gorillas strapped with AK's." Vashon cut in. "They are there just in case shit gets out of hand."

"Word, that's what's up." I replied. "And soon as you see the kitchen lights flash on and off, pull the trucks up to the back door and load the shit up. Once you get what you can, get the fuck outta there. Don't wait for us. Bless, you and the Queens know what to do?"

"Yes, Daddy."

"Cool, then all we do now is wait for T-Money's call."

This whole thing relied on Sean's crew believing we were cops for real or just long enough to catch them off-guard. We needed that element of surprise.

People react three different ways to police raids. Some just start running for no reason. Others just lie down and give up. Then you got the cowboys who want to shoot it out. Those were the ones I wanted to avoid, but to keep it real, I knew they were going to shoot it out. It was common sense to assume that a crew that made millions would be willing to die for theirs.

Each second that passed waiting for T-Money to call seemed like an hour. In situations like these, you have to learn to keep calm. If you didn't, you couldn't focus. People have certain rituals to get themselves up for the moment. Football players yell and smack each other before a big game, boxers pray in the dressing room before a fight, or a nut job who snorts a shit-load of coke before doing a hit.

The same thing applied to stick-up kids. You got to put yourself in the zone. You have to picture your objective from all angles. You have to figure shit out. If this happens, I'm going to do this, or if that happens, I'll do this instead. Then you picture the worst case scenario, and most of the time that means getting killed. Once you accept that, you're ready for whatever.

Lethal, Killer K, Blaze, and Dirty Chuck were listening to Guillotine spitting some gangsta lyrics. Lasandra and Akura were smoking weed. Vashon, Vicious and their crew were doing what they do before a hit. Me, I was getting my dick sucked by

Bless. By the time T-Money called back, everybody was in their zone.

"What's the word, T-Money?" I asked.

"Tonia just called. She's up in the bathroom of one of the stash houses. Sean just walked in on her and Ronnie. They are downstairs beefing. Besides the three cats in the other stash house, there is nobody else around." The excitement in his voice was getting me amped. "Yo, Pharaoh, if you're gonna hit them muthafuckas, do it now!"

"A'ight, yo."

We jumped in the cars and headed out, single-file. I was in the lead car, alone. Task, Guillotine and Blaze, with Akura at the wheel, came next. Lethal, Killer K, and Dirty Chuck, with Lasandra driving, followed them. Bless brought up the rear, alone. Vashon and his crew were already in motion, heading towards the back of the stash houses.

From the direction that we approached Bolten Village, we had to pass the exit first. I was able to get a quick glimpse of the stash house as we passed. T-Money was right, there was nobody in sight.

My palms grew sweaty with anticipation as I made a left into Bolten Village. As I passed the late model Cadillac, I flashed my headlights to give them a heads-up. Racing to the stash houses took forever. Every muscle in my body twitched with excitement. After the cars skidded to a stop, we hopped out and glided into position. The kids and those with guilty consciences ran. When everybody was in position, I pulled out my twin .380s and kissed them for good luck. I nodded, giving everyone the go-ahead. All the doors went crashing in at the same time. Ronnie and Sean were on the floor, tumbling around like two kids in an elementary school fight.

"Freeze! Spread eagle on the floor! Do it now!" I screamed.

"Fuck!" Sean shouted.

"Face-down!" I said.

"Okay, okay!" Ronnie said.

"Put your fucking hands behind your head and interlock your fingers." This was easier than I thought. Both sprawled on the floor without a fight. They didn't even look at my face. The yellow D.E.A. letters was all they had to see. Tonia came down the stairs not long after that.

"Hey Daddy." she said, giving me a kiss.

"Cuff them and go flip the kitchen lights."

"What?" they both said.

"Don't tell me you're a cop!" Sean said with pain in his eyes looking at Tonia. "Come on, Tonia, say it ain't so."

"A cop? Hell, no, Sean. I'm a Gorilla Queen."

"I can't believe this bitch played us both!" Ronnie shouted as he banged his head on the floor.

I looked out the back window and saw Vashon's crew loading up the trucks. When I looked out the front window, I saw a crowd starting to form.

"Do you know who you're fuckin' with?" Sean demanded.

"Enlighten me, Sean. Tell me who I'm fuckin' with." I said, taking a seat across from him and lighting a blunt.

"You ever hear of the Kenji Dragons, muthafucka?"

"You're talking about the Kenji Dragons that come from Shanghai, China?" I said sarcastically.

"Yeah, muthafucka!"

"So that means you're talking about Ming and the boys out of Rhode Island, right?"

"You know who the fuck I'm talking about!"

I said, "Look, you Jon-B-lookin'-ass-bitch. Ming will do business with anybody that can move several kilos of pure dope. You can best believe the bond that you and Ming formed in jail comes second to business."

"Everything is loaded, Daddy."

I went to take a look for myself. When I turned around, Ronnie had made it to his feet and threw himself through the living-room window.

"Yo! It's a stick up. Them muthafuckas ain't police!"

"Shit!" I yelled.

"Oh, yeah, shit's on now, muthafuckas," Sean said with a smirk.

I said, "Pick his bitch-ass up."

Tonia got Sean to his feet as I peeked out the front window. It wasn't looking good, especially when they started pulling out those choppers.

"Back the fuck up!" Tonia screamed. She pushed Sean in front of the door, using him as a shield. "I'll kill him, I swear I will!"

They hesitated a bit, undecided on what to do.

"They ain't gonna kill me. They need me to get out of here!" Sean hollered.

I said, "You think? Tonia, rock his ass to sleep."

"What, hold up a minute."

BOOM! BOOM!

Tonia squeezed two in the back of his head. Sean fell slowly, like a tree. Soon as he hit the ground, a hailstorm of bullets hit the house. I snatched Tonia down by the arm. We scrambled into the kitchen as bullets ripped through the living room.

"Stay low and keep firing at the back door!" I shouted over the gunfire.

"But I can't see!" Tonia squealed.

"As long as you keep firing, they won't try to come in!"

I scrambled back into the living room. Their bullets shredded the sheetrock like it was paper. White powder fell like snow, blurring my vision. Pictures crashed to the floor, glass vases shattered and pieces of glass hit me in the face. The TV exploded like fireworks. Tonia let out a scream that I heard over the chaos.

"Keep shooting!" I yelled.

So many bullets were hitting the house the door fell off its hinges. As I looked to see if Tonia was okay, I saw the kitchen cabinets almost tumble on top of her. Seconds later, the microwave exploded. These dudes were hitting the house with what seemed like a battalion of guns.

All of a sudden, the gunfire stopped. My ears started ringing. Lying in the middle of the living room floor, I had one gun pointed at the door and the other at the window. I was ready to slump anybody brave enough to come through either.

"Shorty, you a'ight?"

"Yes Daddy," Tonia replied.

"Here, take my vest and be ready to move when I say so!"

"No, Daddy, you wear it."

"Bitch, take the muthafuckin' vest."

The barrage of gunfire started back up. But this time, it wasn't as heavy. I crawled to the window to take a quick peek. The mob of gunmen had scattered like roaches. From a distance, I saw Bless emerge from the shadows, blazing her two .38s. Lasandra and Akura fired from the opposite direction. There were still five dudes with automatics focusing on the house. I turned around to get my bearings when a spark from the TV landed on the sofa, setting it ablaze.

"Tonia, come here!" She crawled over to me in a hurry. "The next time they reload, I'm running out to distract them. Be ready. Remember how we practiced at the gun range. Breathe out when you squeeze the trigger."

"Okay, okay, I can do it." she said, shaking.

"Aim for the chest. If you hit two, that's good. I'll get the rest."

"Give me a kiss, Daddy."

We kissed.

In a few seconds, the flames climbed the walls and webbed across the ceiling. It wouldn't be long before the second floor would fall on us. Then came a break in the gunfire.

"Now!"

Diving outside, I landed on my side. The gunmen fumbled with their clips when they saw me hit the ground. I was able to get off three shots. One hit a dude in the chest, one grazed another's shoulder, and the last one missed all of them.

Trying to get to my feet, I tripped over Sean's

body. When I looked up, they had already taken aim. One by one, I watched their heads pop like grapes. Looking over my shoulder, I saw Tonia standing in the window. She had hit all four with only four shots. Seconds later, Task, Lethal, Blaze and the rest of the crew emerged from the other stash house with their guns drawn.

The gunfight moved to the middle of the street. We looked like we were getting the best of them. Then, out of nowhere, came another ten with automatics.

"What the fuck!" Lethal said, diving behind an old Volkswagon Beetle.

"Where are they coming from?" Task shouted.

"I don't know. You got another clip?" Killer K asked, searching in his pants.

"Here!" Task said, tossing him one.

Bless, Akura and Lasandra were trapped behind a dumpster. I couldn't get to them because I was pinned down myself.

"Look!" Dirty Chuck pointed up the street.

The brown Caddy came roaring towards us. Two Gorillas stood up out of the sunroof with AK's while the others hung out the window, automatics in hand.

"Come on!" I waved to Bless and them.

Bless stepped to the side and let Akura and Lasandra go first. They dashed from behind the dumpster. Once they were in the clear, Bless shot out, as well. Halfway to us, Bless was hit in the stomach. As she tumbled around in pain, a few of Sean's boys ran out and snatched her. They dragged her into an abandoned apartment. Without thinking, I went after her.

"Pharaoh, no!" Guillotine shouted.

It was too late, I was already gone. I didn't care about the spray of bullets flying through the air. The thought of dying never once crossed my mind. Nothing seemed more important at the moment than Bless.

I saw Bless's feet kicking just before she disappeared in the door way. No matter how fast I was moving, it seemed like I was running in slow motion. I saw two flashes of light that lit up the dark apartment for a split second. In that moment, as I came up the steps, I saw one of the guys standing over Bless with his gun pointed down at her. Then he squeezed again.

Both Bless's arms and legs flailed in the air and then landed flat on the floor. A trickle of blood dribbled from her mouth. All I saw was red, but I was still focused. Controlled rage.

By the time the first guy spotted me coming through the doorway, I had already killed him in my mind. Just like the other two behind him, reloading their guns. It all happened so fast. One minute I was squeezing my trigger like a mad man. The next minute all I heard were bodies dropping.

I kneeled down to Bless. "Yo! Bless, wake up!"

I slapped her in her face several times before she responded. Then she curled up into a ball, groaning while she grabbed her ribs.

"Fuck, this shit hurts!"

"Be glad you were wearing your vest."

Two seconds later, Task and the rest of the crew appeared in the doorway, guns drawn.

"Yo Pharoah! Don't ever do no crazy shit like that again! That's what you got us for."

"Then get us the fuck out of here!" I shouted.

The Gorillas in the Caddy cleared the streets and pushed Sean's crew behind the houses for cover. That was our only chance for escape, and we took it.

As we sped out of Bolten Village, I hit the button on the remote control. The two bombs Tonia planted in the stash houses exploded. Two balls of flames shot high in the air. That distraction made it easy for us to disappear like ghosts.

Chapter 35

Holyoke looked like a war zone when we were done with it. I told everybody to lie low for the rest of the night. The police were going to be out in full force. Anybody caught slippin' was going to get it in the worst way.

I had all guns melted and the cars sent to the crusher. Anything that could connect us to the craziness of that night I had destroyed. That included having a few people outside of the family slumped. I couldn't have this coming back to haunt me.

Me and my Queens laid up in the bed, watching the news, and damn, Holyoke looked like a war zone. I wondered why no police showed up in Bolten Village. Then as we watched the news, my question was answered. T-Money had detonated the car in the police department's parking lot. He was right when he said they would look after their own first.

The news reporter stood with the burning car just behind her for added effect as she gave her report.

"This is Katie Stew for Channel 5 Action News. Law enforcement are on high alert tonight after a bomb was detonated in the Holyoke Police Department's parking lot. No one was injured. Some suspect that it had something to do with the gangland shootout that took place earlier this evening. The body count as of now is 28 and climbing. The police couldn't respond to the mayhem because their patrol cars were the target of drive-bys."

The screen flashed back and forth from Pine St. to Bolten Village. There were bodies all over the street covered with white blankets.

"There is speculation that what happened tonight was a shifting of power in the streets. Unlike before, when there were many drug organizations that ran the streets, there is only one now. They are called the Gorillas, and their leader is said to be a person who calls himself King Pharaoh."

"That's right, bitch, my Daddy runs shit now!" Tonia screamed at the screen. "Gorillas forever!"

The news continued, "All this comes on the heels of Senator Holten's 'Take Back the Streets Campaign.' I guess the streets have responded, and to them it's business as usual," the reporter concluded. "We'll have more on this late breaking news coming up after the break. I'm Katie Stew for Channel 5 Action News."

Bless came up for air while sucking my dick. "What are we going to do now?"

"Take a vacation."

Chapter 36

This would be my first time aboard an airplane. We boarded a shuttle bus and were quietly driven to the other side of the airstrip. The shuttle left us out front of a huge hangar.

"What are we doing here?" Country asked.

"Waiting," I replied.

"For what?"

Soon as he said that, the door to the hangar slowly opened.

"For that," I said with a smile.

A little golf cart came out first. It had in tow a 15 passenger Executive Class Gulfstream 550. Instead of taking a commercial flight, I decided to do it big.

The 550 came crammed with luxuries. The plush Italian leather seats came with massage buttons. For entertainment, it had two plasma screens with a PlayStation hooked to it and a Bose surround sound system. The whole inside was decked out in black cherrywood, smoked glass, and platinum trimming with a soft, golden glow. The shit was so fly, it even had a bedroom.

"Yo, you bought this?" Country asked.

"Nah, something like this cost like 7.2 million and $200,000 for the flight crew. I'm just renting it for a while."

After we boarded, the jet engines roared to life. As we taxied down the runway, a feeling of relief came over me. I guess I had felt guilty about getting away with all the crazy shit that just went down.

Bless squeezed my hand as the plane shot down the runway. Her grip got tighter as the front wheels lifted into the air. When the back wheels followed and there was that quick rush of weightlessness, Bless crushed the hell out of my fingers. The G-5 roared into the clouds, climbing higher and higher. The sun was bigger and brighter, the tops of the clouds were whiter, and everything felt more peaceful.

At first, everybody wanted to come to South Beach, Miami. Then, at the last minute, some of them changed their minds. Task and his crew decided to go to New York. They rented two weeks worth of studio time at one of the biggest recording studios in the Big Apple.

My Queens, Jessito and his girl, Lavish, decided to go. T-Money brought two girls with him, Country had his girl, Emerald, and Daryl brought some chick I never saw before. The rest of the crew stayed back to make sure everything was straight.

Once the plane leveled off, me, Bless, and Tonia went into the bedroom.

"Yo, Tonia, go get Tiffany. I want to know what happened with Javier."

Seconds later, Tiffany came in, climbing on the bed. "Hi what's up, Daddy?"

"Tell me what exactly went down with Javier and why the fuck he ain't dead?"

Tiffany rolled her eyes and smacked her lips. "Daddy, everything was going fine. I had Javier upstairs, deep inside my pussy. He stopped as soon as he heard a noise and got up. Daryl's clumsy ass tripped over something."

"What happened then?"

"Javier got up, grabbed his gun and started to creep downstairs. No matter how bad I wanted Javier to blow Daryl's stupid face off, I couldn't let that happen. So I followed Javier. I snuck up on him with a butcher's knife I had stashed in the room, you know, just in case."

"Did you stab him?" Tonia asked.

"I got him in the back two times, but he got away."

"Fuck it. As long as we got the deed to his property where the gold rims are, I'm cool." I said.

An hour into the flight, I drifted off to dreamland. I was back in Chestnut Park. I could feel the familiar summer breeze brushing across my face. Spanish clubhouse music banged from the back of E-Love's truck. Everybody was out, enjoying the weather.

"Yo, kid, what's up?"

I turned around to see a man sitting on the bench. He was dressed in black jeans, Timberland constructs, and a white wife beater.

"Yo, you don't remember me?"

I took a couple of steps closer to him. "Who the fuck are you?"

"That's fucked up. You don't remember your boy?"

As I got closer, the stranger's face became familiar. He looked like someone from my past. Someone I was close to.

"Jo-Jo?"

"Yeah, yo, what the fuck, give me some love, yo!"

"But you were a kid when you got hit. How the fuck do you grow up when you're dead?"

"This is your dream, you tell me," Jo-Jo replied with a wink.

"Fuck it, so how have you been?"

"Dead."

We both laughed.

It felt crazy talking to my dead best friend from childhood. He pulled out a blunt and lit it. From there, we started kicking it like old times. We talked for hours about this and that. Laughing at times and getting quiet at other times. I told him everything that had been happening with the Gorillas, and that was when his attitude changed.

"You don't have to tell me what's going on. I can see for myself."

"What do you mean?" I asked him.

"I see your work, kid. Look over there in that abandoned building. See those dudes looking over here at you?"

"The ones with the red eyes?"

"Yeah, those are the Pine Street cats you had massacred. Now, look over there on the corner. I know you know who that is."

"Is that Dante's faggot ass?"

"The one and only," Jo-Jo announced.

"What the fuck is wrong with his face?"

"You put a bullet in it. Check out Sean over there

by the merry-go-round. He got here last week. He told me everything, yo. Look, here come Tito."

"Hey, you fuckin' punk. I'll be here, waiting for you," Tito said, getting in my face.

"I don't know about you." I explained, "But I don't have any plans on seeing you anytime soon. If you want, I can pay a visit to Silena for you. I'm sure she's about two months pregnant now. Just hang in there, you'll be resurrected before you know it."

"FUCK YOU!" Tito roared, bursting into flames.

"So, fuck them mutherfuckas."

"I'm one of the ones you pissed off."

"You?"

"Yeah, me!" Jo-Jo said, raising his voice, while he jumped to his feet. "You're doing all this killing, and you haven't got the cop that killed me!"

"I… I… haven't…"

"What, you don't give a fuck about me, do you?" Jo-Jo interrupted. "How did you forget about me so fast? I was your best friend. I died in your muthafuckin' arms, yo! I can't cross over until you make things right. This park has been my hell ever since!"

All of a sudden, the sky got darker. The clouds rumbled and flashed streaks of lightning across of the sky. Leaves fell off the trees and turned to rats. A crack split down the center of the park and then opened up. From the crack, flames licked the sky, and everybody who died because of me emerged from it.

Blood ran from the bullet holes in the Pine St. crew as they walked like zombies towards me. The whole back of Sean Crass's head was missing. Tito had a hole the size of a softball in his chest.

Jo-Jo snatched me up by one hand and had me suspended in the air. As he choked me, he also laughed at me.

"How does it feel, huh? How do you like it?"

Jo-Jo's clothes peeled away and his skin turned blood-red. Tiny horns grew out of the top of his head. Then a tail oozed from his back. He punched into my chest and pulled out my heart.

"The way you're going on, you won't be needing this anymore."

He tossed it to the rats, and they devoured it.

All I thought was that this couldn't be happening to me. Jo-Jo was my best friend. He choked me until I was about to pass out. Then he threw me to the ground. Something wouldn't let me get up. The next thing I knew, I was covered in rats, nibbling at my flesh. Eventhough, I knew it was a dream, I was scared to death. Everything felt real, a little too real. I couldn't do anything but scream.

When I woke up, Bless was nibbling on my ear and Tonia was suckin' my dick.

"Daddy, you're sweating like crazy. What's up? You okay?"

It took a second for me to realize where I was.

"Yeah, I'm cool."

I heard Jo-Jo's voice fading away. "You got to make it right, Pharaoh. You got to make it right."

Chapter 37

WELCOME TO MIAMI read a huge sign as we walked down the glass tunnel to the main terminal.

"T-Money, go see if the hotel sent the limos yet."

"A'ight."

"We'll be over there in that cafe."

T-Money disappeared into the sea of travelers while the rest of us headed to the cafe. As I walked in, the first thing I thought about was Joey. From the first time he told me, I had been trying to figure out why he wanted one of these spots. Me, personally, I didn't see what was so special about them. Well, there was one thing I noticed, all the cafes we passed were packed. To me, that meant money. I guess Joey knew what he was talking about.

"Yo, son, why you choose Miami for our vacation?" Country asked.

"It's business and pleasure, at the same time. You remember how we would be sitting at home watching MTV Spring Break'?"

"Yeah," he said with a smile.

"We always said we'd go as soon as we made

enough money. So, I figured since we're sitting on millions, fuck it."

"So, what's the business side of the trip?"

"I'm looking for a building for Joey's cafe."

"A cafe?" Daryl replied.

"Isn't that what I said? Me and Joey talked about this before the coma. So I'm taking his cut and mine's and getting us one."

"Hold up, kid. How the fuck did Joey get a cut? I don't remember him bustin' his gun. He's my man and all, but we got to split that, for real."

"What?!" I said, balling my fist up. "If he's your man, for real, you'd be glad I was doing this for him. You acting like he's dead!"

"He might as well be, yo."

If I had my gun on me right then, I would've blew his face off without thinking. How the fuck could he say something like that?

Lasandra saw I was about to flip, and, before I could say another word, she cut in. "Damn, Daryl, shut the fuck up! You never know what to say out your mouth."

"Yo, you keep runnin' your mouth to the wrong muthafucka." Daryl warned.

She said, "And? Like that threat is supposed to mean something to me. You're lucky I don't put toothpaste on my knuckles and punch you in the mouth, with your stank-ass breath."

Everyone laughed. It calmed the situation a little, but the tension was still in the air. It seemed like the more success the Gorillas were having, the shittier Daryl's attitude got.

Before we left, I had to straighten out some shit Daryl had gotten us into. He took his crew and went around, extorting small mom and pop stores for protection money. I didn't know anything about it until Jensenia told me. Her father owned a small store on the corner of Elm and Sergeant Street. We had been going to that store since we were kids, and Daryl went ahead and pulled that shit. I sent Jessito around to the stores to repay everything Daryl took and told them that protection was free.

I was close to letting him go, but one of the Gorilla laws was that a founding member could not be kicked out. He had to leave on his own. The bottom line was that Daryl was becoming a problem, and no matter how much I avoided it, sooner or later, I was going to have to deal with it.

"Yo!" T-Money called from the cafe entrance. "Y'all gonna spend the whole vacation in this cafe, or what?"

"Hell, no!" Lavish replied, jumping to her feet.

"Then let's get the fuck outta here."

The hotel we were staying at sent three glacier-white stretch Bentleys. I felt like royalty riding in them things. South Beach was less than 15 minutes away from the airport, but the hotel we were staying at was farther up the beach. As soon as we hit the highway, I knew I was going to like South Beach. It was like our plane landed in another world.

Nobody said a word; we all were too busy taking in our surroundings. The first thing I noticed was how beautiful the sky was. This was where they probably got the term sky-blue from. Cloudless and endless. I had a feeling this was only the beginning of our paradise.

On the right, I spotted a port for luxurious cruise ships. The highway passed right next to them. I knew they were big, but when you got right up on them, they looked enormous. Next vacation I took was definitely going to be aboard one of those.

"Sex on the beach," Bless said as she nibbled on my ear.

"What did you say?"

"I want you to fuck me on the beach. I want you to fuck me in the daytime, peak beach hours, in front of grandparents, parents, kids, and dogs. I don't give a fuck who sees us. And I don't want no humping shit, either. I want you to fuck me so hard, I pass the fuck out."

"Damn, let me get some of that, too," Lasandra said, high-fiving Bless.

We pulled up to the hotel, but to me it looked more like a glass high-rise you see in the city. T-Money reserved two Presidential suites for him and the rest of the crew, and he reserved the King's suite for me.

I could see why the clerk looked at us crazy. We weren't presidents or kings. I expected to be treated funny. You know how them stuck up, establishment types can be sometimes. So you can bet I was shocked when the opposite happened. Soon as the clerk confirmed that our rooms were paid up, out came the red carpet treatment. Bellboys came out of nowhere, grabbing our bags. The manager came out of his office to personally offer his services.

"My name is Lance Dagot, and let me be the first to welcome you to beautiful Miami."

Lance spoke with a fake-ass British accent, but he

looked the part. He stood a lanky one inch taller than me, had tanned skin, platinum-colored hair, soft blue eyes, and a well-defined chin.

"Anything you need, please contact me personally. My extension is 502. If you'll follow me, I'll show you to your private elevator. And, again, if you need anything, just call."

As I shook Lance's hand, I noticed his eyes were fixed on Lasandra's silver dollar sized nipple imprints.

"Thank you, Mr. Dagot," I said, snapping him back from his perverted thought.

"Uh… oh, please call me Lance."

"Thank you, Lance." my girls said seductively.

Lasandra gave him a wink before the elevator doors closed. When the elevator doors opened to the King's suite, everybody froze. I wasn't expecting what I saw. It was like we stepped into an episode of the "Rich and Famous." Before we left, T-Money showed me a brochure of the suites they were staying in. I thought they were off the chain, but they didn't compare to the King's suite. At the elevator door, two beautiful Latino females met us wearing white thongs and bikini tops.

"Hello, and welcome to the King's suite."

They motioned for us to come in. My Queens walked into the suite as if they were in a trance.

"Oh, my God, this is crazy," Tonia gushed.

"Get the fuck outta here," Lasandra said with her mouth stuck open.

"Is this place real?" Akura asked, just as excited as the others.

The floor was done in green marble with pearl-white swirls. On both sides of the entrance were twenty-foot black onyx statues of naked female angels. Beyond the angels, the green marble floor led to a set of steps that descended. In the center of the spacious floor was a stage with a grand piano. Surrounding the stage were countless plush cream-colored sofas and love seats.

Practically enclosing the whole set up was a huge bar. Off to the side of the bar was a dance area, and then there were more sitting areas. The walls were painted with hundreds of life-size angels, flying upwards. Vaulting to the ceiling along with the angels were seven full-grown palm trees. Besides the three support beams that ran across the ceiling, the entire roof was made out of glass.

"This is your entertainment room," Tata said, coming up on the side of me.

"Yeah?" I asked.

"Yes, if you care to entertain any guest while you're here, we'd be happy to help you arrange everything. If you'd like, me and Tata will give you a tour."

"Yeah, show us what this place is working with," I replied. Bless and the girls were already exploring the suite on their own. I could hear their excitement echoing off the walls.

"This way please."

Tata's deep South American accent enhanced her Latin features. She wore her coal-black hair in a tight ponytail. Her natural coppertone skin looked like it would taste like the richest caramel. My guess, she was no older than 21.

As Tata led the way, I watched as her thong did the disappearing act beautifully between her voluptuous ass cheeks. Her walk was slow, sexy, and deadly. When Tata turned around to say something, my eyes would automatically zero in on her bikini top. The only thing that it covered were her nipples. It left everything else exposed.

"The King's suite is the only one of its kind in the world. It covers the entire top floor of the hotel." Tata explained.

Natala added, "There are five huge bedrooms with their own bathrooms and balconies."

Natala was just as beautiful as Tata. Her white thong also did the disappearing act, but she had a three-inch gap between her legs that I liked. Her curls were bouncy, like Tiff's, but hers were black.

"Plus, there's a 10-person sauna and 10 Jacuzzis throughout the suite. You also have your own basketball court, racquetball court, fitness room, swimming pool, theater and a track is located on the roof. Now, if you follow us, we'll show you your views from the main balconies."

Stepping out onto the balcony, I soaked in the warm weather, closed my eyes and took a deep breath.

"Beautiful isn't it?" Tata asked me.

"Yeah, this shit is tight. Y'all see this all the time, so you must be used to it by now."

"I could never get bored with this. I lose myself in the view every time I come out here." Tata said.

Natala tapped me on the shoulder.

"On this side, you can see downtown Miami, straight ahead, there is a canal that leads to Biscayne Bay. Beautiful, big yachts pass by every day."

"Speaking of yachts," Tata said, "your stay at the King's suite includes full access to the hotel's yacht."

"How big is it?"

"Three hundred feet, I think. It holds 50 passengers. Right now, it's docked at Mango Bay. Just let us know a day in advance if you wish to take it out."

"Damn, is there anything else?"

"No, I think that's about it. Natala and I are next door to the master bedroom. There are intercom systems set up all through the house, so you can call on us for anything, anytime." They turned and walked away.

"Anything, anytime?" I asked.

They turned back around and looked at me. "Yes, Mr. Pharaoh," they said in unison with a smile. "Anything, anytime."

Chapter 38

The next day, I decided to take the girls shopping for some new clothes. Tata recommended some stores in South Beach and downtown Miami. They dressed totally different from up north. They were on their Miami Vice shit hard down there. In Miami, you rock silk, and that was all I bought. We bought so much clothes, the limo had to make three trips back to the hotel.

On top of all the shopping, we also did some sightseeing. As we strolled down Ocean Drive, I could hear Joey's voice describing South Beach to me, all over again. I saw why he did it with so much passion. His words had painted a perfect picture in my head, and now it felt like I was walking through it. From the gentle breeze that rustled leaves on the palm trees to the half-naked shorties everywhere, it was paradise.

What I liked the most were the pastel buildings in the Art Deco district. I took it all in like a pull off a blunt of some real good weed.

We visited the hotel that was in "Scarface." You know, the one with the chainsaw scene in the bathroom. They changed it up a bit, but if you were a true fan of the movie, you would know it was the Flamingo. Further down the street, past Wet Willie's and the News Cafe, was the Versace mansion. I was told he was the one that really made South Beach what it was. It was fucked up the way he went out, but fuck it, that's life.

"Hey, Daddy, look over there," Bless said, pointing to a building across from Versace's place.

"What about it?"

"You said you was looking for a building for a cafe, right?"

"You right, shorty."

It was a pink, six-story, gutted building, next to Versace's crib. It was the only unoccupied building on the street.

"You sure you want to turn that into a cafe?" Tiff asked.

I looked at her. "Why you say that?"

"Because, to me, that building would make a nice beachfront private club. You know, Daddy, one of those exclusive clubs where all the rich people want to go."

"Besides, look at all the cafes on this street alone," Lasandra said. "The last thing this street needs is another one."

"You got a point." I admitted.

Out in the front of the building was a short, fat Cuban, smoking an even fatter cigar. He wore a tight, tan suit with woven sandals.

"What do you mean, you won't be able to make it!" the fat Cuban bellowed. "I've been fuckin' waiting for you for three fuckin' hours! What the hell you mean, the building costs too much! We had a fuckin' deal! What do you mean, the deal is off? Hello! You still there? Shit!!"

We made it to the front of the building just as the fat Cuban was hanging up.

"Hey, what's the asking price for this building?"

The fat Cuban turned around, looked me up and down and said, "You talking to me?"

"Yeah, I'm talking to you. You're trying to sell this building aren't you?" I asked him.

"Look, this ain't no crack house, so run along." he shooed me away like a fly.

"Who the fuck are you telling to run along, you fat piece of shit?" Bless said, getting in the guy's face.

"Chill, baby. I got this." I told her calmly. I turned back to him and said, "Listen, you trying to sell this building or what?"

The chubby Cuban took a puff from his cigar. I could tell he wasn't taking me seriously.

"Okay, you wanna waste my time, let's go."

He reluctantly took us inside the building. Even though most of it was gutted out, there were still a few walls standing. It was a lot bigger than I thought.

"The asking price is three million. It's located on one of the hottest streets in the world, and I don't have to tell you who the neighbor was, or do I? So like I said before, run along," fat boy explained.

"I'll give you $2.5 million for it," I offered.

The fat Cuban broke into a loud, stupid laugh. When he saw I wasn't laughing, he stopped.

"You're serious?"

I nodded. His whole demeanor changed.

"Forgive me. My name is Alejandro Cortez," he said holding his hand out.

I just looked at it.

"Pharaoh." I said.

"So, you want to own a piece of the beach, huh?"

"2.3 million. My next offer will be two million, you dig?"

"Hey, hey, slow down, guy. You got yourself a deal."

"Good." Tiffany was standing right next to me, I looked at her and said, "Tiffany, get his information."

After dealing with Alejandro, we went to a restaurant that offered a view of the setting sun. Man, the shit was off the chain, yo. The weather was beautiful.

Everything was perfect. The sky looked like an ever-changing masterpiece. The way the yellow faded to pink, then orange, then red, then blood red, was amazing. I'd never seen anything like it. Yo, you haven't been anywhere if you haven't been to South Beach. Trust me.

Chapter 39

For the first couple of days, me and my Queens lounged around the suite. I was proud of them bitches, for real. Because of them, the Gorillas became the biggest heroin and coke distributors in Massachusetts. It sounds like I should've been happy with that, right? Well, your average drug dealer would've been, but like I told you, I wasn't your average drug dealer. I had a vision and controlling the West Mass. drug trade was only part of it. My vision cost money, and the drugs were our cash cow. My next move was to acquire power.

Sitting in the Jacuzzi on one of the balconies, I was going over my master plan in my head. Once I had it all worked out, I sent for T-Money.

"Yo, what's up, King Pharaoh?"

"Pull up a chair and smoke this blunt with me."

"A'ight." T-Money took a seat next to the Jacuzzi. "Damn, Pharaoh, I love it down here. This shit is crazy, yo. We need to cop a crib. This would be our getaway spot, you know."

"Yeah, I'm diggin' that, but first we got some more business to deal with."

"What's up?"

"Remember how I wanted you to build a database on all the cops and hustlers?" I asked.

"Yeah, that shit is done." T-Money bragged.

"Good, because I want to take it a step further."

"What do you mean, a step further?"

"I want to include judges, prosecutors, bankers, prominent business owners, congressmen, and senators. I want information on anybody that holds some kind of power."

T-Money sat back and puffed the blunt. "A step further, huh?"

"Yeah, what do you think?"

"I think you're crazy, kid."

"Think about it, T-Money. If we had information that a judge has a thing for kids or that a prosecutor has a slut on the side, or shit, if we found out that the prosecutor had a gay lover on the side, do you know what that would be worth to them to keep it quiet?"

"As always, you're a genius, but the shit you're talking about is going to cost some serous dough son." T-Money confessed.

"How much?"

"Right off the gate, we're gonna need another server. Before, when you gave me that list of names, for each person on that list, we had to do a full profile on them. We got their job history, voices, ex-partners, hobbies, sexual preferences, vacation spots, and their friends and family. Then we did a profile for each of their friends and family. Now on top of all that, you want to take it a step further?"

"What will it take to make it happen?" I asked.

"Well, I know money is not the issue now. I guess it will be how we get that sensitive information. Check it, if we get their credit card information that alone will tell us damn near everything we need to know, like where they shop, what their bills are, and anything else they do on that card. Then if we could go through their trash, it could tell us even more and then even hacking into their computers. We do that, it's a wrap!" T-Money promised.

"How do we go about getting that info on them?" I asked, as I hit the blunt and flicked it over the balcony.

"The bulk of the money should be used to place Gorillas in key positions throughout the city. Females are best. Make it the same way you had your Queens infiltrate drug dealers, just make this more legit. They'll get jobs as filing clerks at the courthouse and City Hall. We can plant them as secretaries in key businesses to seduce the suits and gather information."

"Soon as we get back, make it happen."

Later that night, I had Tata and Natala prepare us a huge Caribbean meal with all sorts of exotic shit from the islands. It was then I told my Queens about their new mission for the family.

"Ladies, ladies, ladies, let me have your attention."

"Damn, who's that man in that fine-ass cream-colored suit?' Lasandra said. "He looks good as fuck!"

"Mmm, Mm, Mm, Daddy, you do look good. You should wear suits more often. They look nice on you."

"Thank you Akura."

I waited for the whistles, claps and howls to subside before I continued. Not to toot my own horn, but the kid was fresh to death. On my feet were Lobb crocodile shoes worth $18,000 a pair. I was wrapped in a slightly baggy, tropical wool blend pinstriped suit by Cesare Attolini. Bless bought me a $300,000 Jaeger Le Coultre watch. To complete the outfit, I had Artey's platinum chain hanging from my neck. With a Partaga cigar full of weed in one hand and a glass of 1865 Lafite in the other, you best believe the kid was fresh.

"Okay, calm down," I began. "Listen, from this day on, your days of setting up drug dealers are over. We are stepping the game up. Besides, there aren't any drug dealers worth robbin' left. But, before I continue, I want you to give yourselves a round of applause because without y'all, none of this would be possible."

Again, I waited for the claps and whistles to subside.

"Instead of money, I want power. Somebody tell me the difference between the two."

Akura said. "Money is power."

"No, Akura it isn't. Money comes second to power. Now, answer me this, what if a person isn't affected by money?" I rose from my seat. "Let's say a Gorilla is arrested for murder, and we want to get him or her off."

"We buy the judge." Bless said.

"But what if the judge isn't fazed by any amount of money we can throw at him?"

"Then we kill him!" Lasandra suggested.

"No, Lasandra, they'll just get another judge, and killing the judge will only make matters worse. The only thing that will affect that judge is a power greater than his."

"Black mail?" Tonia said with uncertainty.

"Bingo. Blackmail is our ticket to power. Bill

Gates can influence people with money, but he has no real power. The Kennedys have real power because they have their hands in politics."

"You want to be a politician now, Daddy?" Tiffany asked.

"No, Tiff, I want the power of one. That's where you girls come in. Everybody has secrets, and politicians are no different. They may have more secrets than the average person. Since they are in the public eye, their secrets can be more damaging to them if they were to get out."

"What if they don't have any secrets?" Lasandra asked.

"Then we give them a dark secret. So when we return things are going to be different. I don't want any of you around the drug side of the family. All them hood bitches you chill with, you better cut them off. I want all of you to infiltrate new circles of friends. The people I want you around now are strictly kids from rich and powerful families. From there, work your way to their parents. I want dirt on the chief of police, the district attorney, judges, the mayor and last but not least, our beloved Senator Holten. Do all of you understand what I want from you?"

"Yes, Daddy," they all replied.

"A'ight then, enough said. Eat up, and go get dressed. Its time to see what's up with this Miami nightlife I heard so much about."

Chapter 40

It was around three in the morning when we got back to the suite. Miami's nightlife was outrageous. Yo, Miamians really know how to get their party on. We had V.I.P passes to all the hottest clubs. We were at this club called B.E.D. and that was exactly what was in it-beds. By the time we got there, I was so high off X, weed and liquor, I didn't give a fuck. I had Tonia and Acura bent over the table with their asses exposed. I took two Moet bottles and shook them up. Soon as the cork popped, I stuffed the neck of the bottle in their assholes and emptied the Moet inside them. Then me and the rest of the girls drank the Moet out of their asses. Yeah, it was one of those nights.

Soon as we walked into the suite, my Queens fell out. Not me, I went and took a shower, and that only woke me up. After I got dressed, I noticed a trail of rose petals leading out to the hallway. The trail brought me to a part of the suite I had yet to see, the roof. When the trail of red, pink, and white rose petals ended, I was standing at the foot of a round bed, surrounded by glowing candles. Tata and Natala waited for me, naked, on top of bamboo green colored sheets.

"In our country, women are drawn to men like you." Tata said.

"And what type of man is that?"

"A man of power." Natala replied.

"The closer I get to you, the more intoxicated I feel." Tata said in a dreamy voice.

"Don't think everybody that stays here gets the treatment that we want to give you. Yes, there have been some rich and powerful men that have stayed here, but they never had that look in their eyes." Natala informed me.

"What look is that?"

"The look that says they are destined for great things. We can see that look in your eyes." Natala said, climbing off the bed.

"There is something about you. Maybe it is the way you talk, the way you're so confident, or maybe it's the way your Queens speak about you. Whatever it is, it makes us want you more." Tata said, rising gracefully out of the bed.

"Make us one of your girls, and let us prove to you that we are worthy of being your Queens." Tata promised.

"We know what you expect of us. Bless told us already, and we promise you, we will not disappoint you, King Pharaoh." Natala added.

Their soft, Latin accents penetrated every nerve in my body. Standing on each side of me, I felt the stiffness of Tata's nipples brush against my arm. On the other side, Natala's hand was caressing my chest. Then Tata's fingers slowly worked their way down over my chest, stopping at my waistline.

"May I?"

"By all means."

Sliding her hands down into my silk pajamas, Tata moaned as if I was inside of her already. She squeezed it a couple of the times before saying, "Mmmmmm, just how I imagined it. Long, thick and black. Mmmmmmm, can I kiss it?"

"Absolutely."

Tata went down on her knees, looking me in the eyes. She pulled the elastic to my pajamas and the boxers down at the same time. Taking me into her mouth she let out a gratified moan. Tata's mouth worked my snake in and out with slow, deep strokes. It was as though her lips made love to my dick.

Natala kneeled next to Tata and tried to lick my balls. "Let me have some too, Tata. Come on, let me taste it."

Tata ignored her like a spoiled brat. Natala got frustrated and snatched my dick out of Tata's mouth. She swallowed as much as she could without gagging.

As they fought over who was going to make me cum, I sipped champagne. The outside world seemed to slip away, bit by bit. Losing myself in the moment, I felt like I was looking at the world through my rearview. They call it astroplaning, or an out-of-body experience. Whatever you call it, I felt it.

The Miami weather was amazing. Here it was, three in the morning on top of a grand hotel, with the ocean on my right, downtown Miami on my left, and the stars as my ceiling, I thought to myself, is this what life was all about? Was it all about the fly women, expensive cars, 25 grand a night hotel suites, and priceless jewelry? Was that it?"

Standing there reminded me of a scene in "Scarface." Remember the part when he had just killed Frank and the detective? Then he went to Frank's house and told Frank's bitch to pack her shit. Well at the end of that scene, Scarface walked out on the balcony. He looked up and saw the Goodyear blimp, and in digital letters, it read,

THE WORLD IS YOURS

That was exactly how I felt at that moment. Just as Tata and Natala were jerking my nut all over their faces, I opened my arms like Jesus on the cross and shouted into the night sky,

"THE WORLD IS MINE!"

Chapter 41

Vashon and Vicious arrived the next afternoon. I sat in the Jacuzzi gazebo on top of the roof, relaxing after last night's fuckfest.

"What up, King Pharaoh?" Vashon said, as he stepped into the gazebo. He took a seat on the sofa across from me.

"What's up, yo, what's the word back home?"

"The police are still buggin' behind what Daryl did. They have been fuckin' with everybody. They aren't letting anybody make any money."

I said, "Yeah, I kind of figured that."

"Senator Holten is holding a press conference to kick off his 'Take Back the Streets' campaign."

"So what's up with the streets?"

"Sean owed the Kenji Dragons a few million, on top of what we took. Ming sent a message. He said since we killed Sean, we took on his debt, and they want to set up a meeting."

"Well, that's a start, I guess."

"I took care of the last of Tito's boys a few days ago. But, I got a call when we landed that the Colombians were in town." Vashon told me.

"Do you think they're gonna be a problem?"

"Not at all. I'll deal with them as soon as I get back."

"What about Javier?" I asked as I took a sip of wine.

"He's in San Juan, like Tiff said he'd be. What do you want me to do about him?"

"Kill him. I don't want any lose ends."

"A'ight then, besides all that, the streets are waiting for the return of their new king."

"That's what's up."

"Ayo, I have a gift for you." Vashon said.

"For me?"

"It's just a little something to show my appreciation for bringing me into the family."

"What is it?"

"It's not a what but a who. It's my girl, Vicious. She's a little wild, but she is loyal as shit. We met at the nuthouse, during one of my visits as a kid. I can tell she likes being around you and your Queens, and I know she would make a perfect Queen for you."

"If she so thorough, why are you giving her to me?"

"I can't give her what she wants. I don't do the love thing, feel me?"

"A'ight, then, where is she at?"

"Vicious!" Vashon shouted.

From downstairs came the beautiful Cape Verden with her brown sugar complexion. Her hazel eyes gave her a mysterious look that I liked.

"You belong to King Pharaoh now."

Her eyes widened with excitement as she cracked a smile. She looked at me, than back at Vashon. She gave him a kiss on the cheek, then turned to face me.

"I'm a Queen?" Vicious she asked me.

"Nah, that shit don't come that easy, shorty. You have to really put in some serious work to get that title. You willing to put in work for me?"

"I'll do whatever you want me to."

"You don't have a problem with Vashon giving you to me?"

"If he said I'm yours, then I'm yours, until you say otherwise."

"If you're with me, it's for life." I emphasized.

"Then that takes care of that. I'm yours."

Vashon was right. Vicious would end up becoming the perfect fit for my harem. Not to mention, Vicious would become one of my deadliest Queens. Fuck what you heard, you know you're doing it big when you're getting girls for presents.

Chapter 42

For the rest of our stay in Miami, we did it big. We took the hotel yacht out for three days, island-hopping through the Caribbean. On other days, we took flights in the helicopter, catching a birds eye view of Miami. Then, at night, we hit all the fliest clubs and ended up sleeping on the beach, so we could watch the sun rise in the morning.

It was totally different from my life in Holyoke. A far cry from the death, drugs, and ghettos of West Mass. Now, don't get me wrong, I know Miami has it's share of death, drugs, and ghettos. But I hadn't seen any. To me, they didn't exist.

As our vacation was coming to an end, Bless wanted to throw a party. And just like everything else she did, Bless went all in. She came up with an Egyptian theme and had everybody dress accordingly. I was Thutmose III, also known as the Warrior Pharaoh. Bless was Cleopatra, and my other Queens were dressed as other well-known Queens of that era.

The King's suite was big enough to put a small pyramid in it, with plenty of room from the two hundred-plus guests. Instead of the normal lights, Bless lit torches attached to the columns. The walls were covered with gigantic murals of the desert. In front of the pyramid, Bless had two thrones seated, side by side. One for me and one for her.

Tata and Natala worked their magic and was able to get a who's who of Miami to attend our party. Tata convinced them that I was a person they needed to meet. That was all she needed to say. Throughout the night, I shook hands with real estate tycoons, bankers, Cuban mobsters, politicians, Arabs, models, stars, and whoever else you could think of.

After mingling for a bit, I took a seat on the throne. T-Money and Jessito stood at my side. Country and his girl decided to stay on the Yacht for the night. Out of the corner of my eye, I saw Daryl and his girl sneeking onto the balcony. There was something familiar about Daryl's girl. I don't know where, but I knew I had seen her somewhere before. The way she had been staring at me the whole trip, you'd think she knew me.

As time passed, I saw the effects of the wine on the guests. The women got looser and the men more aggressive. The naked servants Bless had walking around amped up the mood. Seeing that, I raised my glass, signaling to Natala to start the show. The male servant cleared the dance floor. From the back of the pyramid came 10 naked females, their bodies painted in gold. They took the dance floor and positioned themselves in rows of three, with the leader facing me.

When Sade's "No Ordinary Love" came on, they started seducing the guests with hypnotic movements. They upped the lust factor in the King's suite to the boiling point.

When the dancers were done, the male servants littered the dance floor with huge feather mattresses. They were preparing for the final phase of the party, the royal orgy. Each guy pulled a naked female onto a mattress with him.

Some of the guests left. Some of them chose to stay and watch. I caught a few retreating to different parts of the suite to pursue their carnal delights in private. And some joined the orgy taking place on the mattresses.

African drums thumped in the background, providing the pulse. The faster the beat, the more intense the passion. Flesh of all colors melted together, nobody was left out. Howls of pleasure and grunts of excitement filled the room. The shit was even getting too much for me, so I went looking for my Queens.

Before I made it up stairs, my stomach started bubbling. I made a detour to the bathroom on the first floor. As I was about to go in, I saw Daryl's girl coming up the hall. She had nothing on but an oversized t-shirt.

"Hey, Pharaoh."

"What's up with you?" I asked her.

"Nothing. You really know how to throw a party."

"Yeah, thanks."

She walked up to me and rubbed my chest. "You don't remember me, do you?"

"Nah, am I supposed to?"

"My name is Kiss."

"And?"

"And I been trying to get at you this whole vacation, but your girls are over-protective of their Daddy."

"Why are you trying to get at me?"

"I want to know why these girls are willing to kill for you. Is it that dick?" she asked.

"That's what thorough bitches do for their man. I replied.

"Hmmmmmm, is that right?"

"Yeah, that's right. By the way, where's Daryl?"

"I don't know, and I don't care. I'm where I want to be right now."

"It's like that, shorty?"

"Hmmmmm, you know it is, so stop fakin'. What do you want me to do, beg for your dick?"

"Nah, you don't have to do all that. Just get on your knees and open your mouth. But hurry up because I gotta piss."

Kiss fell to her knees and passed me the wine bottle she was holding. She swallowed what she could of my semi-erection. Then she pulled it out and said, "I'll make you a bet. If you finish the bottle off before I make you cum, you can piss in my mouth."

"I like that, but what if I lose?"

"You fuck me."

"Bet."

I began guzzling the wine. It was half full, so I knocked it out in no time. Kiss was hard at work, sucking, tugging, and squeezing my dick. She was doing her thang, but I had already finished the bottle.

"I guess you won, huh?" Kiss questioned.

"Don't give up just yet. There might be a second-place prize."

Kiss cracked a smile and went back to work. Whatever she was doing was working. I felt my knees getting weak, and my heart started to race. Sweat poured down my face. I was too weak to hold the bottle. My head pounded like a bass drum.

"What the fuck!" I shouted as I slumped to the floor.

"Never thought you'd die like this, did you, King Pharaoh?"

Those was the last words I heard before… I died.

Chapter 43

Poison!

That muthafuckin' bitch poisoned me. Ain't that some shit. She was right, I never thought I'd go out like that. I got up and saw my body sprawled out in the hallway. Kiss continued to suck the shit out of my dick. I tried to kick her, but my foot went right through her.

I don't know how, but I came in her mouth. The bitch spat it back at me. Then she stood up and pissed in my face. Can you believe that shit? First, the bitch poisoned me, spit cum in my face, and then pissed on me. After that, she took a picture of me.

All of a sudden, a bright light appeared at the end of the hallway. Something inside me was drawn to it, so I began walking to it. At the end of what appeared to be an endless tunnel were three figures in white, glowing robes.

"Ma?" I asked.

Two of the figures faded away and only one remained. It was my mother, and she looked more beautiful than ever. My eyes filled with tears, then a strange peace came over me.

"Baby what are you doing here?"

"I… I… got caught slippin.'"

"You're not supposed to be here. It's not your time baby."

"Well, somebody thinks so."

"You still have some good to do."

"Ma, there ain't nothing good about my life. I'm sure you know that."

"Believe it or not, there's good in everybody."

"If there's any good in me, it's doing a really good job of hiding."

"There's still time for change, baby." she said softly.

"Ma, the only thing changing in my life is the seasons."

"Boy, stop being hard-headed, and go on back!" she commanded.

I turned to leave, but then stopped and turned around and said, "What if I want to stay here with you?"

"We'll be together soon enough, but not now. Now, give me some suga, and go on.

"Okay, Ma, I love you."

"I love you too, baby."

"Hey, Ma, is Jesus black?"

"Jesus is all things, my son."

"He wasn't a track star, 'cause if he was, they wouldn't have nailed his ass to the cross."

"Boy, if you don't get out of here."

"Okay Ma I'm gone; I'm gone." I said.

I headed back the same way I came and found myself falling lightly through the clouds. I landed back in my body and woke up.

Chapter 44

The room was dimly lit by a nightlight over my bed. My eyes struggled to focus. Where was I? My throat was dry and sore. Then the smell I hated the most invaded my nostrils. I was in a hospital. Slowly, my hearing cleared up. It felt like I had tubes stuck in every hole in my body.

Looking from side to side, I saw my girls sleeping on chairs, sofas and even on the floor. I heard T-Money, Jessito, and Vashon talking out in the hallway. Bless was lying in the bed with me with her head on my chest, sound asleep. I moved a couple strands of her hair from her face.

She woke instantly. "Daddy? Oh, my God, he's awake!"

Bless smothered me with kisses.

"Water, I need something to drink." I gasped.

Bless rushed into the bathroom, knocking things over trying to get me a cup of water. That brought everybody out of their slumber. They surrounded the bed.

After taking a sip of water, I said, "Get me the fuck out of here!"

They did as I asked.

Back at the King's suite, I lay in the bed, popping pills.

"What the fuck happened to me?"

"That bitch Kiss, poisoned you. She fucked up and didn't put enough poison in the bottle to kill you. The doctor said you're lucky to be alive. She said the amount of poison in your system should've left you brain dead, at least." Bless said, passing me a cup of water.

"How long was I out?"

"Three days." Tonia said.

"Where's that bitch now?" I demanded.

"She disappeared that morning. I sent the girls to the bus stations, airports and the docks, looking for her, but she was long gone by then."

"Tell Daryl to get his bitch ass in here!"

"I already questioned him, Daddy. He said he didn't know that much about her." Tonia replied.

"I don't give a fuck! Get Daryl in here, now! And everybody get the fuck out!"

Shit was getting out of hand. That was the second attempt on my life. How the fuck could Daryl get caught slippin' like that? I knew he was a sucker for a big butt and a smile, but it almost cost me my life.

Then I started thinking, maybe he didn't slip, maybe he was on point and was trying to get me killed. Nah, I dismissed the idea because Daryl was my dude. Even though we weren't seeing eye to eye, I didn't think he would try to kill me.

"What up, son? I see you're alive and well."

Daryl sounded like he couldn't care less that I almost died.

"What other way is there to see me?" I fired back.

"I don't know."

"So you don't know anything about that bitch Kiss?"

"Not really. I met her in the mall with Country. We started kickin' it from there."

"How long have you known her?"

"About a month or so." Daryl admitted.

"Where's she from?" I asked.

"Don't know."

"How old is she?"

"Don't know, didn't care."

"Where does she live?"

"Tell you the truth, I never been to her crib. I always brought her back to my spot."

"You mean you brought a girl on vacation with us that you don't even know? What if she was a cop!?"

Daryl shrugged his shoulders as if to brush it off. "I don't question every bitch I fuck. I just wanted to fuck, for real. It just turned into something else. Why you trippin'? Everybody else brought a bitch!"

"Everybody else's chick didn't try to kill me!"

"Yo, you're alive, though. What are you still complaining about?"

"You know what, yo? Get the fuck out of my face."

"Oh, so you're dismissing me now?" Daryl frowned as he got up and headed for the door.

Just as he was about to exit, he turned around and said, "Ayo, I read somewhere that he who has a thousand friends has not one friend to spare, but he who has one enemy will meet him everywhere. That shit fits you perfect son."

Then he left.

The next time I woke up, it was around 1:30 in the morning. The medication I was on knocked me out. My body felt better, and the headache I had was gone. Tonia and Vicious were at the table, playing cards. When I went to take a sip of water.

"Hold up!" Tonia shouted.

"What?" I asked.

Tonia came over and took a sip first, then handed me a cup.

"Bless said we have to taste everything before you do."

Vicious said, "You can never be too sure."

My cell rang.

"Speak. What! Stop playin'… when?… I'm on my way home now!"

"Daddy, what is it?" Tonia asked.

"Tell everybody to pack up. We're leaving in an hour."

Chapter 45

Fifty minutes later, we were aboard the G-5, climbing into the sky. Once the plane leveled off, I held a series of meetings, starting with my Queens.

"Lasandra, find out where Cool C's keeping those plates. Soon as you know, I'm sending the Gorillas to get them,"

"Okay, Daddy."

"Tonia, I got something special for you."

Tonia smiled as she sat up in the chair.

"What is it ,Daddy?"

"I want you to get close to Senator Holten's stepdaughter, Bethany. I want you to become her new best friend. Same with you Tiff, but I want you to get close to Mayor Santiago's daughter, Selena. They both attend the same high-class private school. That's the school you two are gonna enroll in."

"That should be fun." Tiffany said.

"Bless, I'm gonna leave it up to you to get something on Diane Fletcher. She can be very useful to the family."

"Why you say that?" Bless wondered.

"She's the voice of West Mass. right? Well, what if she would become our voice? We'd be able to influence the masses, and that could lead to something big for the Gorillas."

"Is there anything you want us to do, Daddy?" Tata asked.

"That building I bought I want to turn it into a high-class, members-only club for Miami's super rich. This way, we can lure targets into one spot. Tiff will get with you and set up some accounts. Start spreading the word that it'll be opening soon.

"When we land, Akura, Tiff, Lasandra, and Vicious are getting off," I continued. "The rest of you stay on. Tonia, go wait for me in the bedroom. I got something I want to talk to you about. A'ight, that's all. Bless, send Jessito in."

Moments later, Jessito entered the G-5's conference room.

"What up, King Pharaoh?"

"Have a seat. I think it's time for you to put in some work."

"You know I'm down for whatever, yo!" he insisted.

"Yeah, I know. You know shit is about to change when we get back to the streets. We are the big dogs now."

"Word, that's what's up."

"The thing is, the drug business is only a small part of what the Gorillas are gonna be into. We only fuck with the drugs because it's our cash cow. The other shit the Gorillas will get into will require my full attention. So, basically, after I set everything up, I'm handing over the streets to you. Do you think you can handle it?"

"Without question, I can handle it, but what about Country? You know he's gonna feel fucked up about that." Jessito mentioned.

"Don't worry about Country. I'll deal with him. Besides, I got other shit planned for him."

"Then in that case, don't trip. I got it. I was waiting for this moment for the longest, yo. I already got shit mapped out in my head how I want to do it. Yo, can I pick my own crew?"

"You're a boss now, kid. Besides running the important shit by me, do you."

"A'ight yo." Jessito got up to leave, and as he walked out, Country walked in.

"You alright?"

"Yeah, I'm good. These pills got me feeling nice. What's up with you?" I replied.

"I can't believe Daryl's girl tried to murk you. For real, I'm not trying to drop a bad bone, but Daryl has been acting crazy lately."

"You don't think I noticed that already?"

"I'm saying, how long you gonna let him get away with shit?"

"I'll deal with Daryl when the time comes." I promised.

"Yo, you're the King. What you say goes, but that time will come sooner than you think. I be with Daryl on the reg. I see what type of time he be on."

"Like I said, I'll deal with him when the time comes. He's still my man. He's just going through some shit right now."

"It's whatever with me."

Me and Country chopped it up for a while longer before I joined Tonia in the bedroom. When I walked in, Tonia was ass-naked on the bed in a doggystyle position.

"Is this what you wanted, Daddy?" she purred.

"You know what Daddy wants." I said.

"You want me to tell you a story about my father fuckin' me?"

"Yeah , you know exactly what Daddy wants."

"God, you're so twisted, Daddy. Can I tell you something first?"

"What?"

"I want to be your number one bitch. I know Bless is your number one, but Daddy, she could never love you as much as I love you."

"Why you say that?"

"Do you think she'll kill herself for you?" Tonia questioned.

"You're saying that you'd kill yourself for me?"

"I'll do whatever you ask me to."

I looked at Tonia for a second, then I went into my bag and pulled out Bless's three-eighty. I passed it to Tonia. She took it without hesitation and put it to the side of her head. Her breathing became heavy, her eyes glossed over and sweat poured down her face. I could see the fear in her eyes. She looked like she wanted me to stop her.

When she saw that I wasn't, she screamed, "I LOVE YOU DADDY!"

Click!

Nothing.

Of course, the gun wasn't loaded. What do you think, I was stupid? Tonia had this derange look in her eyes as sweat poured down her face. It made my dick hard as shit. One thing for sure, Tonia's love for me reached new heights that day, so high, in fact, it scared me.

"If I die, Daddy, I'll love you from the grave."

"You better."

"Until then, I'll play my position and do as I'm told. But if Bless fucks up, and you give me the word, I'll kill her and won't think twice about it." Tonia promised.

"I'll keep that in mind, but right now I need some of that sick twisted shit in my life."

Tonia whispered, "You want me to tell you about the time my father fucked me on my birthday?"

"Yeah, tell me about that and don't leave nothing out." I said, as I pulled my dick out and started jerking it.

Chapter 46

When the plane landed, it headed straight for the private hangar on the far side of the runway. A shuttle bus was waiting just outside the hangar, while inside, towards the back, sat a limo, idling. The Massachusetts air was uninvitingly cold. In less than three hours, we went from the heat of the Miami sun to the frost of the New England winter.

Everybody grabbed their luggage and piled onto the shuttle bus. Bless, Tonia, Tata, and Natala were the only ones left on the plane. After the shuttle bus left, the midnight black limo pulled up alongside the jet. A short, fat chauffeur got out and waddled to the back door. And, as if it were a dream, out stepped my man.

"Joey!" I shouted.

"Pharaoh, what's up?" he replied.

Although I was still a little sore, I managed to make it down the steps on my own.

"Damn, it's good to see you, yo," I told him. "Man, shit has been crazy without you around. How you feeling?"

"I'm good, a little weak, but good. So what's with

you? One minute we were pushing twenties out of Chestnut Park, the next minute, you're stepping out of a multi-million dollar G-5 jet. What's really good?"

"Yeah, things have changed, son. We're doing big things now."

"I heard. Your name is ringing bells in the streets like crazy."

"Nah, I can't take all the credit for that. The Gorillas as a whole are ringin' them bells." I said.

"So what's up? Are we going somewhere?" Joey asked.

"Without a doubt."

Just then, Bless stuck her head out the door. "Daddy, the captain needs to know where we're headed, so he can make out a flight plan."

"Tell him we're going to Aruba." I answered.

Before you knew it, the plane was taxied onto the runway. The engines powered up for another take-off. I figured me and Joey had to do some catching up, so why not in Aruba? The girls fell asleep as soon as we were airborne. Me and Joey chilled out and watched "Scarface" while smoking a Garcia of some sick-ass weed from Miami.

An hour into the flight, Joey finally broke his silence. "Yo, I owe you my life, son."

"You don't owe me shit. You my muthafuckin' man. I know without a doubt that you would've done the same for me." I told him.

"I'm just saying thanks, that's all." Joey said.

"You're welcome. Now drop it."

"Yo, remember that cafe idea I had?"

"Oh, shit, I forgot to tell you. We got a building

right on South Beach. The shit is right on Ocean Drive, right next to the Versace mansion."

"Word!"

"Yeah, yo, but there's one thing about that."

"What's that?" he asked.

"There's like a hundred cafes on that street already. My Queens came up with the idea to turn it into a private club." I suggested.

"That shit must've cost some serious dough."

"2.1 million, and that was at a crazy discount."

"2.1 what?!"

When he said that, I knew I would have to start from the beginning. First, I told him about Crazy Eddie and Dante. After that, I told him about my Queens and their targets: Sean, Javier, Cool C, and Tito. He didn't have to say it, but I knew he didn't like the way things went down with Tito and his daughter. Next, I told him about the attempts on my life and how funny Daryl had been acting. I was about to tell him about the database I had T-Money building, but decided against it. Like I told T-Money, not everything is for everybody.

"So what do you think?" I asked.

"Man, when it's all said and done, you need to write a book."

"That's crazy, because I thought about that. I was going to name it KING PHARAOH."

"That shit sounds gangsta."

"That's because my life is gangsta, son."

Joey sat back and let everything I told him soak in. Then he asked, "Where do I fit in, in all of this?"

"You're my right-hand man. You always were, and you always will be. What I got planned for you is something big. I really don't want to tell you, now, because it might fuck up the flow. For now, though, I want you to fall back," I instructed him.

"That's what's up."

A few hours later, the G-5 broke through the clouds and the beautiful Caribbean Sea came into view. Huge cruise ships looked like tiny paddleboats from so far up. Everybody was awake and excited. The captain's deep voice came over the speaker.

"Good morning, ladies and gentlemen. This is your captain speaking. We will be landing shortly in Oranjestad, which is the capital of Aruba and also its largest city. The population is roughly 115,000, and is known as the Las Vegas of the Caribbean. Tourism is the number one source of income. I advise that you stick to the tourist sections of the island. Arubians are known to kidnap Americans and hold them for ransom. Besides that, I hope you enjoy your vacation."

Aruba was even more tropical then South Beach. It had a sexy, Third World appeal to it. It was a mixture of the jungle and paradise. I could only pick out two classes of people, rich and poor. The hotel we stayed in was nice, but it wasn't the King's suite.

For the next week, we explored Aruba. We took pictures of divi divi trees that looked like giant bonsai trees. In Boca Prinsa, we went dune sliding with the locals and hung out with some weed growers. We had lunch at Charley's bar every day we were there. It had third-generation owners. They had this homemade sauce named "Honeymoon" that was straight fire. It left my mouth burning for days. Bless put it on everything like it was nothing.

Our last night in Aruba we spent gambling at the

Casinos. I went through $15,000 in two hours. Bless, on the other hand, won $66,000 in a half-hour. We ate at the finest restaurant in Aruba and drank the finest wine available. What can I say? We lived it up.

"Daddy, let's take a walk on the beach." Bless whispered in my ear. "Just you and me."

"Ayo, Joey, I'll meet y'all back at the hotel. Come on, shorty."

I grabbed Bless's hand. We walked out into the night sky. The weather was perfect. The beach was right across the street and the sound of the ocean made for perfect background music.

"Daddy, you're amazing."

"Yeah, whatever, Bless."

"I'm serious. There's something about you."

"What is it about me?"

"Greatness!"

"You think there is such a thing as a great drug dealer?"

"I don't know, but there is such a thing as a great man."

"So you think that I'm a great man?"

"Yes."

"Why?"

"Because you are ambitious, heartless and full of passion when it comes to money." she explained. "I like the fact that you take what you want, when you want it. You have the power to influence those around you. And another thing, the world through your eyes is much better than it is through ours. We all know that, and we know that through your dreams, we'll reach ours."

"And what are your dreams?"

"I'm livin' it now." Bless confessed.

"Oh, really?"

"Yep," she said with a smile.

"You, know, they say behind every great man is a great woman."

"Yeah, I know." Bless tugged on my arm, and kissed my neck.

The night was beautiful. Stars twinkled, the moon lit up the night sky, and the warm tropical breeze wafted through our paradise. We walked in silence for a while, listening to the ocean wave's crash against the rocks.

Bless looked like she belonged there. Her pearl white silk dress glowed as if she was an angel. She carried her heels in one hand and held my hand with the other. We spent the night on the beach. We didn't fuck. I didn't get my dick sucked. Nothing. We just laid there until we fell asleep.

Finally it was time to leave and everybody had this depressed look on their faces. As much as I wanted to stay, I had to get back to Holyoke. There was a lot of unfinished business to deal with.

We dropped Tata and Natala off in Miami and headed north. It was a quiet flight. I thought about what Bless said about greatness, and for real, I couldn't see myself like that. Someone else had to be the judge of that.

DET. VALENTINE

While I was thousands of feet in the sky, several people were plotting my demise on the ground.

On the other side of town, in the crime-free section of Holyoke, another part of my story starts. Located on the north side of Northampton street in an upper class neighborhood was a two-story Victorian house with a white picket fence.

It stood out from all the other houses on that street. Not because it was bigger and had a new paint job. Not because the lawn was perfectly manicured. Just the opposite, the grass looked as if it hadn't been cut in years. The shrubs had grown so wild they blocked the view of the living room bay window. Fallen leaves clogged the gutter. The neighborhood kids stole pieces of the fence to make ramps, swords and forts. There were patches of rotted wood all over the house from termites.

It wasn't always like this. At one time, this house was the envy of others. The lush, green yard had a beautiful rose garden in the front and a bountiful vegetable garden in the back. In the work shed was an arsenal of tools. Every two years the house was painted a different color. Now, two years later, the house was a reflection of its owner, Detective Valentine.

The alarm clock rang, but it didn't matter, he was already up. He hadn't had a decent night of sleep in two years. Maybe a couple of hours here and there, but never a full night. On the bedside table were sleeping pills that didn't work, packs of Marlboros and a 380. His eyes were bloodshot from lack of sleep. Looking around the room, he sighed.

It was in that bedroom he remembered being the happiest in his life. His daughter Bethany was conceived there. In that same bed, he sought the comfort of his wife after a long night in the streets, fighting crime. Now the Queen-size bed seemed way too big for him. Valentine looked over at her side of the bed. He rubbed her pillow. He imagined the sweet smell that use to linger on that pillow.

Over on the bedside table, his eyes passed over his cowboy killers and paused at his best friend, Wild Irish Rose. Valentine smiled, but then his eyes continued to wander until he saw his service revolver. His smile faded. He reached for it, took it in his hand and looked at it. He opened the cylinder and pulled out the only bullet in the six chambers. He looked at it, kissed it and replaced it. He spun the cylinder twice, then put the gun to his head. What was there to live for? He'd asked himself over and over. It all started with a kid named Angel. He knew he should've handled the situation before it got out of hand. But before he could, his partner took matters into his own hands. Next thing he knew his entire life spiraled downward.

His partner fucked up, and that fucked everything up for Valentine. His wife left him because of the embarrassment and took their daughter with her. His career was put on hold, and he damn near lost his sanity. Middle age was supposed to be better than this, he thought.

He pulled the trigger.

Click.

"Shit!"

Another day of misery.

He tossed the gun back on the bedside table. He grabbed the bottle of Wild Irish Rose and guzzled it. After a few more minutes of sitting there, he finally dragged himself from the bed. He stood in the bathroom mirror. His hair looked grayer and his face looked more wrinkled than normal. His pot belly was bigger than he thought it was.

"No wonder you left me. If I can't stand looking at myself, why would you?"

The sound of his cellphone took him away from thoughts of his miserable life and his ex-wife.

"What!" he shouted into the phone.

"Hey, Valentine, don't bite my head off. I got some good news, old buddy," Detective Cash told him.

"I'm listening," Valentine said wearily.

"What if I told you that your days of sitting behind that desk are over."

"Get to the point Cash."

"I pulled some strings and guess what? The leashes are off boss, and everything is back to normal, with a few extra perks. For one, that spic mayor won't be breathing down our necks."

"What the hell are you talking about Cash?"

"The chief just called me and said they need us back on the street. We're supposed to be part of some task force."

"You sure he said us?"

"Positive! The chief said that the mayor is outranked on this one."

"By who?"

"Senator Holten, and the word is he wants us to do what we do best."

"Where did this all come from all of a sudden?"

"The senator is getting tough on crime, I guess."

"Or he's down in the polls and he needs a boost." Valentine suggested.

"Whatever it is, it freed us in the process. Oh, there's one more thing."

"What's that?"

"The senator picked you to lead the task force."

Valentine paused for a second. All this good news was coming too fast. He tried to find some type of ulterior motive, but the truth was, he didn't care. Anything beats sitting behind a desk in the basement of the police station. Although a desk job was safe, it was slowly killing Valentine. To him, the desk was the equivalent of an old folks' home.

"Hey, Boss, you still there? What do you think?"

"I think it's about fuckin' time. Call Tango, and you both meet me at the station."

"You got it, Boss."

Valentine sat the phone down on the edge of the sink. He looked in the mirror. This time, his reflection was full of life.

"I'm back!"

DETECTIVE CASH

On the other end of the phone, Cash hung up.

"Hey, what the hell are you getting dressed for? I got another hour. Get your ass over here and suck my cock, you whore."

The young prostitute cringed at the thought of putting Cash's filthy penis in her mouth again.

"I said get over here, now!"

Hearing him scream made her jump. Cash had already beat her for not eating his feces when he shitted on her stomach. She didn't want to be beaten unconscious again. As she inched to the mattress. She kept telling herself, just one more hour and this nightmare will be over. If she had known life was anything like this on the street, she wouldn't have run away as a teenager. Her mother's abusive boyfriends were never as bad as this. The most they ever wanted was a blowjob, now and then. What she wouldn't give to be sucking Ted's dick right now.

The worst part was that she wasn't getting paid for this. Cash had made a deal with Terri Lee, Holyoke's only female pimp. As long as Terri Lee provided Cash with a girl every night, he'd let her operate, untouched by the police.

Cash always chose the young girls that had just gotten turned out. He liked scaring them and making them do things that they never thought they would do. Plus, paid pussy was the only way he could enjoy the company of a woman. He had a real bad reputation for beating women. Females at the station avoided him.

Only 33 years old, Cash looked like he was 43. He was already bald on top, except for a horrible looking comb-over. His gut hung so far over his pants, he had to lift up his belly to unbutton his jeans. Every shirt he owned had a gross stain on it, and he smelled like rotten meat all the time.

You could tell he was from North Boston, with his thick Italian accent. He had a Napoleon complex and because he was short, his weight looked exaggerated. He was only a few more greasy hamburgers away from a heart attack. Cash didn't see anything wrong with his life. He lived in a rundown building in South Holyoke that was infested with roaches and rats. His two bedroom apartment looked like a dope fiend's hide out. Empty bottles of Jack Daniels and Budweiser along with hundreds of crushed GPC cigarettes littered the floor.

In the living room was an old black and white, floor model TV. Some milk crates served as chairs. Old newspapers were used as a table cloth and when rolled up, a fly swatter. Piles of empty pizza boxes spilled out of the closet, and were home for the rats and roaches.

You'd hardly expect the youngest detective on the force to live like this. It wasn't a secret that he was well-connected. He came from a family of cops that went back five generations. Because of that, he was the only detective of the trio that wasn't stuck behind a desk.

"Suck that cock... faster, you slut!" Tracey sucked as fast as she could on Cash's tiny penis. She forced herself not to dry heave. The stench from his dick made her dizzy. Not to mention, he farted four times in two minutes.

"You want to eat my shit again, don't you?"

"No pleaseeeee, not that, anything but that." Tracey pleaded.

Cash hit Tracey so hard, her vision blurred for a second.

"Now, I'm gonna ask you one more time. Do you want to eat my shit again?"

Still dizzy from the blow, Tracey nodded her head yes.

He grunted, "I can't hear you!"

"Yes," she whimpered, trying her best not to cry.

"Good, because I gotta shit." Cash climbed over the top of Tracey and squatted over her adolescent breast. It took a couple of seconds of pushing, but it finally came. The first couple of drops were like clay and stuck to her stomach.

"Don't worry, that was just the appetizer, honey. Here comes the main course."

Cash then pushed out a log that was about a foot long.

"Eat it up before it gets cold."

"Pleeease." Tracey whined.

"What?"

"Okay, okay... just don't hit me."

Tracey tried to grab some of the shit log, but it mushed in her hand. She scooped what she could and shoved it in her mouth. She grimaced with complete disgust.

His phone rang.

"Who's this?"

"Hey, buddy, I got your message. What's up?"

"We're back, Tango."

"Are you serious?"

"You're fuckin' right I'm serious. So let that pretty wife of yours know that she won't have to worry about those bills anymore."

"It's about time. So nobody is going to be breathing down our necks?"

"Nope."

"Not even the mayor."

"Tango, I said no. Pick me up in an hour. I just made breakfast for my friend."

"Cash, you don't even cook."

"You'd be surprised at the shit I can whip up."

"That's exactly what it tastes like-shit."

"You don't know how right you are. See you in an hour, Tango."

DETECTIVE TANGO

For Tango, Cash's message was the best news he had heard in two years. It meant he could save his marriage, meet his huge monthly mortgage payments, and his girls would be able to attend that expensive private college in England.

The news was so good, in fact, it got him hard. As he hung up the phone, he turned and looked at his beautiful wife, Trisha. She was asleep on her side, with her back to him. It had been a while since they made love. Things had gotten so bad, he had to slip something in her drink and wait until she passed out to have sex with her.

For the last two years, all they did was argue, fuss and fight. Mainly, the arguments were over money. Trisha came from a wealthy family. She was used to getting what she wanted. Trisha even stipulated before getting married that if Tango couldn't spoil her, she would find somebody who could.

It had been a rough two years since the mayor took them off the streets. Money stopped rolling in, things got tight. He was already living well beyond his means because of Trisha. Her lust for the finer things in life like their 1.6 million dollar house, the two Mercedes and her $10,000 shopping sprees quickly drove them into debt. None of that was a problem before.

Tango knew the two-year suspension was his fault. He just wanted to show Valentine he wasn't afraid to get his hands dirty. He was more worried with impressing his mentor than thinking things through. Tango's intentions were good, but his timing was bad.

Tango pulled the covers off Trisha. She had on red panties and a short t-shirt. Her long, blond hair was pulled back in a ponytail. Tango flashed back to when they first met. He was the high school star quarterback and she was the cheerleading captain. Trisha was Tango's first in everything, but he was hardly her first. The only reason she married him was because she thought he was going to the N.F.L.

Tango eased Trisha's panties down and gently eased three fingers inside her. She was already wet. He frowned. Tango knew Trisha had another man, his best friend, Bruce. They had started sleeping together when Tango was suspended. He wasn't allowed to say anything about it. Sometimes she'd bring him home and make Tango leave the house. Other times Bruce would stay while Tango had to sleep in the spare room. It was all part of the deal. If he couldn't spoil her, she would find someone who could. He pulled his fingers out and then slid his dick in her with ease.

"What the fuck you think you're doing, you fuckin' asshole?"

Trisha pulled away from her husband.

"Hold up, honey. What if I told you that things

are gonna go back to the way they used to be? What if I told you that I'll be able to pay off the house and you'll be able to take vacations whenever and wherever you like."

"Don't fuck with me, Tango. I'm not in the mood for more of your lies today."

"I'm not lying! Cash called earlier and said that we're off suspension. We're back, as of today."

Trisha perked up. She remembered the kind of money Tango was bringing in when he was on the street. A smile spread across her face. "You better not be lying to me, Tango."

"I swear Trisha, it's true. I'm back. So you can tell Bruce to fuck off."

As nice as that sounded, it was already too late. Trisha had fallen in love with Bruce. He was everything she thought Tango was going to be. Bruce was worth over half a billion dollars. He also wasn't weak, like Tango. Where females might've seen Tango's passiveness as sweetness, to Trisha, it was pathetic. It was a complete turn-off. She stayed with Tango only because she was waiting for Bruce to pop the question. Soon as he did, she was gone.

"No, Bruce isn't going anywhere. It's too late for that now. If you can't accept that, you can take your dick out of me right now." Trisha smirked, with her back still to her husband. She got off on talking to him like he was a little boy.

"But… you're my wife." he mumbled.

"If there is no Bruce, there is no me and you. Nothing changes, Tango. Do you understand that?"

There was a long pause, and then finally Tango

gave in to Trisha, like he always did. He mumbled, "Yes."

Trisha's smirk grew. "Do you have a problem with Bruce fucking me?"

"No," Tango said softly.

"I can't hear you."

"No, I don't have a problem with Bruce still fuckin' you."

"Why don't you have a problem with it?"

"Because I'll never be the man you want me to be."

Trisha played to Tango's low self-esteem issues, and because of it she was able to get away with anything. That included openly fucking another man.

"Now take your dick out of me and call Bruce and ask for permission to fuck me."

Tango did what he was told.

"Hey, Bruce, ah, ah I was wondering if it was alright with you if I can fuck my wife. Okay… alright… hey thanks man. I'll let her know."

"What did he say?"

"He said it is alright with him. He said he doesn't want you sucking my dick. Also, he said he's coming over tonight and to have dinner ready."

Trisha sighed, hoping Bruce would have said no as she rolled on her back and opened her legs.

"Hurry up and get it over with Tango. Don't you dare cum in me either. I don't wanna have your baby, you understand? If I'm going to have another baby, it's going to be Bruce's."

"Yes Trisha," Tango said, as he climbed on top of his wife.

THE TWINS, KATE AND KELLY

"What are they doing?"

"Daddy is fucking Mommy," Kate said over her shoulder to her twin sister.

"You sure it's Dad? You sure it ain't Bruce?" Kelly asked.

"It's definitely Dad," Kate replied, looking through the key hole.

"How can you tell?"

"Bruce's dick is bigger than Dad's."

"You can see Dad's dick?"

"Yeah."

"No way. Let me see it." Kate pushed her sister out of the way and kneeled down in front of the key hole. "You're right. Bruce's dick is bigger than Dad's. Plus, Bruce fucks Mom better. Dad looks like he's boring."

"I was thinking the same thing. Hey, you know it's almost time, let's go." Kate grabbed Kelly's arm and yanked her to her feet.

"Do you think he's here already?" Kelly wondered.

"I don't know?"

"What about Mom and Dad?"

"We'll be in the guestroom on the other side of the house. They won't be able to hear us. Come on."

The two sisters hurried down the hall, towards the guestroom. Kate had the only key to the room. They both crept in and locked the door behind them.

"Are you nervous?" Kelly asked.

"Yeah, aren't you?"

"Yes, but I'm glad we're doing it together."

"Me too. Shhhh, I hear something outside."

"Is it him, Kate?"

"Shhhhh." Kate crept over to the open window. When she pulled the curtain back, an enormous black figure dove through.

"It's showtime."

"Jalen, you scared the shit outta me. Did anybody see you?" Kate took a quick peek out the window.

"No, it's cool. I walked through the woods the whole way."

Jalen was from Chestnut Park. Only 17, he was big for his age. He was also a Gorilla and hustled at the coke spot, Friday through Sunday. When he wasn't hustling, you could find him in the mall. That was where he met the twins.

They had only known him for a month, but all they spoke about was having sex with a black guy. Kate and Kelly were 18 year old virgins who didn't want to start college with their cherries. They had planned to lose their virginities together. Plus, the latest fad in their school was fucking black guys. That was why they invited Jalen over.

After they were satisfied that nobody saw Jalen

crawl through the window, Kate asked nervously, "So what are we going to do first, Jalen?"

"Suck dick. If you want to please a black man, you have to learn to suck dick, and I mean a lot of it."

Jalen unzipped his pants and pulled out his dick.

"Oh, my God, that thing won't fit in my mouth. Are you crazy?"

"Chill Kelly, you don't have to try and swallow it all at once. Besides, by the time I leave, you'll both be the best dick-suckin' white bitches in your school." Jalen promised.

That made the twins smile. A few minutes later, they were all naked. Jalen let them play with his dick first. The two squeezed, jerked and sniffed it. While Kate explored his dick, Kelly did the same to his balls.

When it was time for their first lesson, Kelly decided to go first. She crawled up on the bed with Jalen and took his dick in her mouth. Since she didn't have a clue what she was doing, she sucked on it like a straw in a milkshake.

"Work more of it into your mouth. Yeah, like that, now a little more. Owwwcchchh!"

"I'm sorry did that hurt?" Kelly asked him.

"That's the worst thing you could do while sucking dick. Use more tongue and less teeth!" Jalen instructed.

"But it's too big."

"The more dick you suck, the better you'll get. So put it back in your mouth."

Kelly followed instructions and began sucking it again. This time, she used more tongue and less teeth, like Jalen told her to. She fell into a steady rhythm.

"That's it Kelly, Mmmmm, suck that dick." Kate watched in amazement as her sister slobbered all over Jalen's dick. She even bobbed her head up and down with her mouth open like her sister was doing it.

"You think you're ready, Kate?" Jalen asked.

"I think so."

"Kelly, let your sister get some and you lick my balls. You always got to show the balls some love. A lot of girls forget about the balls."

Kelly and Kate took turns sucking Jalen's dick and licking his balls. They both got better with practice.

"See, I told you, white bitches are made for sucking black dicks. It only took twenty minutes and you both got it down."

"So, we're doing it right?" Kate said, coming up for air. Saliva smeared all over her face. "I like sucking dick."

"Me, too. I can see myself doing it a lot."

"That's what's up. Now, most guys like to do this, so get used to it."

Jalen grabbed a handful of Kate's hair and forced her head down on his dick. She gagged and coughed but eventually developed a rhythm.

"Yeah, you got it. When I cum, I want you both to hold it in your mouth and don't swallow. You have to get used to the taste of cum and having it squirted all over your face. Oh, there's one more thing. You gotta swallow, never spit the cum out."

When Jalen finally came, the twins held his cum in their mouths like they were told.

"It's salty," Kelly said.

"It's warm and gooey too." Kate said, smacking

her lips.

"But I could get used to it."

The twins played with Jalen's dick a while longer before he was ready to fuck, "A'ight, a'ight, that's enough of playin' with the dick. Now it's time for some fuckin.'"

"Me first!" Kate blurted as she climbed up on the bed and opened her legs without being told. Slowly Jalen inserted himself in her. The deeper he pushed up inside her, the deeper she clawed into his back.

"Wait , wait, aggggghhhhhh, stop, it hurts." Kate whined. "Oh, my, God, it's too big."

"Don't worry, it's only gonna hurt for a little bit. Put something in her mouth, Kate. I can tell she's gonna be a screamer." Kelly grabbed her panties off the floor, and stuffed them in her sister's mouth.

Kate tried her best to take the pain, but each thrust shot more pain into her stomach. Kelly held her hand, trying to comfort her sister the best she could. The whole time she did, she couldn't take her eyes off Jalen's dick forcing its way up into Kate's tight cunt.

Once Jalen had buried his dick as deep as it could go, he started humping Kate. When she got used to it, he picked up the pace.

"Yo, you taking the dick pretty good for your first time. I'm gonna do it a little harder now," Jalen said.

"Okay," Kate whined ,

FlOP! FLOP! FLOP! FlOP! FLOP!

Jalen didn't just do it a little harder; he started fucking the shit out of Kate. He plowed so deep, he ripped her hymen.

BANG! BANG! BANG! BANG!

The headboard slammed into the wall with so

much force, several pictures fell, but Jalen didn't let up. Kate got dizzy and thought she might throw up. Her eyes rolled back in her head. Her body went limp and her eyes glazed over. This went on for around eight minutes before Jalen pulled out.

Blood oozed onto the sheet.

"Ewwwww, that's nasty," Kelly said.

Instead of changing the sheets, Kelly and Jalen left Kate on the bloody bed and climbed on the bed next to it.

"I want you to pop my cherry like this." Kelly got in the doggy style position and wiggled her ass. "Will it work like this?"

"Fuck , yeah, it'll work."

"Before you put it in me, let me call Bethany. She wanted to be here." Kelly dialed Bethany's number and put the receiver on speaker phone. "Okay, go ahead." Jalen eased in her and started with a couple short strokes.

"Ahhhhhhhh!"

"Hello?"

"Hey, Bethany, Mnmmmmnmn, Oooooww!! Guess what?"

"What?"

"I'm getting my cherry popped as we speak," Kelly announced.

"Whatever. You're such a liar, I swear."

"I'm ahhhh, owwwww! I'm for real."

"Where's Kate at?" Bethany wondered.

"Right here. She lost her's about ten minutes ago. Jalen fucked the shit out of her. She can barely move," Kelly moaned painfully.

"Really?"

"Yep."

"Oh, my God, is he there now?"

"Yep, ooowww, mmmmm He's in me right now."

"Is… he… Big?"

"Big as the black guys on the porn tapes"

"Did you suck it?"

"Mmmmm, ahhhhh, yeah, he let us both suck it. He came in my mouth too. It wasn't gross like you said it was going to be. I liked it."

"What did it taste like?"

"Why don't you come over and see for yourself? Besides, Mmmmmm, it's hard to talk to you with him fucking me at the same time."

"I'm so pissed at you, Kelly. We were all supposed to get our cherry popped at the same time."

"Ahhhhh, we still can if you get your butt over here, right now."

"Come on over, Bethany. I got enough dick to go around." Jalen told her.

"Hi Jalen," Bethany said shyly.

"So, are you coming over or what?" Kelly asked, clawing at the bed sheets as Jalen started fucking her harder. "Owwww, shiiiiitt, he… he'll let you suck it too."

"Either of you take it up the ass, yet?" Bethany inquired.

"No, not yet." Kate replied.

"Okay, I'll come over if I can be the first to get it in the ass."

"Alright, just get your butt over here now!" Kate commanded.

"I'll be over in a few minutes."

BETHANY

Bethany hung up the phone, full of excitement. She had fantasized about this day since she was 13. She was two months away from turning 18 and she couldn't think of a better present than losing her virginity. More important, it was to a black guy.

Sleeping with black guys seemed to be the latest fad for white girls at her private school.

"I can't believe I'm about to do this. This is absolutely crazy!"

Bethany could hardly control herself. Her heartbeat fluttered. Mary J. Blige blared from her computer speakers as she ran back and forth, looking for something to wear.

It seemed that more and more upper-class white kids were becoming attracted to the street life. They started listening to rap and R&B, dressing in baggy clothes and speaking with a street slang.

Bethany and the twins took it a step further and watched hours and hours of interracial porn. Big, black guys fucking little, white teenaged girls. Now it was her turn and she couldn't wait.

Running down the stairs, Bethany blew past the maid, Maressa.

"Slow down Bethany, you're going to hurt somebody."

"I can't. This is going to be the best day of my life!"

"Hey, stop right there young lady! Where are you off to dressed like that?" another voice demanded.

Bethany sighed because she knew she was in for a lecture.

"What?" she said, stepping in to the living room.

"It is rude to answer someone with a "what." Now, where are you going dressed like a whore?"

Bethany glared at her stepfather. This was their relationship. They hated each other. They constantly argued. It drove her mother crazy at times. She even considered sending Bethany to live with her father. But there was another side to Bethany and her stepfather's relationship.

On several occasions, she caught him staring at her inappropriately. Most girls would have been grossed out by an old man gawking at them. Not Bethany, it made her feel sexy, womanly even. When she knew her mother wasn't around, she would sunbathe out back by the pool, nude. Other times, she would masturbate with her door open and moan loud enough for her stepfather to hear and come investigate. He'd just stand there and watch her. She'd pretend she didn't know he was there.

Bethany stepped into the living room and said, "How would you know what a whore looked like, unless you had a few, stepdad?"

"Watch your mouth young lady. Guys only think

of one thing when they see a girl dressed like that."

"And what's that, stepdad?"

"Whore. And it wouldn't hurt just to call me dad."

Bethany turned around and looked at herself in the full length mirror. She smiled because she did look like a whore. It was the look she was going for. The red lipstick was a bit too much and so was the pink eye shadow. The black mini-skirt was way too short, her shirt was too tight and she didn't have on panties or a bra.

Maybe it was the fact that she was about to lose her virginity or maybe it was how Frank called her a whore because of her clothes. Whatever it was, it had Bethany feeling slutty and she wanted to up the ante in the silent game they played with each other. Today was as good a day as any.

Bethany turned to face her stepdad. She pulled her red hair into a ponytail. Doing that made her arc her back and push her tits out. She started towards him again.

"Do you really think I'm a whore, Frank?"

The question caught Frank by surprise. "I… mean, ah, I mean. I just don't want anything to happen to you." Frank tried not to stare at her nipples, but he couldn't resist.

"Is that what you're thinking when you see me laying naked by the side of the pool? Is that what you're thinking when you're standing at my door watching me play with myself?"

Frank's eyes bulged. His face turned beet red. His mouth opened but nothing came out. Frank squirmed uneasily in his chair.

"Ah… ah, I don't know what you're talking about,

Bethany." Frank opened the newspaper to hide his embarrassment.

"It's okay, Frank, I'm not going to tell anybody. I can keep a secret. I mean, I've kept it for this long, right? Besides, I like it when you look at me like that. It turns me on."

Frank still hid behind the newspaper.

"I… masturbate about you coming into my room at night and fucking me."

That was a lie, but Bethany didn't care. She wanted to see how far she could take it. Bethany heard a moan creep from behind the trembling newspaper, the same moan she heard when he watched her play with herself. She took a few steps closer to him. The excitement of it all was driving her crazy. There was a scene just like this on one of the porn tapes Jalen gave her. The girl in the video was trying to seduce her black stepfather.

"Don't you want to touch me, Frank? I'll let you touch me anywhere you want." Bethany stood between Frank's legs, sucking her thumb, just like the white girl did in the porn tape.

Frank closed the newspaper and sighed. "What are you talking about, Bethany?"

He tried to sound stern, but it didn't work.

"Come on, Frank, you really don't know what I'm talking about?"

"No I don't."

"Maybe I should show you." Bethany pulled her shirt over her tits and she pulled the front of her skirt up.

"Do you know what I'm talking about now?"

"Ah… ah, dear God." Frank mumbled.

Bethany sensed Frank's defeat and went in for the kill. She grabbed his hand and placed it in the inside of her thigh, then she slowly moved it up her leg.

Frank's heart pounded. It felt strange to him because he was a man of power, he was used to being in control. He was also a man with a dangerous, dark past.

Bethany let go of his hand and it shamefully continued up her thigh until it reached her pubic hairs. She parted her legs so Frank's hand could continue its journey. For the first time, Bethany experienced the power of her sexuality. The feeling was so intoxicating, her pussy instantly got wet.

"You know you can't tell anybody about this." Frank whimpered.

"I told you, I can keep a secret," Bethany said as she sat on his lap.

Her skirt was well above her waist. Her shirt was around her neck. Frank grunted and moaned as he greedily groped Bethany's tits and fingered her pussy. Bethany's breathing got heavy as she grinded her soft, round bottom into the bulge in his pants.

Frank became so worked up that he pushed Bethany to the floor, stood up, unzipped his pants and pulled himself out.

"Put it in your mouth you... you... whore."

Bethany's eyes lit up. Being called a whore was a badge of honor, Jalen once told her. She didn't have the slightest clue of what to do but she wasn't going to let that stop her. She just imitated the girls on the porn movies. It seemed to work because Frank threw his head back and let out a loud moan.

Both of them were too into it and didn't hear the

front door open or close.

"Hello, where is everybody? Maressa, where's my husband?"

"Last I saw, he was in the living room with Bethany."

"Here, take these bags up to my room please."

Claudia passed Maressa several shopping bags and headed for the living room.

She thought, I hope them two aren't fighting. I'm not in the mood for that today.

It took twenty or so dramatic steps to reach the living room entrance. What she saw was the last thing she expected to see. Her mouth fell open. Her eyes teared up.

"Oh my God!"

SENATOR FRANK HOLTEN

"What the hell is going on in here?" Frank and Bethany broke their embrace.

"Oh, hey mom." Bethany said as she turned around nonchalantly.

"Is everything all right?" Claudia asked.

"Claudia, darling, everything is fine." Frank assured her.

"No, it isn't fine. Not when you two are normally at each other's throats, and when I walk in, you two are hugging. Is the world coming to an end?"

"Claudia, please. I guess you can say that Bethany and I have found a common ground."

"Yeah, mom, I guess Frank isn't so bad." Bethany said, walking over to her mother and giving her a kiss as she exited the living room.

"Well, I'm glad to hear that." Claudia walked over to Frank and gave him a hug and a kiss.

Bethany then poked her head back inside the living room. Her mother's back was to her so she flashed Frank her pussy before leaving once more.

"So are you ready for your press conference darling?" Claudia said, breaking their embrace.

"Of course, I'm ready. How was your day?"

"Me and Lois went shopping in Boston. She was telling me how she caught her maid smoking crack in their basement. Can you believe that woman? I hope Bethany is smart enough to stay away from that stuff."

"Crack is a problem for the lower-class, dear. You don't have to worry about it coming into the Highlands. That's why we live in a gated community."

"That's good to know." Claudia poured two glasses of wine and passed one to Frank. "You know, you've been getting good reviews about your Take Back the Streets Campaign.

"Guess who I got to head the task force?"

"Who's that?"

"Your ex-husband, Valentine."

Claudia's smile turned to a frown. "That's an interesting choice. Is he sober enough to do the job?"

"I suppose. He's the only one qualified for the job. We can't play fair with these drug dealers, and we need someone who knows the streets."

"Well, in that case, he's your man. Hopefully, it can give meaning to his pathetic life."

"Now Claudia, that's not a nice thing to say about your ex."

"The worst years of my life were spent with that man. I have a right to say what I want about him."

Frank came up behind Claudia and wrapped his arms around her. Claudia felt his warmth and melted in to him. "Well, you don't have to worry about that anymore. The rest of your life will be spent with me."

"And that's why I married you, Frank, you always

know what to say."

"I should at least be able to do that, I'm a politician, remember."

Frank gave Claudia a playful squeeze. As he did, he felt his bulge press into his wife's backside. With thoughts of Bethany still on his mind, Frank started groping his wife.

"Well, somebody is feeling frisky." Claudia remarked.

Frank walked Claudia over to his desk. He unzipped her dress from the back and let it fall to the floor.

"I love you Claudia."

"Frank, what are you doing?" Claudia blushed.

"Somebody could see us."

"So? This is my house and you're my wife. I'll do as I damn well please."

"What has gotten into you?" Claudia tried to cover herself with her hands. She hadn't been naked in front of Frank for so long it didn't feel right. She even tried to pull away. "Frank, please stop."

Frank grabbed her arm and yanked her back to his desk as he forcefully bent her over. He held her there by the back of her neck and with his free hand he snatched her panties down. Then he pulled his dick out and positioned himself to penetrate her.

"Frank, stop it! Frank pleasssse, oh, God!"

Her pleas only encouraged her husband. Something was wrong, terribly wrong. This wasn't her Frank. He never had been this rough with her before. They barely had sex once a month. This wasn't the man she married. This was someone else.

"Mr. Holten!" Maressa screamed from the doorway.

Frank snapped out of his trance. He glanced around lost. His eyes looked like they were going to drop out of his head. Then he looked down at his wife, who was naked and slumped over his desk, sobbing. He saw he was fully exposed and erect. It only took a second but he realized what happened.

Frank stumbled back and collapsed into his chair. He covered his face. Images of bloody clothes filled his head. He heard screams, their screams. He saw their faces. Faces he never wanted to ever see again because they reminded him of the person he once was.

Then what color he had left completely drained from his face when his alter ego started whispering in his ear.

"Hey, Frankie boy. It's about time you let me out of my cage. Ooooh, what do we have here? She's a little too old for our taste. You know how we like them young and tender right Frankie boy?"

"No, I don't like young girls." Frank's voice was childlike.

"Yes we do Frankie boy. We love the young ones. You don't remember? Do you need me to remind you? Do you want to see the things we did together?"

"No! Please no, no, no, no."

"I didn't think so. Now, let's fuck this old whore in the ass Frankie boy. We need to get our mojo back."

Frank looked at his wife who was still slumped over his desk crying. His eyes narrowed and a wicked grin was etched on his face. He stood up, grabbed himself and stroked it as he approached his wife.

"That's it Frankie boy. That's it. Fuck the whore. She's a whore Frankie boy. They're all whores!"

"Yesss, they are all whores."

On the outside, Frank was the upright senator. Everybody loved him even his enemies admired him. Little did anyone know, Frank had more skeletons in his closet than Arlington Cemetery. Skeletons that cost his wealthy parents millions to bury. The skeletons that returned after his encounter with Bethany.

Chapter 47

Downtown at the police station, news crews were setting up. It looked more like a circus with cameramen fighting for the best spots to set up. This press conference brought out all the bigwigs. But there was one big wig that wasn't happy with the campaign, Mayor Juan Santiago. He was against having Valentine run the task force. Although he couldn't prove it, he knew Valentine and his crew were corrupt. He pushed to have them fired, but since there was no proof the worst he could do was stick them behind a couple of desks.

Now after two years Valentine managed to weasel his way back into the streets. As much as he hated it, he couldn't do anything about it. Senator Holten outranked him on this one, plus his city was getting worse by the day. For that reason alone, he had no choice but to side with the Senator. Not to mention election season was coming up soon.

****

Outside it was a warm winter afternoon. The roads were clear but the snow dunes on the sidewalks were ten feet high. The sky was cloudless, and the sun was out as if it was summer already. Tango picked Cash up and headed for the station.

"You know, I never thought I would say this, but I missed all these niggers and spics." Cash said, as they passed through the slums of Holyoke.

"You weren't the one chained to a desk."

"I know, but it wasn't the same without you and Valentine."

"I know what you mean. It feels good to be back out on the streets."

Cash rolled down the window and screamed to a group of thugs standing on the corner. "Hey, you niggers and spics we're back!"

Tango shook his head, "Same ole Cash huh."

"How the fuck do they live like this?"

"Like what?"

"I think these niggers were better off as slaves. Fucking monkies, they are a waste of flesh. What kinda person sells crack to their mother? They have no respect, forget about it."

"Hey, they are what they are, don't get yourself all worked up on your first day back."

"You're right, how's the family?"

"Better now that the money is going to start rolling in. Trisha has been distant lately, but today she finally came around." Tango said, with a smile.

"That's good, what about the twins?"

"Oh, they're growing fast, listening to rap music and talking funny."

"Hey partner, you better nip that in the bud quick. If not, before you know it one of these young monkies will be driving a fuckin' foot long up their little asses."

Tango's face turned as red as his Corvette. He looked at his Italian partner. "Don't you ever talk about my girls like that, ever!"

"Okay, okay, sorry man," Cash knew he crossed the line. "I love those girls like they were my own. All I am saying is be careful."

"My girls aren't stupid, they know right from wrong."

Cash remained silent and thought. If they are anything like their slutty ass mother, you're in for some big trouble buddy.

At the same time their conversation was taking place, Kate was clawing at her sheets like a wild animal. She was taking all of Jalen's foot long up her ass and loving it.

"Hey, when I called Valentine he didn't sound so good." Cash said, lighting another GPC and letting out another fart.

"You wouldn't be either if your wife left you for your best friend, who would later turn out to become the Senator."

"Yeah, you're right, it must kill him to know she's sucking that asshole's wrinkly prick."

They laughed as they pulled in to the police parking garage. A young Spanish female attendant in the booth pressed a button and the gate opened. When the red Corvette passed through, she wrote down the license plate number and stuffed it inside her bra.

Valentine waited on the hood of his car drinking

coffee and smoking a cowboy killer. Tango and Cash looked at their boss and saw how the two year layoff took its toll on him. Everything about him looked tired. His gray hair looked white and his stomach made his leather jacket that much of a tighter fit. Tango swallowed a lump of guilt, knowing it was all his fault.

"What's the plan boss?" Tango said.

"First, we deal with this damn press conference and let all the important people get their pictures taken. After that, we hit the streets and find our old snitches. If we can't find them we spread some money around, and get some new ones. I want to know who got the deepest pockets now. We shake their pockets and everybody else will fall in line. This time around we will take in a few million a piece. Cash, spread the word that we are back."

"Gotcha, boss."

"Tango, find out who else on my task force likes to make some extra cash on the side."

"No problem, boss."

"Alright then, let's go get this bullshit out of the way, so we can do what we do best."

The three detectives strolled into the station like veteran cowboys. They received all kinds of looks, some good, some bad. Things had been a lot quieter since they were put behind the desk. Anybody that knew the trio knew that was about to change. They entered the conference room right as Chief O'Mally introduced the Senator. Valentine's stomach knotted up as the Senator took the podium.

"Back stabbing son of a bitch," he mumbled.

"Today starts a new day in Holyoke. Today is the

day we take back our streets!"

The room erupted in applause.

"No longer will our children be afraid to play on the playgrounds. No longer will our senior citizens be afraid to walk the streets at night. Those days are over. We've warned the drug dealers and they have ignored us. Now we've declared war on them and that is something they can't ignore!"

Again the crowd erupted in applause while flashes from the cameras lit up the room.

"Senator! Senator! One question please!"

"Sure Diane."

"Is it safe to say that this is your preamble to the march on the White House? We all know you're a sure win for the democratic nominee."

"One fight at a time Diane, one fight at a time." He replied with his patent politician smile.

****

After the press conference back in Chief O'Mally's office, the real meeting took place.

"Okay, my part is done. You have the funding you need, all the men you need and the right to operate as you please. Am I missing anything?"

"No, Senator." Mayor Santiago replied.

"I should expect to see results in less than a month's time. Will you have a problem with that Det. Valentine?"

Not backing down or flinching an inch, Valentine answered, "No sir, not at all."

"Good, gentlemen I want results. I've put my neck out on the line for this one. Don't make me look like a clown. If you do, I'll personally see to it that none of you work in law enforcement again. Are we clear on that?"

Everybody nodded in agreement.

"Very well then, I'll leave you gentlemen to the details."

"I'll see you out Frank." Chief O'Mally said, following the Senator.

Valentine also got up to leave when the mayor grabbed his arm.

"Let me have a word with you."

"Sure." Valentine replied with a shit eating grin, "What can I do for you Santiago?"

"Don't think this lets you off the hook. This task force bullshit don't change anything."

"Oh, yes it does and you can't do anything about it, can you?"

Santiago's nose flared as he clenched his fist. "Don't push me. I still got a couple of strings I can pull."

"I tell you what you do with your strings, wrap them around your neck and choke yourself to death."

Santiago got face to face with Valentine. "You think the Senator, who by the way is banging your ex-wife like a rag doll, is on your side? No, Mr. Valentine, this task force is temporary. After the Senator's crusade blows over it'll be back to business as usual, and I'll make sure your ass will be back behind that desk!"

"Do you think just because you are the mayor that bad things can't happen to you? You don't think that a bunch of A.I.D.S infected junkies couldn't kidnap your daughter and fuck her like a Brazilian prostitute? The streets are filled with all kinds of sicko's."

"I'm not afraid of you Valentine. We can make this personal if you want to."

"It's already personal, isn't it mayor."

Santiago paused for a second, "You're right, it already is."

"Now if you'll excuse me, I got work to do. I'm sure you have better things to do then bore me with your threats."

Valentine shoved passed the mayor and exited the office smiling. In the parking garage he gave Tango and Cash their final instructions before they left. Sitting on the hood of his car, Valentine took a moment to let the days events catch up with him.

So far so good. It shouldn't be long before the money starts rolling in again, he thought. I wonder if Claudia had anything to do with getting me back in the streets?

Valentine's phone rang.

"Who's this?" Valentine said, answering his phone.

"Is this Valentine?"

"Yeah, who's this?"

"Somebody with a deal of a life time for you."

"I don't have time for games, what the hell do you want?"

"I just seen the Senator's press conference on TV and the word is you're going to be heading the task force."

"So, and?"

"I was thinking we could help each other."

"How's that?"

"Is it safe to talk?"

"Yeah, go head."

"It's no secret what you're going to be into when you hit the streets. That's all everybody is talking about. I figure I can help you out."

"Why would I want your help?"

"Come on Valentine, you've been gone for two years, things are different nowadays, you're going to need someone to show you who's who. I can show you who the big cats are."

"And who might that be?"

"Well, for starters, there's Pharaoh and his Gorillas."

MELVIN

On the other end of the phone, Melvin hung up with a smile. A devilish feeling passed through him as he hopped out of his ebony colored Denali. He walked about a block and a half before turning towards a four-story building.

A'ight, that's taken care of. Now it's time to see what's up with these dudes. If everything goes right, I'll be the new King of West Mass., Melvin thought.

As he approached the door, three young thugs stood up and reached into their North Face jackets.

"Hold up, son. Where do you think you're going?" The smallest of the three said.

"I'm here to see Quick."

"Who the fuck are you?" another said.

"Tell him Melvin is here and I have some information on Pharaoh he might like."

The smallest of the three looked Melvin up and down as if he wanted to slump him right there on the spot. He then pulled out his Nextel and hit the intercom button.

"Yo Quick, somebody name Melvin is here to see

you. He says he has information on Pharaoh."

"Send him up."

"A'ight."

The door buzzed then clicked. The little dude step to the side and let Melvin pass.

"All the way to the top floor."

As Melvin climbed the stairs, a million things swam through his head. If I'm gonna pull this off, I'll need a crew. Infiltrating Quick's crew is perfect because they're from out of town and nobody really knows them. If I can get in and turn a couple of key members against him, the rest should be no problem. Getting in with Quick shouldn't be a problem, either. He hated Pharaoh just as much as I did. Yeah, my enemy's enemy is my friend.

Although Melvin came to forge a partnership with Quick, he pulled out his Desert Eagle, took the safety off and put it back in his jacket. Things could go opposite to what he had in mind, if so, he was taking a few with him.

"This way," a Big Pun-looking Spanish dude said as Melvin made it to the fourth floor. Before Melvin could sit down the fat man motioned him to the wall, patted him down and took his only sense of security.

"Have a seat. He'll be out to see you in a minute."

Feeling butt-naked, Melvin took a seat, a little more nervous than before. Looking around the apartment, Melvin saw Quick had a taste for the finer things in life from the Persian rugs to the Gucci furniture, even down to the custom-made wallpaper. All this told him about his partner-to-be.

"What type of info do you got on Pharaoh?"

Melvin turned to see a tall, high-yellow, young-looking cat with golden dreadlocks. Even with the dreads, you couldn't tell Quick was Jamaican. It wasn't until he spoke that you knew for sure.

"Before we get to that, I got an offer that I think you might like." Melvin said.

"What makes you think I might like it?" Quick asked.

"It involves controlling the coke and heroin distribution in West Mass. and getting rid of Pharaoh for good."

"How are you gonna get rid of Pharaoh?" Quick wondered.

"You mean we. We're gonna get rid of Pharaoh together." Melvin replied.

"We? What do you mean we?"

"If I deliver what I'm saying, I want to become a partner. I'll turn your little $100,000 a month operation to a million dollar a month operation."

The sound of a million dollar operation caught Quick's attention.

"How do I know you're not a cop?"

"I don't got no problem putting in work, if that's what it takes."

Quick sat in silence for a minute and thought.

Who the fuck is this nigga that shows up out of nowhere and wants to join my crew? He pondered. *He's saying all the right shit like he can read my mind. What do this bloodclot pussyfoot know that I don't? Then again, I can let him do my dirty work and then do him when I don't need him no more.*

"So what's up we got a deal or what?" Melvin

asked.

"I need to hear your plan first." Quick told him.

"Check it. I got someone in his crew that can't stand him. The only reason he hasn't killed him is because he's afraid of the blowback. He figures he can make money on selling information about what Pharaoh got."

"How deep is he in Pharaoh's crew?"

"Deep! He's one of Pharaoh's right-hand men. It don't get no deeper than that. He's in a position to tell us everything we need to know, for a price." Melvin explained.

"What's this boy's name?"

"Nah, you know I can't tell you that. He's my insurance policy that you hold up your part of the deal. Another thing I can also bring to the table is the fact that we can operate without the police fuckin' with us, you feel me?"

"I feel you star, but I don't want to kill Pharaoh off the rip. He's pissed off some very powerful people. They want to do some crazy shit to him." Quick mentioned.

"I like the sound of that."

"Yeah, so tell me why his right hand man wants him dead."

"Me, I have my reasons and they're personal. His man can't stand him because Pharaoh has this king complex. He seriously thinks he's the king of West Mass. His right-hand man was there when it all started and now Pharaoh is acting like he put the whole thing together himself."

"A'ight, we'll see if you're for real. If not I'll feed

you to my pitbulls." Quick warned him.

"So does that petty-ass threat mean we have a deal?"

"Yeah star, we have a deal."

Chapter 48

Later that night, after Claudia feel asleep, Frank crept from his bed and made his way down the hallway. His cock throbbed with excitement. He felt young again, full of life. Stopping at Bethany's bedroom door, he hesitated. He asked himself if it was all a dream, did it really happen?

Bethany had awakened something in Frank, something he had buried. He had done so good for so long. But all he had to do was walk away from Bethany's door. It was that simple. Everything came down to turning that door knob; his career, his marriage, his morals and his self-respect. The consequences of this ever getting out would ruin him. Everything he worked so hard for would be lost. A few times, he tried to walk away but he couldn't. Deep down inside, he didn't want to walk away. He grabbed the doorknob and anxiety ran through him like icewater. Just opening the door harden his erection.

"Bethany."

"Frank?"

Frank walked to the edge of the bed where Bethany met him. She got up on her knees and pulled her nightgown over her head. He untied his robe and let it fall to the floor. Next, he pulled his boxers down while Bethany removed her panties.

Neither of them said a word but the excitement between them could've lit up the whole house. When they were fully naked they stared at each other for a minute. The anticipation of breaking the taboo proved to be more erotic than the act.

Bethany laid on her back as Frank gently climbed onto her. She parted her legs and braced herself as Frank guided himself into her. At first it didn't hurt, but the deeper he went the more that changed. Bethany tried not to make any noise but occasionally a moan would escape. The pain she felt wasn't from Frank's size but from the punishment she took earlier from Jalen.

She wrapped her arms around his neck, clawing at his back with her legs around his waist, pulling him deeper into her.

She wanted to show him she could take it. Frank humped faster and faster. He tried not to slam into her but he couldn't control himself. He ended up pounding Bethany like a sledgehammer. It had been so long since he fucked like this. It felt good, really good.

The moaning and grunting got louder. Frank covered Bethany's mouth. Bethany covered his mouth. Frank came quicker than she wanted to. Pulling out, he jerked it all over her adolescent nipples. She smeared it over her body like lotion and stared into his eyes.

They said nothing to each other as they got dressed. Frank kissed her lips and left. When he was gone, she pressed stop on the camcorder she had hidden in her closet, rewound it and watched it over and over again as she fingered herself.

    Little did she know that recording was going to get a lot of people killed one day.

Back at Tango's house

"Ahhhh! Ahhhhhhh! Yesssss, Bruce. Fuck meee!"
FLOP! FLOP! FLOP! FLOP! FLOP! FLOP!
Bruce pounded Trisha from behind on her bed like a maniac but that was nothing new. He called her all kinds of foul names, whore and slut but that was nothing new either.

What was new was Tango sitting in the Lazy Boy naked, watching Bruce fuck his wife.

"Look at him Tango, look ahhh, look at the way he's fucking meee! Ahhhhh! Look at that fuckin' cock of his! Look at it you weak little boy! You'll never be the man Bruce is!"

FLOP! FLOP! FLOP! FLOP! FLOP! FLOP!

Tango watched for over an hour while Bruce had his way with his wife. He watched her take it up the ass, swallow Bruce's dick and act like the whore she screamed she was. The things she said to him, Tango had heard before from his father. His drunk, abusive father.

"You're a momma's boy! You little weak shit! You'll never be a man you sissy boy!" his father would bark.

Tango could remember crying himself to sleep as a child every night. His father's words hurt more than if he had beaten him. Now those same words had a different effect. The humiliation now aroused him.

What the hell is wrong with me? Tango thought as he shamefully started jerking his dick.

Cash closed the night out by breaking in a new prostitute and Valentine ended his by jerking off to his old wedding video.

I was just getting to sleep myself at the time. I had been branded Public Enemy Number One. Hey, you know when you're watching a movie and when someone's going to die, you always hear the creepy music first? Like in the movie, *Jaws*. Once you heard the music you knew somebody was gonna die. Well, if this book was a movie, this would be the part you'd hear that music, because a lot of people were about to die.

TO BE CONTINUED...

LOG ON TO:
www.bebpub.com
FOR THE RELEASE
DATE OF
KING PHARAOH PT2

www.ingramcontent.com/pod-product-compliance
Lightning Source LLC
Chambersburg PA
CBHW071300110426
42743CB00042B/1122